Perfect Children

PERFECT CHILDREN

Growing Up on the Religious Fringe

AMANDA VAN ECK
DUYMAER VAN TWIST

UNIVERSITY PRESS

OXFORD
UNIVERSITY PRESS

Oxford University Press is a department of the
University of Oxford. It furthers the University's objective
of excellence in research, scholarship, and education
by publishing worldwide.

Oxford   New York
Auckland   Cape Town   Dar es Salaam   Hong Kong   Karachi
Kuala Lumpur   Madrid   Melbourne   Mexico City   Nairobi
New Delhi   Shanghai   Taipei   Toronto

With offices in
Argentina   Austria   Brazil   Chile   Czech Republic   France   Greece
Guatemala   Hungary   Italy   Japan   Poland   Portugal   Singapore
South Korea   Switzerland   Thailand   Turkey   Ukraine   Vietnam

Oxford is a registered trade mark of Oxford University Press
in the UK and in certain other countries.

Published in the United States of America by
Oxford University Press
198 Madison Avenue, New York, NY 10016, United States of America

© Oxford University Press 2015

All rights reserved. No part of this publication may be reproduced,
stored in a retrieval system, or transmitted, in any form or by any means,
without the prior permission in writing of Oxford University Press,
or as expressly permitted by law, by license, or under terms agreed with
the appropriate reproduction rights organization. Inquiries concerning
reproduction outside the scope of the above should be sent to the
Rights Department, Oxford University Press, at the address above.

You must not circulate this work in any other form
and you must impose this same condition on any acquirer.

Library of Congress Cataloging-in-Publication Data
Van Eck Duymaer Van Twist, Amanda.
Perfect children : growing up on the religious fringe /
Amanda van Eck Duymaer van Twist.
pages cm
Includes bibliographical references and index.
ISBN 978-0-19-982780-0 (pbk.)—
ISBN 978-0-19-982778-7 (hardcover)—
ISBN 978-0-19-982779-4 (ebook)
ISBN 978-0-19-021473-9 (ebook)
1. Cults.   2. Children—Religious life.   3. Families—Religious life.   I. Title.
BP603.V35   2015
200.83—dc23   2014015980

Contents

Acknowledgments	vii
Introduction: What Happens to the Children?	3

PART ONE *Sects and Their Children*

1. Sects, Children, and Society	13
2. Leadership and Discipline	42
3. Points of Conflict: The Children of God and the State	67

PART TWO *What Happened?*

4. When Perfect Children Grow Up	103
5. The Young Members Who Stay	113

PART THREE *On the Outside*

6. The Young Members Who Leave	141
7. In the Wilderness	188
Conclusion	211
Appendix	217
Notes	221
References	249
Index	259

Acknowledgments

I thank all those who have read previous versions of this book and have given me valuable feedback: San Kim, Sarah Harvey, Larry Greil, Sibyl Macfarlane, Barbie Underwood, and the peer reviewers. Special mention should go to Paul Rock, who gave essential theoretical advice (and reads at the speed of light), and to Eileen Barker, an inspiring mentor who always pushes toward unbounded sociological curiosity.

Special gratitude goes to all those who have shared with me the aspects of their inner lives, experiences, and thoughts that are at the heart of this book. It wasn't always easy, and I commend their courage.

Perfect Children

Introduction

WHAT HAPPENS TO THE CHILDREN?

OFTEN, THOSE WHO travel outside the mainstream and into a fringe religion, or a "cult," are assumed to have proverbially lost their minds—perhaps even been victims of brainwashing by an unscrupulous but powerful leader. As an outsider, observing the dynamics between new religions and their critics, I always marveled at the accusations of brainwashing being bandied about, with the concept of normality narrowed and stretched accordingly to include the accuser but never the accused. Those who turn their backs on what they consider a society-gone-wrong, on the other hand, often view those who populate the mainstream world as brainwashed by the ruling elite, and are proud of their own revolutionary lifestyles. On either side, these are adults who choose particular lives (albeit sometimes with unforeseen elements and consequences).

But what happens to those who are born into such fringe or even revolutionary lifestyles? They haven't chosen this life; will they grow up to wear it with pride and weather the criticism? Will they carry the same stigma? Will they be brainwashed? Can children be brainwashed, or are they just socialized in a different culture? For previous research I interviewed second-generation members of the Family International (formerly the Children of God), a radical millenarian group, and asked them about the end times. I was fascinated to find out that although the children had, by and large, learned the same teachings as their parents, they tended to push the date of the end time back a bit to make time for things they wanted to experience first. This interested me and I embarked on further research to delve into what happens to those who have been raised with strong beliefs that are considered unusual, radical, or even ridiculous by the mainstream.

In order to do this I had to explore the radical fringes of religion, specifically groups that had a generation of their own children whom they had shielded in some way from the outside world and raised within their worldview. Hence I chose to focus on controversial new religions that had a strong communal element to them and that had raised a new generation of young members.

I will describe the groups and their histories, beliefs, and practices, as well as their pedagogical choices, in chapter 1. Since such religious groups, although considered on the fringe of society, are still very much part of it, I also looked at the reaction of society (civil and statutory), as this affects the groups and the individuals in them.

This book is the result of an exploration and analysis of the variables involved in the socialization of children in sectarian communities, and the interplay between the changing constituents involved: that is, between children, sects, and society (the state and civil society). Part of the analysis is also an exploration of which aspects of the socialization have been considered to be "successful," and which have "failed," and according to whom, as well as discussion of whether these are realistic concepts. The groups that I have focused on are the Bruderhof, the Church of Scientology, the Family International, the Unification Church, and the International Society for Krishna Consciousness (also known as the Hare Krishnas). These are the specific groups considered in detail in chapter 1.

I relied on a variety of resources for the research, ranging from face-to-face interviews with former as well as current second-generation members, (foster) parents, and teachers, in some cases written communication when distance precluded a meeting, participant observation, analysis of on-line discussion forums for former members of certain sectarian groups, and attendance at relevant conferences. I interviewed thirty second-generation former members and current members, teachers, and (foster) parents, as well as nine children and teenagers (between the ages of seven and sixteen) between 1997 and 2006.[1] Furthermore, I have also used case notes of seventeen inquiries to Inform from former members of religious groups (all but one fit my definition of sectarian). Inform is an independent charity founded in 1988 with the support of the British Home Office and the mainstream churches to obtain and make available objective and up-to-date information about new religious movements, also known as sects or cults.[2] It has an inquiry line and receives questions from a variety of individuals and public and private institutions. Many of the inquirers are former members of religious groups; some have been born and raised in these groups. I have included these cases because they have been a part of my general learning and the formation of this research—I have been working for Inform since 1998 and was the staff member who dealt with most of these cases.

The young former members in my research were raised in a subculture different from the rest of the surrounding society. Some stayed within it, considering it better than what was on offer outside. Others left and suffered some sort of crisis as a result of their mixed identity, occasionally being geographically diasporic following the missionary work of their parents, usually being cognitively different from children who had a sectarian upbringing and education. A further similarity is the stigmatization suffered by those who left who were negatively labeled by their parents and community (for not "fitting in"), and who feel stigmatized by others around them (again, for not "fitting in"). Having left, they straddled both worlds, much of their identity based in one while attempting to fit in the other, which often left them feeling like "misfits."

Segregated Socialization

Sectarian upbringing by its very definition begets segregated socialization. The young members are raised in a particular subculture, and those who choose to leave frequently have difficulty adjusting to the norms, values, and culture outside. But it is important to keep in mind that sects, and the childhoods of those in sects, are not static. There is an inevitable process of change and adaptation in a quest to manufacture the perfect environment conducive to the aims of the community.[3] The birth of a second generation puts pressure on existing practices, dynamics, and resources. The sect may have to adjust practices to comply with standards set by the wider society. All this challenges the "group" as defined by Mary Douglas (1970), changing the balance between social boundaries and internal hierarchy simultaneously. Some sects initiate changes to try to keep the status quo despite challenges from outside and within. In others this change is an effort to adapt to changing circumstances, to go with the flow as it were and sacrifice some previous priorities in favor of a new priority—be it the well-being of the children, reduced tension with the wider society, or both. Change toward adaptation is usually in response to outside scrutiny, inside disagreement, or disputes regarding controversial missions, practices, or revolutions that are frequently experimental and short-lived, and to demands by the maturing members of the second generation.

I relied on Brian Wilson's concept of sects, defined as being in opposition to society, as setting themselves apart as a result of a divergent faith.

In Wilson's words, sects are "a self-consciously and deliberately separated religious minority which espouses a faith divergent from that of other religious bodies.... [The term] is employed to encompass also those minority movements sometimes referred to as 'cults' or as 'new religious movements'. Each sect is, in greater or lesser degree, unique" (1990: 47). Chapter 1 introduces the concept of sectarianism in more detail, as well as the groups that I focus on and their key beliefs about the new generation within their fold. I purposefully use the term "sect," as Wilson did, to denote specific group dynamics. Sects arise out of opposition, and are in tension with their surroundings. This is not necessarily, or definitionally, an aspect of all new religious movements (NRMs).[4] Sects, on the other hand, have moved from being in opposition to "church" to being in opposition to "society"—hence less combatants in religious issues than deviant and abnormal religious threats to conventional, generally a-religious social practice. "Sects thus become an issue of social rather than of explicitly religious concern," Wilson asserts (1990: 47). Sects challenge the ethos and practice of other religious bodies and of society. They are often contrary and radical, yet have to find ways of existing in the society they oppose. Over time they find ways of doing this, and the sects will choose and adjust their relationships with other groups, organizations, institutions, and currents of ideas in society according to their own beliefs and practices. James Beckford (1985) has outlined such strategies, which he refers to as "modes of insertion," a term that describes the ways in which members are individually and collectively related to other groups and social processes. Of course Eileen Barker's work on NRMs and the "cult scene" has also been a significant influence, and I refer to much of this throughout—and discuss all these ideas in more detail in chapter 1.

Change, as I mentioned before, is another important variable—nothing stays the same. I discuss the important changes that affected the groups and their children in chapter 2. Over time the attitudes vis-à-vis "the outside" change, along with the structure and makeup of the sects. The birth of a second generation forces certain adjustments. However, although change is inevitable, the ways in which each group changes is different. Furthermore, it is dependent on events particular to each group. In some cases the state intervened in order to safeguard the rights and well-being of the minors—for whom it has a responsibility. Although parents have the right to raise their children within their religious beliefs, the children have rights as well, and the two sets of rights are occasionally in an imperfect balance. The point at which a state intervenes is influenced by a society's history of diversity and attitude to minority religions.⁵ In chapter 3 I discuss, at length, the interactions and dynamics between the group then known as the Children of God, the members' children, and the authorities in charge of child welfare. It is an important part of the group's history that gravely affected many of its children.

What Happened?

Chapter 4 centers around a discussion of what happened once the children grew up to make their own choices. Had they been socialized into the groups in which they grew up, or were there acts of rebellion? As always, this depends. As discussed in chapter 3, change is a process, which means that the first cohort of young members usually has a significantly different childhood from that of those members' younger siblings. The first cohort's members, in a sense, "break in" their parents, the leaders, and the structure and initiate the modifications and pave the way for their younger siblings. This work they do has often given them a reputation, a label, or even a stigma, ranging from "goodies" and "rebels" to "baddies." Throughout chapters 4–6 I discuss these labels within the context of the life stories of some young people who left and some who stayed.

Rebels and baddies will have challenged the boundaries—often before leaving. This, however, puts a wedge between the first and later cohorts, as they have had different childhoods and different experiences as young adults. The first cohort of children may have had more tumultuous childhoods as a result of trial and error and a process of adaptation by the group to those children's presence and the resulting new responsibilities. Also, leaving for them has often been more of a challenge, as the sect had not faced this issue before, hence there may have been less support and understanding. Chapter 6 concentrates on the young members who left and the struggles they faced.

The later cohorts typically left under different circumstances; the sect adapted and became more experienced in this respect. It may have established new levels of membership for those young members who did not want to be governed by the same rules as their parents were, or who wanted to work outside yet still have contact within. Or there may be ways in which the members can gradually leave, adjusting to outside while receiving support from inside.⁶ This affected the labeling; in some cases there was more room for rebels among later cohorts. This issue of stigma is important, and it is discussed throughout the later chapters of the book.

The labels given to the young members within the group have become internalized over time, and those who left felt stigmatized "outside" as well—they carry these stigmas with them.

Support

The process of leaving has been a different experience for the young members depending on which cohort they belonged to within the history of their group. This is discussed in chapters 6 and 7. The first cohort of leavers within the second generation often chartered their own passage; they became their own "agents" on a do-it-yourself basis. Later cohorts frequently had the opportunity of choosing an agent within the self-help movement created outside who could help them through the status passage (discussed later). Furthermore, the first cohorts often received little material or structural support from the group, whereas the latter cohorts were more likely to. Specialized support outside has, so far, been mostly organized by those who have had previous experience with the groups—be it as former members or relatives of members. In many cases, this self-help support came with theological, doctrinal, and moral criticism toward the communities of their childhood. The young former members often joined the opposition to the groups that they had been exiled from, by whom they were stigmatized. The opposition (social networks, often online), aside from providing support, often had a secondary role of providing a new socialization, providing a different worldview and explanations to ultimate questions.

These self-help groups are significant. The young people were often fearful of the world they were entering, and it is helpful for them to join a group where they are recognized, where the people understand who they are, where they are coming from, and what they have gone through—a group where they do not have to explain themselves.[7] Yet connecting themselves to such groups (by communicating with the group, joining the network, attending meetings) often alienates them from their relatives and others in the sects in which they were raised. The dualistic world of "us" versus "them" that is part of the sectarian stance does not often tolerate contact with those who have gone to "them." The young former members going outside and joining other subcultures, and creating their own, has changed the outside. Hence, for the later cohorts who leave, the world outside is a slightly different place.

Former members have created their own self-help groups outside because they experienced a lack of support useful to their situation when they left. As one young former member commented when calling Inform, there is support for parents who have difficult children, there is support for gay people who are not understood by their parents—why is there no support for people like her whose parents do not accept their child for who she is?[8] (She had rung a few help lines for children and young people, but had found them neither knowledgeable nor helpful for her particular situation, and there was no particular ex-member support for young people leaving her particular group.) She argued she was suffering from religious intolerance from her parents and religious leaders, because they did not accept her desire to leave the religion, and were pressuring her to stay. She felt there was nobody to turn to for help and support. Existing secular and religious support was not desirable to people like her, who believed the majority of counselors lack understanding about the particular worldview, language, and cognitive framework of young ex-members. Also, the young ex-members often worry that they may be ridiculed for what they realize, by then, to be unconventional worries and fears ("will I get it wrong?"; "what if they were right and the world is going to end?").

Counselors may be unaware of the special institutional, social, interpersonal, emotional, and spiritual dynamics that may be the norm in particular sects but unusual in the wider society. And if a young former member has difficulty formulating her or his concerns and troubles, then this may be a significant challenge to counselors who are not familiar with the language and conceptual world the young former member has come from.[9] It is exactly for this reason that the self-help groups are attractive and helpful. These are organizations and individuals who offer more specialized support to those leaving sects, and who "understand." They have the motivation to establish support organizations to help young former members like the one described above (and often also to keep them going on a shoestring budget). But this help frequently comes with a bias. This bias has a significant polarizing effect in the general cult scene, and on interfaith relations within the diversity of culture, as the discourse widens the gap between sects and their critics rather than create a bridge toward communication and possibly understanding (if not reconciliation). Such reconciliation, at the moment, appears to be a far-fetched ideal. The different cohorts of children were, in some cases, divided as well. The first cohort frequently had to choose more starkly between either relations with the group or relations with other former members—jumping, in a sense, from one community to another. The later cohorts had the opportunity of using first cohort leavers as agents to help them adjust to the outside. Yet this wasn't always an easy choice. The later cohorts tended to have better relations with the parents and the group, but often at the cost of relations with their elder siblings, whom they saw as being against the group and the parents and as being potentially disruptive to their own bridge with the community. Hence, for the later cohorts, using a first-cohort leaver as agent could have too high a price.

Consequently a complicated map of allegiances and divisions has been established. Independent and secular organizations, which aim to chart a middle way in this complicated map, occasionally even mediating between different factions, struggle to get the funding to undertake the work they deem necessary. In this polarized debate between sects and their critics, independent organizations are frequently challenged and regarded with suspicion by those who take an ideological position on either one side or the other. The religious diversity found in many Western societies is hardly one of peaceful coexistence as yet. Although I have chosen to concentrate, in this book, on sectarian groups with problematic pasts, it is important to point out that not all minority religions are in tension with their surroundings. But it is equally important to note that sectarianism continues to exist, with a continuous stream of new minority groups that disagree with the status quo. In this environment, people occasionally struggle to build a bridge between absolutist subcultures that, rather than representing hybridized cosmopolitanism, represent clashing parochialisms. It is important to research the ways in which such environments can affect the children raised and socialized in them.

PART ONE

Sects and Their Children

> FOR THIS CHILD SHALL SHINE AMONGST MEN, *for he is a prince to be called a prince amongst men. And he shall stand before his people and his God to deliver them out of great sorrow and bondage. For he is to become a prince that shall become a prince amongst men to become a standard bearer before God*
> —BERG 1977b

Davidito was born in 1975 to Maria. As the first child born to the leadership of the Family, following a special ministry, he was to be the harbinger of the end, a soldier for Christ. He along with his younger sister Techi, inspired a series of publications, including the *Davidito Letters*, later compiled into *The Story of Davidito*, and the *Techi's Battles and Victories* series.

Other children within the movement followed intently the stories about the trials and tribulations of Davidito and Techi, the future royalty in the Kingdom of God.

I
Sects, Children, and Society

THE SECTARIAN GROUPS I focus on throughout this book are placed within the wider context of sectarianism and introduced below. But it is important to keep in mind that, although I discuss aspects of sectarianism as a context, the particular groups I discuss in detail are not necessarily general examples of sectarianism. I focus on these groups in particular because they are or were communal or provide communal living for a portion of their membership, have special child-rearing philosophies and facilities, and at some point in their history experienced an occurrence (a particular teaching, practice, or a coming together of events), short-lived or prolonged, that affected a generation of children in a significant way. Furthermore, although I discuss some aspects the groups have in common with other contemporary and historical sectarian groups and with each other (e.g., structure, leadership), I do not provide a clear and clean comparison between the groups, as their histories have not run parallel in a way to make such a comparison useful or meaningful. I focus on the events and processes that affected the children, and analyze and discuss these, in five groups that were sectarian and radical.

Sects and Society

The ways in which a sect fits within the surrounding society often depends on its priorities, how members think these can be attained, and how they relate to the rest of society. Concurrently, society's perception of the sect will relegate it to a position within society that reflects the extent to which the group is accepted by its surrounding population—be it uncontroversial and integrated or derided and marginalized. James Beckford (1985: 85), when analyzing the controversies surrounding new religious movements, asked: "How are NRMs inserted into their societies?" and analyzed their social relationships in order to build up a picture of their "modes of insertion." An NRM's mode of insertion into society highlights ways in which members of

NRMs are individually and collectively related to other people, groups, institutions, and social processes (85). Beckford here distinguishes between an internal and an external axis—the former refers to relations within an NRM and the latter refers to relations between the NRM members and "outside" people, institutions, and social processes. The focus on social relationships allows for a variety and range of modes of interactions with outsiders—individuals and institutions. Hence a group could have an isolated core of members who keep to themselves while also having missionaries and businesses that interact daily with the outside world. Beckford's framework combines social and ideological aspects, with the social elements standing out. Previous work on the topic has concentrated on ideological aspects, and how these have influenced social behavior.[1] Indeed, beliefs are important, and certain salvation beliefs can set a group of people apart from the rest—the elect, such as the 144,000 (Revelation 7:3–8, 14:1, 14:3)—those who are enlightened versus those who are not, those who are free from *maya* (illusion that stands in the way of one perceiving "reality") as opposed to those who live in illusion and indulge in "sense gratification." Salvation beliefs can range from physical or mental healing to elaborate prospects of the transmigration of the soul, or reincarnation. The common denominator is always the promise of present reassurance in the face of malevolent or troublesome phenomena or events (Wilson 1990). Salvation beliefs can be strong motivators for behavior and practice. Conditions for the attainment of salvation imply a range of "restrictions" in the form of taboos and injunctions for everyday life, as well as a range of "additions" in the form of tasks and responsibilities. Such laws to live by can make for unusual daily routines, as is visibly obvious in communities such as the Amish or ultra-Orthodox Jews; these communities are considered marginal at best.

Religious and cultural diversity makes concepts such as "mainstream," "normative," and "marginal" somewhat problematic. Of course everybody, to some extent, lives his or her life by rejecting some ideas and practices while choosing others. Furthermore, in a globalized world the possibilities are ever growing, and the concepts of mainstream and marginal, or "normal" and "abnormal," keep expanding. Everyone has a concept of a "mainstream,", yet all these mainstreams do not perfectly overlap as one singular reality. Despite this, there is a generalized, or imagined, concept of mainstream ("the norm") and of religious groups that are in tension with this mainstream ("abnormal"), as well as being communities of like-minded people who pick and choose ideas from the cultic milieu while discounting the ideas prevalent in the mainstream (and who are often labeled as living "alternative lifestyles"). One can identify groups of people who turn their backs on the lifestyle enjoyed by their parents in order to embrace another—be it an invented, reinvented, or imported lifestyle or a syncretistic amalgamation. Of course norms are continually shifting as well. Vegetarianism and saris and dhotis (Indian clothing) are not traditionally part of Western society, yet today being a vegetarian and wearing clothing similar to saris or dhotis does not mean one is a follower of Vishnu or any other of the Hindu gods. Meanwhile, groups like the Amish and the Exclusive Brethren are the West's cultural and religious creations, yet joining them now would be far from a mainstream activity. Some of their salvation beliefs and practices have resulted in them having little interaction with those who are not part of their community—they are considered to be, as they consider themselves to be, different from the norm. This marginal position comes with distinctions between "them" and "us," and social boundaries protecting the chosen from the likes of "them" and their ideas and practices—considered to be depraved or otherwise immoral.

Protecting the flock from negative influences, and creating an environment conducive to the beliefs and practices necessary for salvation, tends to become an important priority for sectarian groups. Consequently, the modes of insertion in society are purposefully limited. Or, as Kai Erikson argued in *Wayward Puritans*, such communities are "boundary maintaining" in the sense that they place symbolic parentheses around their members: "When one describes any system as boundary maintaining, one is saying that it controls the fluctuation of its constituent parts so that the whole retains a limited range of activity, a given pattern of constancy and stability, within the larger environment" (1966: 10). A short synopsis of five of the main sectarian groups discussed throughout this book follows, and it will serve as an introduction to illustrations and examples throughout the following chapters.

The Bruderhof

The Bruderhof is a collection of pacifist communities following Anabaptist precepts that at several points in their early history sought to be associated with the Hutterites. In 1990 some Hutterite congregations excommunicated the Bruderhof for what they perceived as doctrinal deviations, and eventually the Bruderhof broke the remaining ties with the Hutterite tradition. The Bruderhof, which means "community of brothers," consists of over twenty-six hundred members, living in over twenty communal settlements ranging from self-contained villages to, in a more recent development, some smaller households in urban areas.[2] Eberhard Arnold (1883–1935) founded the Bruderhof in the 1920s in Germany, and the group has "hofs" (communities) in the United States, the United Kingdom, and Australia. Upon joining, members hand over their belongings to the community, after which they are meant to reject what community members consider the divisiveness of private property and power. One of the main rules in place to help maintain the brotherly communal atmosphere is the "law of Sannerz," named after the first community. The spirit of the "law" is that disputes or disagreements are settled between individuals, face to face, without the mediation of third parties. This discourages talking about third parties behind their backs, gossip, and other behavior seen to be out of step with the "spirit of love":

> There is no law but that of love. Love means having joy in others. Then what does being annoyed with them mean? Words of love convey the joy we have in the presence of brothers and sisters. By the same token it is out of the question to speak about a Bruderhof member in a spirit of irritation or vexation. There must never be talk, either in open remarks or by insinuation, against a brother or sister, against their individual characteristics—under no circumstances behind the person's back. Talking in one's own family is no exception. (Oved 1996: 25)

The Sermon on the Mount serves as the biblical foundation for the Bruderhof communities. The members become radical disciples of Jesus after adult baptism, and lead a life of pacifism. Conduct is strictly regulated; transgressions are handled with public confession and repentance of sin, and sometimes exclusion of the sinner from the day-to-day life in the community, until she or he has found "the path" again.

Being a pacifist community, the Bruderhof left prewar Germany for England, which the members later left for Paraguay, where they created three separate communities at a settlement they called "Primavera." There the members formed a self-sufficient commune, isolated from the Spanish-speaking Paraguayan population. After the war, members established communities outside Paraguay. But even in English-speaking countries, the communities were relatively isolated from the rest of society. The hofs were intentional communities, created out of a desire to live according to Christian and humanistic ideals. However, the 1960s saw a crisis (referred to as the "Great Crisis") within the Bruderhof.[3] The crisis was due mainly to a schism in the leadership between Hans Zumpe (Eberhard Arnold's son-in-law) and the European leaders, on one side, and the Arnolds (Eberhard Arnold's sons) in the United States. The American leaders accused the communities in Paraguay of being "cold-hearted" and of having moved away from the Hutterite ideals they held at the time. The "cold-hearted" were the people who had joined because of a shared humanist ideology, and who sought social and economic relations with the wider community. The "warm-hearted," on the other hand, had joined as a result of their belief in Jesus Christ and the Holy Spirit, and favored a closed community in order to focus on this devotion.[4] Hence they favored self-sustaining communities. There was a feeling, among the Arnold followers, that the movement had moved away from what were perceived as the "warm-hearted" days in Sannerz, and the original leadership under Arnold) toward a more liberal and ideological stance (which was perceived as legalistic rather than spiritual) under the Zumpe leadership. Under these circumstances the communities in Paraguay were dissolved, as were several other hofs (in England and North America), and over six hundred people left or were expelled. The "warm-hearted" devotion won over the more liberal ideals, and the Bruderhof became a closed Christian community with like-minded "brethren."

In the West, the Bruderhof have never been considered as unfamiliar and exotic as some of the foreign sects that arrived in the West around the same time. The members and their traditional ways—sober and traditional dress, manual agricultural and artisan labor, and communal sharing of goods—were generally seen as quaint and romantic.[5] Their sectarian stance toward society was intensified and highlighted only once exiles from the Great Crisis started voicing their discontent.[6]

The Church of Scientology

In 1950, the publication of *Dianetics: The Modern Science of Mental Health*, written by Lafayette Ron Hubbard (1911–1986), introduced new ideas regarding the human mind and the goal of "Man"; the book gained a certain level of popularity. Four years later, a religious organization was established around the themes of Dianetics, called Scientology. The aims of Scientology are to solve the problems perceived to be affecting society, such as crime, drugs, and illiteracy. The essential tenets of Scientology are that people are immortal spiritual beings, whose experience extends well beyond a single lifetime, and whose capabilities are unlimited—even if not presently realized.⁷ The spiritual being is called a "Thetan," which is believed to be basically good and seeking to survive. But the Thetan is impeded. People, according to Scientology, lack self-awareness, and have come to believe that they are their bodies, rather than their Thetans. This is a result of the mind, which, according to Scientology, is an accumulation of "mental image pictures" (what we often think of as memory) from current and previous lives. But the mind can have a confining effect. The mind consists of the analytical mind and the reactive mind. The former is the rational, conscious, and aware mind that thinks, observes data, remembers these data, and resolves problems (Jentzsch 1994: 60). The latter is the accumulation of negative images and experiences, which have a harmful effect. Some of these negative experiences are recorded unconsciously; they are stored not as memories, but as "engrams." Engrams are thought to have mass, and act as blockages in the mind. The reactive mind is unconscious, and not normally under our volitional control. But Scientologists believe that Hubbard found the key to unlock this reactive mind, and a method to learn to control its allegedly debilitating effects. Members and clients are meant to become aware of their reactive mind through auditing, a form of cocounseling (Scientologists stress that it is a system through which someone is allowed to find his or her own answers, without outside suggestions or solutions), aided by an "electropsychometer" (e-meter). This meter measures changes in energy flow. The goal of auditing is to erase the engrams from the reactive mind and re-store them as standard memories in the analytical mind. Once this goal has been realized an individual is "clear," and may proceed through training to become an "operating Thetan," not burdened by the alleged restrictive forces of the reactive mind. The doctrine focuses on the human mind, what impedes it, and what would reportedly set it free. This route to freedom, to the state of clearness and through the operating Thetan levels, is called the Bridge.⁸

Aside from helping people cross the Bridge to "total freedom," Scientology aims to heal what it perceives as the ills of society. Hence the organization consists of many affiliated organizations that target society's perceived problem areas, such as Narconon (drug rehabilitation), Criminon (crime rehabilitation), and Applied Scholastics International (improving education through the application of Hubbard's "study technology"), all governed by the Association for Better Living and Education International. These organizations rely heavily on the book *The Way to Happiness* by Hubbard. Other social reform programs include the Citizens' Commission on Human Rights, which aims to expose what Scientologists consider psychiatric abuse, and the National Commission on Law Enforcement and Social Justice, which aims to clean government files of false reports. Since 1981 all of the churches and organizations of Scientology have been brought together under the Church of Scientology International.[9]

The size of membership of the Church of Scientology is difficult to establish. There are clients who take courses now and then, more dedicated adherents, staff, and full-time members who have devoted their lives to Scientology and signed a contract extending well beyond their biological life span—a billion-year contract.[10] The latter are members of the Sea Org, an elite group of people who live communally and regard Scientology as the main priority in their lives. Sea Org members have to step down once they have children, but can rejoin when their children are ten and have agreed to join as well, as "little cadets."[11] These cadets are then schooled—in England this happens at the Little Cadet School, at the Saint Hill community where they also live. There is also a cadet school at Scientology's US headquarters in Florida. In 2009 Scientology claimed to have 10 million followers worldwide and 120,000 in the United Kingdom—these numbers are likely to be exaggerated.[12] Scientology has centers throughout the world.

Scientology teachings include aspects typically associated with religion, psychology, philosophy, and science, yet the organization is not fully recognized and accepted by any of these disciplines. This is partly because Scientology defies easy categorization—it charges money for services other religions might offer free of charge, and it is structured (and operates) bureaucratically.[13] It has been accused of swindling and brainwashing followers, and the movement in return has harassed its critics.[14] Scientology strongly adheres to a set of values that has been formalized into an ethics policy to which followers adhere.[15] The purpose of adhering to ethics is to ensure continued survival across the dimensions of self, ranging from the self to the family unit and groups, mankind to all living things, the universe, and infinity.[16] The follower is encouraged to maximize chances of survival by bettering understanding of and accomplishments within these areas of the self—which will consequently enable better understanding of the "tech" (the learning tools). A follower who fails to achieve this is "out ethics," and should be reported to a senior member for further training to again achieve the position of being "in ethics." The areas of "self" recognized by Scientologists include dynamics that are generally considered to be outside the self, such as social groups, all living things, and the physical universe. Hence, followers' path to betterment extends beyond the organization, where "ethics" and Scientology standards are applied as well. Consequently outsiders can create a situation of out ethics, such as people who give the movement a bad name in public by testifying against it in court, by publicizing negative information, and so forth. People who are seen as actively trying to suppress or damage Scientology are referred to as "suppressive persons," and those who are in contact with suppressive persons are seen as "potential trouble sources" (Bednarowski 1995: 388). Scientology's relations with government officials are not necessarily much better than their relations with individual critics. In 1977, eleven senior members of the Guardian's Office (set up to deal with perceived threats to Scientology), including Hubbard's wife, were convicted of stealing government documents from the US Internal Revenue Service after finding out about plans of a raid on the movement by the agency.[17] The organization waged a twenty-year battle with the Internal Revenue Service in the United States before it was awarded tax-exempt status. Similarly, it has been trying to get charitable status in the United Kingdom, which was denied in 1999 (although it was allowed by the Supreme Court to register its chapels as places of worship in 2013). Scientology has an inconsistent status throughout Europe, although the European Court of Human Rights has considered Russia's denial to register Scientology as a religious community as a violation of aspects of the Human Rights Convention (Church of Scientology Moscow 2007). There have been many court cases, including several US grand jury investigations. In the last few years several high-profile members have left the organization and divulged details of their life inside, while some investigative journalists have published scathing and in-depth reports.[18] Children of Scientologists, including the niece of the leader, have left, and created a website compiling the accounts of other second-generation members who have left.[19] These developments have created another dent in the public perception of Scientology.

The Family International

The Family International, formerly known as the Children of God and later as the Family of Love, emerged during the countercultural Jesus Revolution of the 1960s. In 1967 David Berg (a.k.a. Father David, Moses David 1919–1994) preached a message of salvation to hippies in Huntington Beach, California—he and his predominantly young followers were known as the Teens for Christ. David Berg came from a southern American Protestant background infused with fundamentalist and millennial beliefs. His idea was to set up a "heavenly community" where members would practice a "godly socialism." As Berg's following grew, communities were set up in Texas and Los Angeles. There, members developed the skills of provisioning (soliciting funds and goods from institutions and the public), an important aspect of the group's life. As with other communities, most belongings were shared, and the full-time members were expected to offer their commitment, adopt biblically inspired names, live in a Family "home" (i.e., community), and work for the movement. An important aspect of their work was "witnessing," telling the world about the Lord. Throughout the years the movement has gone through many changes, including different styles of leadership. The majority of the full-time Family members lived communally until 2010, although the communities became smaller and spread all over the world, and individual families often moved from country to country as missionaries. Thus in any given home there was a constant flux of families moving in and out. In 2010 the movement began a new era with a structural shake-up, a so-called reboot, where individuals were given freedom to choose their own lifestyle (including employment, relationships with non-members, and outside education for their children) while the Family's governing structure was greatly reduced.[20] This is a significant change in the Family, with some wondering whether the movement has disbanded. I won't discuss it much here as my research predates the reboot.

Members of the Family have a definite belief in the end time. Berg took the millennial beliefs popular in American fundamentalist Christianity literally—he believed that the Bible could be read as a virtual textbook of the events leading up to the end of the world (Millikan 1994: 203). He believed he was the last of God's great prophets. The Family expects that a dictator will rise in the East and try to rule the world. At first he will appear to be bringing peace. The world will continue to modernize, and people will be able to buy goods and services without monetary interaction. The majority will have accepted a microchip implanted under the skin. After three and a half years of success the dictator will declare himself as "God," although others will recognize him as the Antichrist. Then will follow three and a half years of trial and tribulation, as the Antichrist persecutes all who refuse to worship him, and who refuse the microchip (which will have the number of the Beast, 666). After these seven years Jesus will come down from heaven, in a white light, exactly as he ascended according to scripture. His believers will be resurrected and fly up to his Heavenly City with new bodies and supernatural powers. As the Antichrist starts the battle of Armageddon, Jesus and all his saints (members of the Family and other Christians who have received the Lord) will destroy the worshippers of the Beast, and capture the Beast. Then the period of one thousand years of peace on earth, known as the Millennium, will begin. Jesus's supernatural helpers will clean up all the debris of the battle and rule over the people who remain—those who refused the mark of the Beast, but who had not received Jesus into their hearts. The earth will be restored to its original beauty of the Garden of Eden.

Members believe the world is currently evil, which confirms the Bible's prophecy that we are in the end time. David Berg, as God's prophet for the end time, declared a war on the wicked ways of the world, and a renunciation of this world, which he referred to as the "system." Berg received much of his authority through his alleged contact with certain "spirit helpers" such as David (King of Israel in the Old Testament) and Moses. Moses David, as Berg was often called, used to speak in tongues and relate-translate their messages. His messages were written and distributed as Family literature (known as Mo letters). Although independent of the Bible, they were considered to be messages from God by the members. In 1994 Berg passed away. But he is still considered to be present in spirit, channeled through Maria, his common-law wife, who, together with Peter Amsterdam (whom she married after Berg had passed away), took over the leadership position.

The West is not unfamiliar with Christian groups witnessing and reaching out to the down and out. David Millikan, a theologian, describes the Family's theology as a mix of apocalypticism, evangelical southern American Protestantism, and universalism (1994: 191). Despite its relatively familiar doctrine, the group was controversial, and allegations of brainwashing and cultism were spread, mainly by critics and concerned parents, through the media in the United States. The first anticult group, The Parents' Committee to Free Our Children from the Children of God (later shortened to FreeCOG), was created in reaction to David Berg and his followers. The situation worsened when Berg started writing about new witnessing experiments that he and Maria had been exploring: the "Flirty Fishing" ministry.

In 1974 Berg sent out a Mo letter to followers describing how Maria had witnessed successfully in a revolutionary way; she had engaged in a sexual relationship with a man to show him God's love, and he had joined the group. Berg urged his female readers to approach lonely men and show them God's love, using sexual contact if necessary. Over the next few years, Flirty Fishing (or FF-ing) became an important evangelistic tool. At roughly the same time, Berg was elaborating his teachings on sexuality in general, referring to the biblical "Law of Love." Berg emphasized a doctrine of positive sexuality—he considered the credo that "sex is sin" a false doctrine. He argued that the Law of Love supersedes all other laws. Using the parable of the good Samaritan, he taught that love and compassion must be put into action. And the greatest manifestation of love is the sharing of the self (Melton 1994b: 77). Over time the Family's Law of Love came to teach that love could cross such boundaries as marriage; spouses, if willing, should share one another with others "in need." Aside from FF-ing, there was also sexual sharing within many Family homes and communities.[21]

The perception of the Family in middle-class Anglo-Saxon North America was not favorable, and this eventually informed the perception in other countries where the Family had a presence. The fervently millennial and evangelical attitude of the followers, and their negative attitude to society, did not leave them with many friends in the wider community. The FF-ing ministry made matters worse. Female members were often described as "hookers for Jesus," "prostitutes for Christ," and other such terms. The group was generally described as a "sex cult."[22]

The Family Federation for World Peace and Unification

The Family Federation for World Peace and Unification was formerly known as the Holy Spirit Association for the Unification of World Christianity, and members were often referred to as "Moonies," after the name of the Korean founder and leader, the late Reverend Sun Myung Moon (1920–2012). I shall use the more familiar terms "Unificationists" and "Unification Church" (UC). The movement was founded in 1954 in South Korea, and in the early 1970s Moon and his wife moved to the United States, where the UC became one of the new religions with the highest profile throughout the West (Barker 1995c: 223). Over time the UC has developed into an organization with many subsidiaries and projects, including educational institutions (from school to university postgraduate level), political organizations, and businesses, as well as valuable property. These institutions and businesses are propelled by the internationalism of the UC, which stresses "unification" of the world. In 1982 Moon was convicted of conspiracy to evade taxes and sent to prison. After his release, he spent most of his time in the East and the United States, because he was banned from entering the United Kingdom and all the nations participating in the Schengen Agreement, which reduced border controls between participating European countries. In 2005, however, Moon was allowed to visit the United Kingdom for twenty-four hours, and a few other Schengen states, and as of 2007 the ban was lifted in several countries. Membership estimates range between 250,000 and over 4 million followers worldwide (of which 10,000 are said to be in Western nations).[23] Toward the end of his life, Moon began involving his children more in leadership positions, which has been followed by reports of internal disputes and rivalries.

To his followers, the Reverend Sun Myung Moon was the messiah. Moon's teachings have been compiled by followers in the *Divine Principle*, which argues that Adam and Eve were meant to establish a God-centered family. Yet Lucifer seduced Eve, who in turn physically seduced Adam; they "fell from grace." From then on, according to the UC, all children have been born with what Moon referred to as "fallen nature," which is a state of being resulting from a "Lucifer-centered" union as opposed to a "God-centered" union. For Unificationists, purity before marriage is very important, and adultery is the most horrendous sin among human beings—it is at the root of all sinfulness (Fichter 1985: 30). Eve's transgression with Lucifer has enabled him to hold sovereignty over this world, rather than God. Jesus was meant to restore the world according to God's plan, but he was killed before he was able to marry, hence he could not restore the Kingdom of Heaven on earth. Unificationists believe that Moon was the messiah who has managed to lay the foundation for the restoration of the "Kingdom of Heaven" on earth through his marriage in 1960 (Barker 1995c: 224). Marriage and family are seen as the keys to salvation. For the first generation of converts, the most important ritual was to be "matched" to a partner by Moon, after which a "blessing" would take place. This was seen as the only way in which eventually fallen nature could be eradicated (in mass wedding ceremonies that could involve thousands of couples). Preceding the blessing there is a "holy wine" ceremony, during which, it is believed, the matched couples' bloodline is purified, enabling them to bear children untainted by fallen nature (Barker 1995c: 225). After the blessing ceremony the couples often separate in order to continue their church activities; this used to be for several years, although over time this separation period has shortened. Once the couple is reunited, more rituals follow in order to ensure that the wife will give birth to so-called blessed children. This includes a three-day ceremony starting on the night the marriage is consummated, which includes prescribed sexual positions that are meant to symbolically expunge the devil and re-create a God-centered family.

The importance of the blessing carries through to the next generation of blessed children, who have the task of continuing building on the foundation to the Kingdom of God laid down by their parents. This means that a Unificationist "sister" can only marry a Unificationist "brother."[24] The movement is considered to be one big unified family, and blessed children must marry within the movement so as not to break down this foundation to God's Kingdom created by Moon's blessings. Moon's plan was salvation through the creation of God-centered families, where a perfect relationship with God helps to establish a perfect relationship between husband and wife, and then between parents and children (Fichter 1985).[25] There were certain requirements before a couple could be blessed in marriage. The first-generation converts were generally required to have been members for at least three years, and to have each recruited three new members ("spiritual children") to the church.[26] Also, a required financial contribution to the "indemnity fund" was necessary. Indemnity is a very important concept within Unification theology. The belief behind it is that all of humanity shares in the debt owed for the fall of mankind and the betrayal of Jesus, and all must pay, spiritually, for this collective sin. But a good deed can cancel the debt; hence this payment can be done through good, sacrificial deeds. But different value is bestowed on deeds depending on the actor. Indemnity, according to Moon, is the result of an event that happened between three individuals—but not all bear equal responsibility. Lucifer seduced Eve, but Eve in turn seduced Adam. As a result of this causal dynamic, Eve bears more responsibility than Adam. This resulting asymmetrical responsibility continues throughout history. Cain and Abel, for example, were in mirror positions of good and evil. Cain should, according to Moon, have fulfilled the indemnity condition and removed the fallen nature; he should have humbled himself to Abel. Instead, he killed Abel, and thus allowed the condition to continue.[27] This lopsided relationship is represented between individuals, groups, nations, states, and political positions and between the physical and the spiritual. Women have to pay more indemnity than men, (former) communist states more than noncommunist states (the former are seen as Satan-led and antonyms to Moon's ideal of heaven on earth), and humanity has to pay indemnity toward the spiritual realm (mankind has failed to achieve spiritual salvation).[28] For Moon's followers, paying indemnity, one's own as well as the indemnity for others' misdeeds, is a contribution to the restoration of the Kingdom of Heaven on earth.

Largely because of the variety of businesses, Moon's alleged wealth, and other accusations by the media and anticult groups regarding the church's recruitment methods and the supposed brainwashing of members, the

UC has been very controversial. Individual rank-and-file members were often seen as victims, recruited into a corrupt organization involved in illegal behavior such as, for example, weapons manufacturing.[29] Not only did many Christians have difficulty accepting Moon's interpretation of biblical history, many Western Christians had difficulty imagining the messiah as a Korean man. Friends and relatives of members and former members have also found it difficult to accept Moon's large and wealthy empire (much emphasized by the media) compared to the relative poverty of rank-and-file members. Most governments remained wary of receiving him, and closely monitored the expansion of his domain.[30]

The International Society for Krishna Consciousness

A. C. Bhaktivedanta Swami Prabhupada (1896–1977) brought the International Society for Krishna Consciousness (ISKCON) to the United States from India in 1965 and to London in 1969. Srila Prabhupada, as his followers called him, had founded a worldwide movement within a decade of starting the first temple in New York City. In 2002 the group claimed to have approximately 10,000 temple devotees and 250,000 congregational devotees, 350 centers, and 60 rural communities worldwide.[31] ISKCON eventually began attracting followers from immigrant Indian backgrounds, and its membership stabilized, with peaks of attendance at its temples during religious festivals. The movement has its roots in the fifteenth-century Krishna Bhakti (devotional) movement founded by Sri Caitanya Mahaprabhu (1486–1534), who had revived a devotional form of Hinduism, emphasizing that love and service to God were the means through which one could gain spiritual realization (Goswami in Gelberg 1983; Rochford 1995: 216). Caitanya, and later his followers, considered Krishna the supreme manifestation of God, instead of seeing him as one of many gods. Caitanya preached that all people, regardless of their caste or station in life, could be self-realized through their activities performed in the service of Krishna. This was a major split from other forms of Hinduism (Rochford 1995: 216). Caitanya also introduced another practice, *sankirtan*, for which ISKCON has become notorious:[32] "Growing out of his intense religious passion, Caitanya initiated *sankirtana*, a practice requiring his followers to venture out into the streets to dance and sing their praises of Lord Krishna. When Prabhupada began his movement in America, *sankirtana* (preaching, book distribution, and chanting in public) became the principal means of spreading Krishna Consciousness" (Rochford 1995: 216). According to Prabhupada, devotion to Krishna and sankirtan were imperative for devotees to reach their goal: to escape the cycle of rebirth and return to Godhead.[33] In order to avoid the material world and return to Godhead devotees must escape the laws of karma, by controlling their senses and perfecting their spiritual lives. Devotees commit themselves to chanting the *Hare Krishna* mantra daily (*Hare Krishna, Hare Krishna, Krishna Krishna, Hare Hare, Hare Rama, Hare Rama, Rama Rama, Hare Hare*) with a string of 108 prayer beads, called *japa* beads (one mantra per bead, sixteen rounds per day) and living a life of devotion. This devotion includes a specific dress code, following a special diet (no meat or foods that are considered to tantalize the senses, or that grow in shadow or darkness, such as mushrooms), and abstaining from alcohol, drugs, caffeine, and gambling. Devotees should also abstain from sex, except for procreation within marriage.

The life of ritual and devotion is crucial to achieving Krishna consciousness. The chanting and worship of the deities can actively raise one toward Godhead, and keep the devotee from maya, illusion, the soul being misled by matter and, consequently, entrapped.[34] Such devotion might take someone from the world of the "conditioned souls" to the world of the liberated entities. Followers believe that the soul transmigrates through millions of bodily forms on its way toward perfection. It is only those who have attained Krishna consciousness who are truly liberated, and no longer subject to continual reincarnation (in human or animal forms). Likewise, the universe passes through different stages, *yugas*. The universe in its various stages will last for 4 billion, 300 million years. When it comes to an end, all creation (including hundreds of thousands of universes) is inhaled back into the body of Vishnu (an expansion of Krishna), and reborn with Vishnu's next breath. At present, according to ISKCON, we are in the *Kali yuga*, the *yuga* of death and destruction. Followers are taught that Krishna has shown a special mercy by entering this world in the shape of Caitanya Mahaprabhu—and human beings have received the rare opportunity to attain spiritual fulfillment despite being in such a destructive age.

For most Western countries during the 1960s, this was a new message, hence ISKCON stood out. Likewise, devotees stood out because of their dress and style of worship, and the practice of sankirtan brought them into the public eye. At the time the general public was wary of new religions, which it considered to be cultic. Cults were perceived to be a challenge to churches, the state, family life, and the general well-being of individuals.[35] ISKCON, especially, being an exotic import and espousing an unusual lifestyle, was treated with apprehension. Guru-disciple relations were regarded with suspicion, especially when some gurus within ISKCON started abusing their positions of power and involved themselves with sexual misconduct, drug dealing, and in one case, murder (Muster 1997). Yet ISKCON was attractive to many people, who were generally young, dissatisfied with society, and ready to turn their backs on it and embrace something new. They were ready to devote their lives to Krishna, and did so with fervor.[36]

Sects and Children

The generation of firstborns within the sectarian community is often considered a special milestone by parents and religious leaders, and a reason for structural changes aimed at increasing protection of this new generation by keeping out negative influences while holding in positive ones. Of course this sentiment is shared by most parents, whether they are part of a sectarian community or not. Yet for a sectarian group the birth of a new generation can greatly affect the sect's previous priorities and lifestyle as parents have to divide their time, energy, and resources.[37] The lifestyle of young revolutionaries with relatively few responsibilities is different from that of parents who need to provide for children. It is likely that they will need to alter the previously manufactured environment to make it appropriate for children. Groups might even find they need to reevaluate certain beliefs and practices. The ways in which sectarian groups adapt to this change, and the degree to which they do so, depends on how they choose to combine their new responsibilities with their previous priorities. How these priorities are juggled depends on the way in which the new generation is regarded. Children might be perceived to have a special and doctrinal importance, or an intrinsic importance. In most cases they are thought to be different from "other" children—this difference may result from prophecy, by association, by birth location, or even by biology. Hence one can distinguish between doctrinal importance bestowed on children (i.e., they are deemed special as a result of a prophecy, perceived biblical parallels, assigned spiritual roles, and so forth) and intrinsic importance (i.e., they are deemed essentially special—biologically rather than spiritually). Such distinctions are found within sects as well as within other religious collectivities; however, for sectarian communities such beliefs are likely to affect the entire community and culture, as individual nuclear families within the larger communal structure are more likely to share ideas and ideals and mutually reinforce these on a daily basis.

Children of the Millennium

For Christian-inspired millennial groups the doctrinal importance bestowed on children is likely to revolve around the return of Jesus. The parents in the Family, for example, believed their children were special because they were the last generation to be born before the return of Christ, a chosen generation—God's anointed children. They believed Jesus's return was imminent, and saw their children as harbingers of events to come. This was intensified when Maria, Berg's common-law wife, had children—Davidito and Techi were depicted in the Family's literature as having a millenarian role in the group's apocalyptic expectations (Palmer 1994: 16). Berg and Maria believed that Davidito and Techi would lead the group's other children as rulers during the millennium. Children in the Family are raised in preparation for the spiritual battle the group believes will take place when Jesus returns. No matter where they are in the world, the children are taught that they will be his helpers, fighting alongside him with newly developed supernatural powers. Interestingly, during the millennium their doctrinal importance will develop into an intrinsic one as well, according to the teachings, as their biological bodies change for the occasion. Many believe they will learn how to fly and walk through walls—they will consist of pure energy. Their task will be to rebuild the world after the great battle. The Family's children will be the judges and kings over the people who were saved.[38] They have been raised as the "end-time teens," revolutionaries for Jesus, and generally believe they have a very important role to play in the future of the world. They believe they are spiritually advanced.[39]

The children in the Bruderhof are considered to be special for doctrinal reasons as well—in this case connected to the place and circumstance in which they were born. Born within community, in the spirit of the Sermon on the Mount, they are referred to as the *sabra* youth, like the children born in the State of Israel. The term "sabra" is derived from the Hebrew word for the prickly pear (a cactus fruit) and was used by the Zionist movement to describe the "new Jews" born in Israel—the native-born rather than the immigrants. Similarly, Bruderhof members believe that their children form a new and special generation, as they were born in the right circumstances, within a peaceful community. They might still stray, but their brethren will be there to put them back on track. Hence during the Great Crisis, the sabras were allowed to stay, whereas many of their parents were expelled. The sabras are special, and they need to be spared from outside influences considered to be detrimental to their character by the Bruderhof.

This is similar for the children in ISKCON and Scientology's Sea Org. In the case of the former, children can be guarded from maya. Prabhupada (1978: 10) taught his devotees that all people are born in Krishna consciousness; it is external interference from our lives, which are filled with material concerns, which muddy the clear waters of the soul. If you filter all the mud out of the water, it again becomes clear and transparent. And if you separate the mud from the clear water to begin with, filtering it will not be necessary. Hence the children would retain their Krishna consciousness as long as they were raised in an environment conducive to the required lifestyle and practice. The children born to Sea Org members in Scientology do not have a comparative spiritual staring point to those born in ISKCON; they aren't born "clear." However, children raised in Scientology are believed (by followers) to be at a significant advantage, being raised with Hubbard's "study tech" (a methodology of learning developed by Hubbard) and kept from "wog material"—"wog" is a term used to describe non-Scientologists and is generally used in a derogatory way for those who reject the Scientology methods.[40] Little cadets have their own school, and their curriculum consists mainly of Hubbard's study tech. In other cases Scientology children also have the opportunity to go to schools that have leased Scientology's Applied Scholastics for use in the classroom. John Atack (1990: 392), a former member who wrote a book outlining the history of Hubbard's rise, Dianetics, and the Scientology organization, argues that Scientologists consider it good practice for these children to learn to interact with non-Scientology children; they are trained to become world leaders, and at the same time they gain experience in dealing with so-called wogs.

The New Children

For some religious groups the exceptional nature of their children surpasses doctrine and circumstance; they see their children as inherently special. The holy wine ceremony in the Unification Church allegedly clears the bloodline of the parents, so that the children are born blessed—without fallen nature. Not only have they been born without fallen nature, they also appear to have, or at least are meant to have, other special abilities. According to Moon, his children Hyo Jin, Ye Jin, and Eun Jin have spiritual abilities and strong premonitions that are innate. Moon (1998: 25) claimed that if children are born with such gifts on a "good foundation" and use them limitlessly, these gifts will develop infinitely. In Moon's own terms:

Knowing that you were born on such a foundation of the Unification Church, you should, before your father and mother have thought of it, decide the way you want to go by the age of ten or twenty. If you have such a resolve, even though you may go in a different direction, your body will turn towards the proper way. Everything will be guided. For example, although you are sleeping facing the east and thinking to go east the next morning, if it is wrong to go east your body will turn toward the south. Your body itself knows that. It is very sensitive. Do you understand what I mean? If you do not reach such a level, you cannot be a great leader in the future. Accordingly, you would not be able to stand in front of me and fulfil the mission as responsible persons of the second generation. The time will come when your spiritual level will be evaluated automatically. It is gradually coming closer. Among ten people in a village, three people will have spiritual power. They will all know what the others are thinking. You should know that this time will come. Therefore, now you must have the right attitude and devote yourselves. (1998: 22)

Children within the UC who are not from blessed parents, hence are not blessed themselves, allegedly do not have these qualities—this is a significant distinction. Moon is not alone in his belief in the spiritual abilities of his children. As mentioned previously, the children in the Family will allegedly have similar spiritual abilities, if not further developed ones, after the return of Jesus.[41]

Parents tend to think their child is special, but in some sects and parts of the cultic milieu such beliefs are viewed through a framework of doctrines and worldviews that is atypical. Children in the Family are taught that they will develop supernatural powers and abilities that will help them once they become soldiers for Christ. Blessed children are taught they are free from fallen nature. They are children born within the paradigm of their parents. Such beliefs are likely to affect the childhoods and socialization of the new generations born into these sects and spiritual communities. The beliefs that these children are special, and different from other children, may have significant consequences in sectarian communities that are unlikely to arise in nonsectarian collectivities. In sectarian communities parents and religious leaders are more likely to manufacture an environment where they can control the socializing forces and set their children apart from potentially negative peer influences and teachings they consider harmful. This is reminiscent of Douglas's (1966) symbolic interpretation of dirt and rules surrounding hygiene described in *Purity and Danger*, where she concluded that all societies classify the world around them and assign as social taboos those things and concepts considered to be challenging established boundaries. Similarly, some sects organize themselves in ways to keep "clean" and away from polluting influences—especially those polluting influences most dangerous to them. Some sects aim for a relatively high level of protection for their children, consequently tightly managing their insertion into society. Their sectarianism is purposeful. Sects aim to establish their own cultural identity, cultural codes and identity spaces independent of, and often resistant to, dominant cultural codes, and structures.[42] I aimed to identify sects that manufactured an environment conducive to the socialization of their special children and, in a sense, constructed childhoods and socializations for their purposes. The influence on their followers has been profound, and the influence on their children even more so.

Establishing Priorities

Among sectarian groups there is a wide range of attitudes to children; some groups see all children as gifts from God, others are celibate and urge members to renounce family ties and any form of dependency. Yet this does not mean that groups that practice celibacy will not have a next generation; children can be adopted, or the importance of celibacy can be questioned in light of the continuation of the group. For example, the Oneida Perfectionists and Ananda Marga changed to incorporate a second generation.[43] The leader of the Oneida Perfectionists changed his mind on celibacy and the group moved to a system of sexual sharing, enabling some couples to have children according to a system of eugenics specified by him. Celibacy proved to be a temporary practice as other issues, such as sexual sharing and a second generation, became more important. Some Ananda Margis remain celibate, and in some countries the group runs orphanages and raises the children as members. Krishna devotees can be celibate, be married, or return to celibacy after having children. Devotees generally aim to progress through four life stages, or *ashramas*, according to Hindu tradition. They begin their devotional paths as *brahmacharyas*, students in an apprenticeship focused on celibacy and character building within the context of their spiritual path. In the second stage the devotee marries and becomes a "householder," *grihasta*. The third stage, *vanaprastha*, involves gradual withdrawal from family life (once the children have reached the appropriate age) and retirement into solitary life—it is seen as a gradual withdrawal from the "egotistic" life of the student and the householder, both seen to involve levels of indulgence. The fourth stage, when achieved, takes the devotee to a life of renunciation, *sannyas*. This renunciate is a monk who has taken vows to denounce material goods in favor of spiritual gain. Men and women can also choose to proceed from the first stage directly to the fourth stage. During the early years in ISKCON, devotees were by and large *brahmacharyas*, devoted to a life of celibacy.[44] Prabhupada, at the time, clearly thought this was preferable to marriage, which he described as the appropriate option for those who could not ignore their desires (Rochford 1997).

Scientology also has a clear standard of priorities for its Sea Org members, who must leave the organization when they have children, but can rejoin once the child decides to join as well—or once the child has reached adulthood. These premises are in stark contrast to groups that completely involve the children in the day-to-day life of the community, such as, for example, the Family and the Bruderhof. However, the integration of children, or their perceived doctrinal importance, does not necessarily mean that these children will become the group's priority. Even when children are considered to be an important aspect of the group's physical and spiritual future, they can be seen to stand in the way of other priorities—such as self-realization, devotion, political agendas, social work, and so on. But priorities can be juggled and responsibility shared; in a community of like-minded people, resources can be stretched to cover child care as well as other necessary jobs. And this might be seen as beneficial to both parents and children; separation of parent and child might be deemed necessary for a variety of reasons—for a greater good, justifiable in relation to a bigger picture, or perceived as better for the parent, the child, or both. Both parents and children might be perceived to have special needs that should be prioritized, and this perceived need might entail separation from each other. Some groups believe that the parents are a negative influence on their children, and that the children are better off socializing with their peer group, under the supervision of specially trained carers. And parents might have tasks, responsibilities, or predispositions that need to be prioritized over child care.

In the Sullivan Institute, a psychotherapy commune, the question of whether or not to have children, and how to raise them, hinged on psychological issues.[45] Not all members were deemed ready to have children. Parents were seen as having a negative influence on their children—they had to reach a level of maturity before they could procreate, and had to consult with their psychotherapists before doing so (Siskind 1999: 56). True to a Freudian legacy, members believed that mothers usually behave in an "envious and hateful manner towards their children," and, in this more emancipated era, that no parent should be under an obligation to look after a child full-time (56). Hence, for the few who were allowed to have children, there were full-time babysitters. These were sometimes hired from outside, although some members volunteered their time—limited time spent with children, they believed, could help the adult gain insights into his or her own personality and encourage personal growth (56). And for the children, it was thought that the less exposure they had to their parents, the better a child's mental health would be (56).

Whereas in the Sullivan Institute separation of parents and children was encouraged for psychological reasons, in other cases this is encouraged for spiritual reasons. Sri Mataji, the founder of Sahaja Yoga, a movement she started to teach her meditation techniques, recommends that children be sent to one of the Sahaja Yoga schools as early as possible so they can avoid their parents' "vibrational problems."[46] Similarly, Osho, a spiritual teacher who founded communes in India and the United States, taught that the nuclear family was the main corrupting influence in life, followed by schools and churches.[47] Elizabeth Puttick has selected from several of Osho's writings:

> With all good intentions, all parents are murderers of their own children. You see all over the world only dead people walking, who have lost their souls even before they had any notion of what it is.... The most outdated thing is the family. It has done its work, it is no more needed. In fact, now it is the most hindering phenomenon for human progress.... The family is the root cause of all our neurosis. (1999: 90)

Such attitudes are in stark contrast to the perceived importance of family values as put forward by many mainstream religious groups and, indeed, other sects, such as the Bruderhof. Yet despite their marginal and alternative position vis-à-vis the Western cultural acceptance of the nuclear family, alternative child-rearing philosophies can be very important to the functioning of a sectarian community. Aside from the psychological and spiritual reasons mentioned above, there can be significant ideological or economic reasons. For example, in the early kibbutzim the children spent a significant amount of time apart from the parents, and this was perceived to be beneficial for both parties. The parents could do their work, and the children could grow up without what was perceived as "interference" from their parents. The commitment to the ideal of communal work and ownership in the early kibbutzim extended to communal upbringing of the children. It was strongly believed that the bourgeois family was at the root of individualistic impulses and that communal child rearing would inculcate cooperative and communal values. There was, however, a strong economic basis as well: with communal child care most parents would be freed to work. Furthermore, the children would not be economically attached to the parents, freeing them emotionally as well as structurally. There were also egalitarian reasons; the sharing of child care is crucial to the involvement of women as participants in the "building of the dream." Indeed, the kibbutzniks believed that equally sharing all work engenders equality.[48]

Any beliefs regarding what is best either for the child or the parent's spiritual path (or both), however, must tie in with a more material reality of what is actually possible and realistic—the structural resources have to underpin the psychological and spiritual demands. Separating children from the parents requires alternative child care, as does involving mothers in day-to-day work. Offering day-long parental guidance, in turn, requires alternative resources, as the caretakers will not be partaking full-time in other tasks necessary for the community. These are similar issues to the ones faced by all families where both parents work, throughout society. Yet in this case the issues must be solved within communities that are often trying to "reinvent the wheel" and improve on the existing social systems. In communities efforts can be pooled, making more resources available to the members—although this usually involves the shifting of priorities and existing resources.

Parents and sects have to weigh their priorities regarding their child-rearing philosophies (and how these match with those available in the mainstream), as well as the available resources necessary for child rearing, the group's needs, and members' spiritual paths. Sectarian groups generally aim to have control over the socializing influences their children encounter—after all, the sectarian stance results from dissatisfaction with society and its hegemonic cultures, and sects are concerned with the production, maintenance, and transmission of distinctive beliefs. They adapt their social boundaries to strike a balance between keeping in the "good" while blocking out the "bad." Hence groups might need to focus on teaching children special practices, training them in certain skills, and passing on to them specific norms and values that are not generally part of the "outside" socialization process. At the same time, groups might aim to keep their children safe from perceived danger associated with outside institutions or influences. For example, Prabhupada considered outside schools to be "slaughterhouses for children," teaching them sense gratification rather than the necessary practices to reach Krishna consciousness (Goswami 1984). Prabhupada was troubled by the sense gratification pervasive in society, hence he created the *gurukulas*, where the children could grow up untainted by maya and taught a Krishnaized curriculum.[49] There are many other groups (as well as individuals) who refuse to send their children to schools, because they are troubled by the information floating freely within society, the techniques or the technology used in schools, the other socializing forces, and many other reasons. Depending on the beliefs and preferences of the parents, there are usually a variety of other options available. Examples are Montessori education and Waldorf Steiner schools, which both offer a more child-centered approach as an alternative to "mainstream" education.[50] Children of Scientology parents might attend a school that uses Applied Scholastics, and cadets, children of Sea Org members, have their own schools. There they can be taught using Hubbard's tech, while "wog material" can be censored. The Bruderhof in the past offered primary education within its community, but for secondary education some communities would send the children by bus to state schools. After school these children were picked up again and driven back to the community. Over time the communities developed their own schools through to secondary education.[51] The Amish send their children to school until the age of twelve, either state schools or their own, depending on the resources available, after which the young members are taught the skills they need for life in the community. Similarly, the Family chose to homeschool and bring its children along to the mission field, where they would simultaneously be trained in the skills necessary for missionary and community life. Sectarian groups do form a physical community, and tend to create special structures in order to direct, as much as possible, the socialization of their children. However, the integration of children into the existing social structure of the group has to be balanced with other priorities. The children might be desirable and welcome, but not necessarily easily integrated; and the parents might have to make important decisions as to how the priorities will be balanced. The ease of the integration of children into the group's lifestyle depends on the structure of the group as well as its resources.

The Advantages of Communalism

Communal life can have many advantages; the pooling of efforts and energy maximizes resources. If a few people look after all the children, the others can work and raise funds—this division of labor makes sense economically. Many are the ways, however, in which labor can be divided. These ways are generally determined by the group's beliefs and subsequent attitudes to gender, sexuality, marriage, and ethnicity, as well as the authority structure in which such beliefs are translated into practice. A strong authoritarian and top-down decision-making process leaves little room for individual variation of doctrinal interpretation and practice. This is especially the case with small sects.

The extent to which sexuality is regulated in sects has a strong influence on the ways in which men and women coexist within the community, and where the children will fit in. However, attitude to gender and sexuality, usually deeply embedded in the group's worldview and philosophy, is often part of the group's attraction. Someone who is attracted to the idea of renouncing material desires in exchange for salvation, for instance, is not likely to be surprised by the concept of overcoming physical desire along the way. A person who joins a group where racial identity is entrenched in the doctrine and teachings will probably expect certain social attitudes. And a person who joins a revolutionary group with the aim of helping to break down the established social order might also embrace opportunities to break down other social norms and personal boundaries. Rosabeth Moss Kanter, whose current work at Harvard Business School focuses on the transformation of major institutions, began her career analyzing communes and how they create and manage their collective life (1972, 1973). In *Commitment and Community: Communes and Utopias in Sociological Perspective* (1972) she described communes as social laboratories, experimental places where the rules of engagement could be changed. There is ample evidence that members of sectarian communities are prepared to lead personal lives in line with what they perceive to be a greater good. For example, Stuart Wright (1986) has documented cases where followers married, separated, or divorced following the desires of the leader. Inhabitants of the Oneida Community switched from celibacy to a system of organized sexual sharing once the leader declared that this was for the general well-being of the community (Kephart 1982). Members of the Family have seen the rules of the Law of Love change quite dramatically over the last three decades. Rules regarding sexuality are not set in stone, although they do tend to remain within certain parameters—the perceived similarities and differences between men and women.

The regulation of couplings and sexuality is based on attitudes to gender and theories of the nature of interaction between men and women.[52] Such attitudes to gender and sexuality are important to understand a group's division of labor. The early kibbutzim, egalitarian and often socialist communes, were adamant that women should share equally in the labor. In the UC and the Family, women partake in missionary work and provisioning (Family) or fund-raising (UC) as much as the men do, although with their own specialties—under the assumption that men and women are "different but equal."[53] In the Bruderhof, labor is divided according to traditional lines with women as homemakers and men in charge of the manual labor—their work considered different but equally important. These relationship dynamics between the members, and between the members and the leadership, as well as the resulting division of labor, are necessary background information for understanding how community dynamics influence the choice of primary caretaker: mother, father, both, or neither. Top-down, a system of relationships and a hierarchy of priorities are decided, and the children are integrated into the resulting social structure accordingly. This structure, in a sense, channels the socializing forces. The leadership prescribes the structure of relationships and the division of labor. The next important question then is: from where do the resources come?

The critical stance sects tend to have toward society often involves a resistance to participation, hence a resistance to mixing in it and contributing to it through secular work, at least for the core members.[54] Most religious traditions have a core of renunciates, or religious professionals, for whom adherence and religious practice is a full-time occupation. This adherence and practice can involve full-time work within the movement, through, for example, fund-raising or administration. Within Scientology one can distinguish (at a basic level) between clients who pay for courses and buy some of the materials and merchandise and Sea Org members, who have chosen to devote their lives to the organization and have signed a contract extending well beyond their biological life span. The latter work for Scientology full-time, live in community with other Sea Org members, and have their primary needs (housing, food, etc.) met by Scientology. For many sectarian groups, however, especially new groups consisting mostly of first-generation converts, renouncing secular jobs can be a requisite to joining—a sign of belief and devotion as well as a political message to the wider society. ISKCON's monks and nuns have to be in the temple and practice *bhakti* devotion several times throughout the day, as well as practicing sankirtan. The latter is part of their devotion, and it also forms a substantial part of the temple's income. Similarly, fund-raising is an important part of the lifestyle of members of the Unification Church; and it has its spiritual uses as well—through fund-raising a member can pay off some of the indemnity he or she might carry. For members of the Family dropping out of the system included not being tied to that system through material means. They could accept gifts and donations, but generally did not have salaried jobs.[55] Hence provisioning had practically become a full-time occupation, with each home having a few people who specialized in providing the household with donated goods, and, ideally, also sending some to other homes in the mission field. These donated goods ranged from food to clothes, furniture, and machinery to money. The Family has been known to arrange, through provisioning, hospital equipment or other necessities for third-world countries. Despite the financial uncertainty for the group that comes with having to rely on fund-raising and provisioning, there was some security for the individual in knowing that the community would provide (aside from the belief that God will provide). This is especially the case for members of the Bruderhof. They have handed over all possessions to the community upon joining, and it becomes the responsibility of the community as a whole to provide for its brethren. Community life provides a sense of security not only on a material level, as mentioned above, but also on a social level. For example, in Family homes there was always someone in charge of the children while other adults would go out witnessing, "litnessing" (witnessing through the use of literature), and provisioning. Especially when the Family had large communities, sometimes consisting of over two hundred members, there was organized child care. Both ISKCON and Scientology have organized child care and schooling while the parents take care of their responsibilities.[56]

Groups and Adjustments

Theoretical frameworks mentioned at the start of this chapter that outline distinctions between, to use Mary Douglas's (1970) language, group and grid structures are useful for identifying significant structural differences between sects and other collectivities where religious beliefs provide a prism through which to interpret events and organize one's life. As a result of their group structure the sectarian groups had to adjust on a variety of levels to integrate their children within the ideological and spiritual framework, yet do it without sacrificing core beliefs and practices. The perceived importance of the children directs where the children will be located within the structure of the group. The Bruderhof integrate the children into community life and the ethic of the Sermon on the Mount, which is facilitated by their communal structure in which resources and responsibilities are shared. The first generation of children was easily integrated, both into the parents' homes and into the hofs, without undue disruption to previous institutional habits.[57] The Family integrated members' children into the missionary lifestyle from a young age, making them part of witnessing, which often happened through song and dance. When the first generation of children was born, child care and other necessities were incorporated with relative ease as the lifestyle of the members had been flexible.[58] For the Family and the Bruderhof, children are considered "gifts from God." For the Unification Church, they are believed to be a special and atypical generation. In all three cases, they were doctrinally important. For the Unification Church, however, there was another dimension, as salvation hinges on these children—they had a special role. However, in practice the first generation of children born into the movement was not always an immediate priority in the sense that other priorities continued to be of high importance and parents had to juggle them. Moon appeared to put equal importance on fund-raising and missions to reduce indemnity and to build the Kingdom of God, and parents were often called to leave their children in the hands of other community members for such missions. Consequently the children were not completely integrated into the movement's everyday life; rather there was a division of labor where some members concentrated on long-term missions while their spouses or other families concentrated on child care. For Scientology's Sea Org and ISKCON, the children were neither doctrinally important (for the salvation of the parents or the continuation of the community—it still relied heavily on converts) nor a priority. In fact, in both cases the sects' leadership seemed reluctant about the presence of children. As a result, the children never completely integrated within the day-to-day life of the community. Special structures were created for them, quite separate from the life of the adult practitioners. This was possible with the group's resources, and was not very challenging to the overall group structure.

This book focuses on the groups that have chosen to reinvent the wheel, as it were, and create new childhoods for their special children. These groups, as a result of their decisions, have increased their sectarianism in order to accommodate their new generation in new and special ways. Yet attitudes to the second generation, and the resultant integration of the children, are not static. The interplay between society, sects, and their children creates an environment of pushes and pulls which are potent sources of change. Chapters 2 and 3 analyze these changes.

2

Leadership and Discipline

THIS CHAPTER ILLUSTRATES the discussion of change with reference to the leadership of several sects and the decisions made regarding each group's priorities, its mission, and the raising of children. I focus on challenges encountered in the disciplining practices of some groups, and the changes they made, or resisted making. But first I discuss, in brief, leadership structures. A sect's leadership structure is likely to predispose the group's attitude toward change or stasis; whether there is a charismatic leadership or reverence to a particular tradition is a significant variable.

Changes over Time

Over time, groups often find they have to make a choice: adapt to the new generation and its associated responsibilities at the cost of some aspects of their current lifestyle (such as religious practices, rituals, and missions considered essential to achieving spiritual goals) or hold on to their traditional ways and aim to minimize the impact of the new generation. These choices are crucial to first-generation movements, whose initial structure generally does not involve children. When adapting the structure and culture of the community to children, groups risk alienating some of the founding members, who might believe the group is losing its initial vision and revolutionary ethos. The group's choice—change or stasis—is likely to depend on a number of factors, such as the group's social organization, resources, tradition, beliefs, and worldview. Whichever path the group follows, the result will alter the dynamics, changing the group's modes of insertion (to use Beckford's phrasing) within society as well as the internal relations between the founding members and the second generation.

Authority structures have their social and organizational consequences; as Max Weber argued, charismatic authority is inherently unstable compared to other authority structures, because of its lack of tradition and reliance on a single authority figure. The charismatic leader has not been elected as a result of proven expertise through training or examination, nor is that leader a successor in a traditional line of rulers—the charismatic leader can stand independent of tradition and official recognition. This leader is accepted by followers because of a perceived special nature, talents, or skills, or a so-called gift of grace (Gerth and Mills 1946: 245–50). As a result, this leader's legitimacy is unbounded by tradition and norms. Traditional authority, on the other hand, relies on preexisting structures and a history of rules, hence is likely to be more rigid (Gerth and Mills 1946). There is a precedent that directs the way things are done.

Charismatic Leadership and Change

New religions and sectarian groups are more likely to have charismatic leaders, and as a result they tend to be more inclined to change (Barker 1995a). Consequently changes within new religions and sectarian groups can occur within a relatively short time compared to more institutionalized and established religions. Possibly the largest catalyst to change is the birth of the second generation (Barker 1995a). Sectarian communities, or "laboratories for social experiments," as Kanter saw them (1972), often aspire to a lifestyle that is new, different, or "pure": an alternative to the status quo of the mainstream. An environment of social experimentation among consenting adults is a different matter, however, from one that includes minors. In the latter scenario a process of "trial and error," through social experimentation and attempts to reinvent the wheel pedagogically, may have a developmental impact with altogether more significant consequences.[1] Consenting adults require relatively little guidance; minors require someone to take responsibility for their social, pedagogical, emotional, and medical care, among other things. Hence social experiments are often reconsidered in the light of different responsibilities; rituals are adapted and practices altered. But this process of change is vulnerable to a number of dynamics, such as competing priorities and possibly resistance from the initial religious avant-garde (who will eventually become the *arrière-garde* to the maturing second generation).

Followers of Sun Myung Moon regard him as the Messiah. Although he placed himself in the Christian tradition, following in the footsteps of Jesus, his message and doctrine are strongly based on personal interpretation rather than generally and historically accepted Christian tradition. Discredited by the majority of Christian churches, Moon can be considered a charismatic leader within a tradition he created. And as the spiritual father to his followers, he decided on the movement's general course of action.[2]

This, however, has not always been a straight course, but rather one where Moon appeared to be changing the focus frequently and rapidly—called by one former member "short-termism."[3] The 1970s and 1980s were a time of large-scale outreach on a global level, with groups of members moving to different countries and spreading the message in a very open and public manner. The movement was largely communal; most members lived together in the centers where they enjoyed mutual support, as well as the sharing of resources and child-care responsibilities for the first cohort of children. But in the early 1990s Moon decided to change the focus from the global level to the family level, and started the "Hometown Providence." Members were urged to go back to their hometowns and convert their own family and childhood community. As a result, members moved away from the centers where they had emotional and structural support from fellow members to live closer to their biological families—with whom they often had strained relations after joining what was largely perceived as a "cult." What was supposed to be an exercise in tribal messiahship, a change from a life of service to the world to service with the followers' own family and relatives in order to save their own "tribes" first, often turned out to be a lonely and strenuous task. In many cases, old bridges had been badly burned, and members found themselves isolated and without a support network among family and old friends. Approximately five years after Hometown Providence, followers were introduced to the National Messiahs Providence. Groups consisting of three couples from different nations were sent to countries throughout the world, according to rules of indemnity; one couple from an "Eve nation," one from an "Adam nation," and one from an "Archangel nation."[4] Usually this coupled a Korean couple (who have relatively less indemnity to pay) with couples from Japan and from a Western country (who have relatively more indemnity to pay), who were meant to establish themselves in this new country and remain there for three generations. Many couples who were assigned to be national messiahs did not go, or did not stay, partly because a new plan, revolving around work toward the reunification of Korea, required a number of women to go to Korea for a period of up to three years. As a result the husbands would often remain wherever they could rely on child care. Alongside the major mission changes from global to family level to national messiahs, there were smaller ones that could periodically uproot the members from the conventional kinship structures. Spouses were often sent on separate witnessing missions to different countries, or urged to attend training sessions (lasting for weeks) in Korea for important providential missions. At times when both spouses had to go abroad, children were sent to other families or to a boarding school; the latter often organized special summer programs for the children.

Throughout the 1970s and 1980s, the majority of followers were working for the church full-time. The church, however, did not provide financially for all the members. National leaders, business leaders, and departmental leaders could expect a stipend, but rank-and-file members, including missionaries, were expected to raise funds for the movement as well as for their own day-to-day living costs. As one former member explains: "The ethos was: we are volunteers for building the Kingdom of God, and you don't place a burden on the church."[5] In the early days, when members lived together and shared child care, resources were shared in order that as much time as possible could be given to the mission. But with the Hometown Providence members did not have this extended UC family around them for support. Simultaneously, there was no extended UC network exercising social control. Hence, more followers started looking for work in order to support themselves—especially individuals who did not like the strain and insecurity of fund-raising. "Short-termism" may thus have undermined the stability of the Unificationists by perpetual change, a constantly diffusing focus, and the breaking apart of support structures. Moon's status as a messiah, however, legitimized the constant changes as divinely inspired.

The Power of Traditional Ties

Charismatic groups are not necessarily devoid of traditional ties. But groups with strong traditional ties do tend to be more resistant to change, because of, as Weber wrote, a "piety for what actually, allegedly, or presumably has always existed" (qtd. in Gerth and Mills 1946: 296). Both the Bruderhof and ISKCON, for example, have based their authority structures and beliefs firmly on an existing tradition, and both groups have shown resistance to deviating from their respective traditions.[6] Yet they are not easily pigeonholed, as their development has been paired with a constant tension between charismatic innovation and tradition. ISKCON was brought to the West by Prabhupada, who aimed to transport the old bhakti tradition of Caitanya. Before he died, Prabhupada established a system of eleven regional gurus who would, together with the organizational management of the Governing Body Commission (GBC), continue the spiritual leadership of the movement. Each guru was to be treated with the same respect formerly paid to Prabhupada, and each guru had complete authority over his regional zone—together they were to be the "collective body" of Prabhupada (Muster 1997: 30–31). The guru system had its problems, but it could not easily be changed because followers were reluctant to change Prabhupada's (charismatic) legacy and the gurus, personally selected by Prabhupada, held a lot of power.

The Bruderhof started as a charismatic community under Arnold, but this charisma was routinized through his adoption and incorporation of the Hutterite tradition—he received ordination as a Hutterite minister and aligned his community's practices to those of the Hutterites (Rubin 1993; Oved 1996). In the Bruderhof's authoritarian hierarchy of leadership, following Hutterite tradition, God and the Holy Spirit stand at the top, and they inspire the *Vorsteher*, or bishop, who is the spiritual and administrative leader of all the communities. The *Vorsteher*, as a servant of the Lord, interprets divine mandate and decides on the direction of the global community, as well as internal hierarchy. Each individual community has its own servant of the Word, who acts like the chief executive officer as well as a preacher; he is elected by a consensus of all baptized men. The servant of the Word is assisted by five to seven witness brothers, who act as an administrative council. These include community stewards and controllers as well as foremen of the different work departments and elderly spiritual leaders. In addition to the Hutterite hierarchy, the Bruderhof distinguishes between fully baptized members who enjoy participation in the prayer circles and are allowed to vote, single members who are excluded from certain decisions, and non-decision-making Brotherhood members. The latter are believed to be suffering limitations as a result of old age or physical or emotional impairments (Zablocki 1971: 204). As a result, members in good standing are part of the decision-making process, and members who are not, such as critics and questioning members in the *kleiner* or *grosser Ausschluss*, are excluded from the decision-making process. In a letter quoted in *Torches Rekindled*, Heini Arnold, the son of the founder, asserted: "We are definitely not democratic, since we believe in a King, and our surrender must be without limitation."[7] The Bruderhof leaders believe that all attempts to live in community by human efforts alone will fail; only through the rule of the Holy Spirit can it be achieved.

In the Bruderhof there is a hereditary succession of office; the *Vorstehers* are generally the sons of the leader. After Eberhard Arnold's death in 1935, however, this was not immediately the case; his sons were not in Germany at the time and could not travel for fear of being conscripted into the army. Upon Eberhard's death, his son-in-law Hans Zumpe was installed as servant of the Word, and from this position of leadership Zumpe made changes to the Bruderhof's hierarchy of leadership and relationship with the Hutterites (Oved 1996: 20). The Arnolds protested against this change, but Zumpe's followers accused them of being overly emotional and rigid in their insistence on following in Eberhard's footsteps (20). A few years later, however, Zumpe was deposed by the Hutterite leaders (with whom the Bruderhof was affiliated at the time) and excluded from his community, and other servants of the Lord were installed, including Heini Arnold, by Hutterite leaders in line with their usual authority structure.

The years that followed were marked by disruption and moves; because of the changing regimes in and around prewar Germany the communities were scattered. But the communities were governed under a collective leadership in line with Hutterite methods. The Paraguayan hof, however, was isolated, and the primitive lifestyle significantly different from other hofs; over time, the new generation of members there grew up lacking in the observation of the Hutterite way of life and the general Bruderhof standard of living.[8] Both Heini Arnold and Hans Zumpe were in Paraguay. Heini fell ill and Hans Zumpe was reinstated as servant of the Word. The balance of authority had changed again. A leadership crisis as well as a spiritual crisis ensued, as leading brotherhood members were divided in their allegiances to Arnold and Zumpe—the former believing that the community was moving away from the Hutterite ideals and the latter meting out harsh punishments of exclusion to the dissenters. This was the beginning of the "cold-hearted" versus "warm-hearted" division that eventually led to the Great Crisis, in which Heini (reportedly feeling bitter as a result of his exclusion) accused Zumpe of having moved away from Hutterite principles and the God-led lifestyle and of being, instead, cold-hearted—led by day-to-day responsibilities (and rationalism) rather than spiritual ideals.[9] The rift deepened in the following years as Heini moved to North American communities and Zumpe to Europe, where they both sought to expand the Bruderhof. Since the Great Crisis, the Bruderhof's authority structure changed, with Heini Arnold elected to the office of elder of the entire Bruderhof flock (in line with Hutterite tradition), while Hans Zumpe was in exclusion. Heini Arnold was eventually succeeded by his son Christoph.

Although the Bruderhof leadership has a strong sense of tradition, there are also charismatic elements to the leadership and its decision-making process. One aspect of the rift during the Great Crisis was the perception that parts of the community rejected the (warm-hearted) spiritual legacy created by Eberhard Arnold. The rift between the warm-hearted and the cold-hearted was a top-down initiated purification, an identification and elimination of those considered to be spiritually weak and unfit for Heini Arnold's view of the Christ-centered community—what Julius Rubin (1993), a professor of sociology who has written a number of books and articles on the Bruderhof, refers to as "Heini-ism":[10]

> The members of the Bruderhof institutionalized, by their own account, 'a dictatorship of the Holy Spirit', and a system of religious totalism that requires the undivided loyalty of their members. The concentration of spiritual and political power into an elite leadership group of servants, ever-obsessed with unity, has resulted in the continued and systematic abuse of Church discipline as a political device to expel members, who because of individual conscience, question or oppose community policy. Such persons stand charged with sins of pride, selfishness and egoism, and are said to be motivated by 'the wrong spirit', or to have luke-warm zeal. The abuse of Church discipline as a political tool to stifle dissent or to redirect the movement, as in the periodic crises and purges, most notably the Great Crisis, has marked Bruderhof history. (Rubin 1997: 88–89)

Heini's son, Christoph, who followed in his father's footsteps as *Vorsteher*, also worked toward cooperation and association with the Hutterites, but this failed as the Bruderhof were eventually rejected in 1990 by the more orthodox branch of the Hutterites (who claimed that the Bruderhof communities were modernizing), and as Christoph (in line with charismatic authority) eventually broke with the less orthodox branch of the Hutterites for what he saw as their internal deterioration.[11] The Bruderhof communities still aim to live in Christ-centred community, following the Sermon on the Mount, and they continue to shun those who are not considered to be "living in the spirit." Other traditions that were initially deeply ingrained, however, have been dropped. The Bruderhof's commitment to pacifism has been adjusted since the leadership has chosen to fight its critics through the courts.[12] In several cases this has deepened rifts; and the Bruderhof has acquired a vocal community of detractors since the Great Crisis.[13] Consequently, the communities have built strong social boundaries to protect the children from their detractors, and increased their isolation from the wider community. The communities' modes of insertion into society have changed over time, as they have businesses, charitable organizations, and outreach efforts, and use "outside" courts for legal disputes (decreasing their level of sectarianism) while strictly monitoring social interactions between members and children and "outsiders" (increasing their level of sectarianism).[14]

Modifications in Leadership

Change is inevitable, but in charismatic groups it is likely to arise with greater frequency. David Berg and Sun Myung Moon initiated many changes within their movements. And in a different way, the leadership in the Bruderhof and ISKCON initiated changes in order to hold on to certain parts of a respected tradition—they changed in order to not change. For the Bruderhof this was the Great Crisis in favor of the Arnold legacy and warm-heartedness, for ISKCON they were adjustments (changes nonetheless) in favor of Prabhupada's legacy and the guru tradition. Modifications in leadership are influential on the structure of the group and the decision-making process, practices, and decisions regarding what aspects of doctrine are emphasized or deemphasized. The battle within the Bruderhof to prioritize the perceived warm-hearted Arnold leadership over the cold-hearted Zumpe leadership was achieved at the cost of approximately six hundred members, who were deemed to be in the wrong spirit and exiled. This affected the children and young adults, who generally were kept on, as sabras, to form the base of new communities while their parents were in exclusion. In ISKCON, the guru system was maintained despite the problematic (and in some cases even criminal) behavior of some of the gurus.[15] In helping Prabhupada establish the guru system, the GBC limited its own executive power. The Family also aimed to continue Berg's legacy after his death with minimal changes. When David Berg died, Maria took over as leader of the Family, together with Peter Amsterdam. Maria and Peter claim to be in spiritual contact with Berg, and thus continued his legacy by channeling his messages. Hence, the group's tradition did not change significantly as a result of Berg's death.[16] Consequently, the Family was resistant to changing aspects of the doctrine that Berg had supported and preached while alive, unless change was supported by postmortem messages from the spirit world.

The decision-making process involved in negotiating change is important to understand, as experimental communities are likely to go through a process of trial and error in their efforts to manufacture what they consider to be an ideal environment for their purposes. There may be unusual tension between rigidity regarding "the word" or "the book" and flexibility as new prophecies or revelations put this "word" in a different light. Yet how is a group likely to react when a social experiment has not worked out as planned? With first-generation groups in particular, the enthusiasm of the converts and their desire to change the world can make for communities with unusual and revolutionary practices. These are not always appropriate for children. Hence, the birth of children can trigger tension between founding members (in some cases especially between parents and nonparents) and intense discussions over doctrine and practice. I discuss this next in light of some disciplining practices that proved revolutionary, and controversial.

Disciplining

The disciplining of children is a contentious topic; there are many theories regarding the methods and values of punishment, but there is no consensus.[17] Despite the United Nations Convention on the Rights of the Child, a range of arguments exists between cultures, groups, and individuals: on the one hand some argue that children "need" to be disciplined within the context of love ("spare the rod and spoil the child") and corporal punishment is biblically condoned, while on the other hand some argue that children cannot defend themselves within such an unequal power relation and all violence toward children should be avoided. Over half the American states have banned the use of corporal punishment in schools, and the use of corporal punishment has been banned in both public and private schools in England since 1999.[18] Britain was the last country in Europe to ban corporal punishment in schools. Yet many parents and religious groups still argue for the right to spank their children as a method of disciplining. Disciplining can be an important aspect of the socialization of children, in order to prepare them for the lifestyle and conduct they are expected to mature into. But disciplining can also be part of the process of trial and error when a community, in the desire to create an environment conducive to its religious ideals, prioritizes certain objectives over the well-being of all the members in the spirit of "the end justifies the means." Furthermore, a community of enthusiastic converts may have rigid expectations regarding the spirituality and purity of children, and discipline them for behavior that would otherwise be accepted as within the general range of children's development.

The Family's Victor Program

By the late 1980s there were concerns in various Family field homes with regard to junior end time teens (aged eleven to thirteen). They did not seem to have the enthusiasm and commitment their parents had expressed when they joined. The Victor Program was established for these teens who, leadership believed, were in need of monitoring, discipline, and intense retraining in the word of Berg and the Bible (Kent 1997). The idea was that they needed to find their path again and become victors over their perceived bad habits. The leaders tried to provide the teenagers with a sense of enthusiasm and a sense of excitement and adventure, and to enlarge their goals and the vision of what it means to be in the Family (Ward 1995: 163). The Victor Program was envisaged as enabling the necessary close shepherding, the spiritual equivalent of rehabilitation programs. In reality, adolescents were separated from everyday Family activities and, instead, submitted to a strict discipline of manual work and "word" study.[19] Disciplining involved extended periods of silence restriction or isolation, as well as corporal punishment. The Family's organized disciplining efforts started in 1986 with the creation of a Mexican teen training camp, which was followed by the teens' detention camp in Macao—which was referred to as a camp for "determined teens" (Ward 1995: 152)—and in 1989 the establishment of the first Victor Program for teens (139). Victor Programs operated in Macao, Thailand, Mexico, Denmark, Italy, Switzerland, Scotland, and England. There were also Victor-style disciplining programs in the Philippines and Japan—the latter was referred to as the "rotten apple" camp (Ward 1995: 139). The largest disciplining program was the Jumbo in the Philippines, a walled complex that housed between 200 and 350 people from early 1988 until 1989 (Kent 1997).

Life in a Victor Program was regimented. The teens' time, according to one former Victor, was filled with a workload of manual labor that involved building and renovating (in some cases digging trenches for the sake of physical activity), other physical exercise, such as calisthenics, studying Mo letters, and the writing of open heart reports.[20] The latter are reports of thoughts and confessions of doubts and criticisms that are submitted to the shepherds and leaders.[21] The Right Honorable Lord Justice Alan Ward, who presided over a case against the Family brought in the family court in England, wrote of this program: "OHRs—open heart reports—were widely used as a means of forcing confession with the result that children were made to feel guilty if they did not confess. If they had no NOW (Needs Work On) they were said to be self-righteous and proud: if they expressed their doubts and antipathies, then they were murmuring. Either way they could not win" (1995: 97). Aside from the regular regimen, disciplining methods were used when teens were thought to digress from the leadership's expectations. Digressions were measured by assigning "demerits." Demerits could be picked up from talking during quiet time (time to think about spiritual matters), murmuring, complaining, or criticizing.[22] In most cases, seven demerits resulted in disciplinary action—spanking or being deprived of parent time (Ward 1995: 89). In the Victor Programs, however, there were few parents present, hence the latter was usually not applicable. Consequently, disciplinary action consisted largely of increased physical labor or exercise, silence restrictions, isolation, or corporal punishment—depending on the amount of demerits accumulated. Teenagers under silence restriction were to wear signs around their necks stating they were on silence restriction, so that peers knew that these teenagers were not supposed to speak or be spoken to unless by an adult in charge. In some cases teens were on silence restrictions for weeks. Isolation involved physical separation from the other teenagers; in some cases the teenager was locked in a room in order to fast, with a bucket as a toilet.[23] If these methods failed, a teenager was put on intensive care status, which amounted to separation from other Victors and round-the-clock supervision from an adult for personal counseling and Word study.[24] Corporal punishment involved beatings with a fly swatter, switch, or wooden paddle with holes in it—in the Philippines a bamboo cane was used. The beatings were witnessed by the other teenagers. Ward was in no doubt that corporal punishment was widespread and endemic, especially in Victor Camps in Macao, where children were bruised and injured (Ward 1995: 105–106); Kent (1997) describes the corporal punishment as "physical maltreatment."

David Berg's granddaughter Merry Berg, known as Mene within the Family, developed doubts in her teenage years about the group and some members whose behavior she considered to be contradictory to the Bible.[25] She was, as a result, disciplined, and eventually sent to the Victor Camp in Macao. Before and while at the Macao camp, Mene was subject to exorcisms.[26] In the case of Mene, some of these exorcisms have been recorded and described at length in internal Family publications, namely *The Last State? The Dangers of Demonism!* (D. Berg 1987) and *It's Up to You! Mene's Farewell from the King's House!* (D. Berg n.d.).[27] *The Last State* describes one of Mene's exorcisms by Berg; Berg violently shakes her, shouts at the devil to leave, and rebukes Mene for "letting the Devil in."

> God is angry! He is angry with you! I mean he is really angry! The power of God's spirit curse that devil and curse you for allowing him in.... I've never put up with anything like this ever from the

very first beginning of this Family, from my own first children, I have beaten them with the rod, I have beaten them until they cry for mercy.... From now on I'm going to knock the devil out of you if I have to.... How can you my own granddaughter supposed to be one of my saved children, how could you invite Satan in and put curses on others, send little devils to other people? I don't ever want to hear about that again! (D. Berg 1987)

As part of her exorcism Mene was subject to corporal punishment, food and silence restrictions, and solitary confinement. The exorcisms and disciplining led to Mene suffering a breakdown, after which she was sent to an institution and subsequently sent to stay with her grandmother. Mene eventually left the movement, after which she spoke out against the harsh disciplining in Macao. She recalled:

When I was finally allowed out of confinement, they began to bring other teenagers to the same house with me that were also "having problems". Most of these teenagers had questioned or criticized the leadership so they were considered "rebellious, proud, self-righteous, having a critical spirit and in need of major deliverance". Many of the same tactics began to be used on them as they used on me: Fear, restrictions (i.e. absolute silence), severe paddlings, and solitary confinement for "serious cases". They added hard labor to the list. There were also long, exhausting exorcisms over many of these kids. (M. Berg 1992)

The early 1990s was a turbulent time for the Family, as allegations of child abuse and child sexual abuse motivated authorities to interfere. In 1990 a home in Barcelona was raided by regional authorities and the children taken away, and in 1991 and 1992 homes in the United Kingdom were investigated by social services. In 1991 Maria instituted the Discipleship Training Revolution, designed to reevaluate and revamp the way the movement was treating and handling its teenagers. This included integrating the methods of the Victor Program in every home, appointing a child-care team or worker in every community, weekly child-care parenting meetings, and family time (one hour a day for parents and their children), as well as a family day—one day a week for parents and children to spend together. Maria also set disciplining standards for children and adults within the Family, and mandatory guidelines for homeschooling

(Ward 1995: 139–40). In 1992 Family homes in Sydney and Melbourne, Australia, were raided by police and officials from the Department of Community Services, and the Ward custody case began in the United Kingdom. The Family was changing as a result of these events, especially in response to the British custody case. In 1993 Maria encouraged worldwide open-forum discussions between leadership and teenagers to hear about their desires, needs, and complaints. She also requested that teenagers write to her personally (141). In 1994 the Family published *The Family Discipline Guidelines*. Disciplining of children since the publication of these guidelines included "conversation restriction," but could not involve physical restraint such as placing tape over a child's mouth, and ought not to last longer than three hours at any time or in a day—a few minutes to half an hour being preferable. "Time out," or isolation, was to last from five minutes to three days depending on age and behavior. There were age-specific guidelines for corporal punishment (142).

Maria described the teenagers as undertaking a "revolutionary boot camp training programme" (Ward 1995: 90). They were supposed to become teen soldiers. In its millennial fervor the Family aimed to create an army of Christian soldiers, but the draconian regime and penalties, in turn, left the Family with many so-called rebellious teenagers who carried a grudge and eventually left the movement behind. The Family's idea of how their children ought to be did not conform with how the children frequently turned out to be; which started a battle of wills between leadership and rebellious teenagers. Ward concluded that the children had been subjected to a "regime of physical and psychological brutality" (92). But Ward was also convinced that the Family could change, and had changed. And he pressed the group for further changes. Thus where the Family was first determined to change its teenagers, eventually the movement had to adapt to internal and external pressure, and was forced to change because of and by its teenagers.

ISKCON's Gurukulas

The gurukulas, in their task to raise the children into the bhakti practice necessary for a life lived in Krishna consciousness, developed a disciplinary atmosphere similar to some of the Family's Victor Programs.[28] Gurukulas were specifically meant to train pupils in the spiritual life through a "Krishnaized" curriculum and focus on practice. Children needed to be trained in "sense control," hence they were removed from parents from the age of four or five, to avoid the "ropes of affection" between parents and child.[29] Children attended the gurukula on a year-round basis, residing in ashrams with other children of similar age and sex. Visits to their parents tended to be sporadic.

There is evidence, however, that the gurukulas functioned as strict residential centers for children rather than schools—education arguably not always being the leadership's priority. ISKCON started as a communal organization of monks and nuns, but was eventually transformed into a loosely organized congregation of financially independent householders and their children. Despite this expansion of family life, the organization's attitude remained, at first, biased toward celibate monastic life. As the numbers of marriages and births began to grow in the mid-70s, householder life was redefined by ISKCON's renunciate elite as a symbol of spiritual weakness. The height of this organizational discrepancy was reached in 1976, with a "fratricidal war" in North America, a clash between householder temple presidents and *sannyasis* and *brahmacaries*—the latter had a preaching campaign against householders and women, who were seen as a threat to a man's spiritual advancement (Rochford and Heinlein 1998: 49–50). E. Burke Rochford Jr, a professor of sociology of religion who has studied ISKCON for the past twenty-five years, and student assistant Jennifer Heinlein argue that, as a result, householders were a stigmatized and politically marginal group within ISKCON, and powerless to assert their parental authority over the lives of their children. Hence there was an atmosphere where children were not valued by leaders, nor by their own parents, who accepted theological and practical justifications offered by the leadership for remaining uninvolved in the lives of their children (43–44).

The first gurukula was established in Dallas in 1971, one year after Prabhupada had established the GBC. By 1972 Prabhupada was, allegedly, aware that child abuse (including sexual abuse) was occurring in the gurukula.[30] By 1978, when ISKCON airport and street soliciting were at their peak, there were eleven gurukulas in North America and one each in Vrindavana and Mayapur in India. Three years later there were twenty-four gurukulas running in eighteen countries, with approximately seven hundred students, and only one year after that ISKCON publications listed thirty gurukulas worldwide.[31] By this time there were about as many married devotees as celibates; airport and street soliciting were at half the peak of 1978, and parents were pushed outside the communities to find employment to support themselves and their families (Rochford and Heinlein 1998: 55). The movement was changing rapidly, but the changes came too late for some. During the early 1980s a two-year-old boy died from battering in New Vrindaban. One year later, in 1984, child abuse was exposed at the Los Angeles temple nursery school, two more boys died in an abandoned refrigerator in New Vrindaban, and a devotee was prosecuted and imprisoned for abusing children in Dallas.[32] The child abuse appeared to be widespread and endemic. In 1985 the GBC received an anonymous letter describing child sexual abuse at the hands of Bhavananda, one of the gurus. Meanwhile, another guru, Kirtananda, was also known to be sexually molesting children. Evidence of child abuse continued to surface, and in 1986 the majority of gurukulas closed, except for the India ashram gurukulas and a few day schools (Rochford and Heinlein 1998: 46–47). Yet the ISKCON press was still in denial (Muster 1997), and ISKCON leaders were complaining that their children were turning out to be *karmi*es (outsiders, people living within maya), and wondering why that should be so (Rochford and Heinlein 1998: 50). ISKCON authorities had been slow in addressing this problem. For the gurukulis (gurukula pupils) the turning point did not come until 1990, when Raghunatha, a former gurukuli himself, organized a gurukula alumni reunion and the *ISKCON Youth Veterans Newsletter*, in which he published an autobiographical story about physical and sexual abuse during his childhood in the gurukula, titled "Children of the Ashram."[33] That same year the GBC passed a series of resolutions dealing with child abuse, but for many young members harm had already been done.

In June 2000, forty-four young adults filed a $400 million damage suit against ISKCON for sexual, physical, and emotional abuse inflicted on them as children in gurukulas. By May 2003 the suit had expanded to ninety-one complainants.[34] Estimates of abuse range from 20 percent of all students who attended an ashram gurukula suffering from "some form of abuse," to as many as 75 percent of the boys enrolled at the Vrindavan, India, gurukula having been sexually molested during the late 1970s and early 1980s (Rochford and Heinlein 1998: 47). The bias against married life and the priorities of the leadership led to a general environment of neglect for the children. The latter felt unwanted and abandoned by their parents. The majority believed they were in gurukula so that their parents could continue sankirtan—"dump the load and hit the road" (52–53). The function of the gurukulas, in reality, had been child minding rather than education. Consequently, there was insufficient staffing, funding, and general oversight. Rochford and Heinlein argue that it became an institution defined by neglect, isolation, and marginalization (53). There was a shortage of trained and qualified staff, and the majority of staff were ill prepared for working with children. The gurukula became, indeed, the "dumping ground" for staff who were not reaching the preferred sankirtan quotas (53). Sankirtan brought recognition within the devotee community, working in the gurukulas brought invisibility and a loss of status. Hence there was a high turnover rate of untrained, unqualified, and unmotivated teachers. The second generation had been marginalized within ISKCON, and this was now reaping consequences.

Throughout the 1990s, after Raghunatha had published his memoir and organized reunions for the disenfranchised second generation, the ISKCON leadership initiated changes to support the gurukulis.[35] Simultaneously, the gurukulis continued to meet at the alumni reunions and continued to voice their complaints. The opposing voices did not agree on the speed and usefulness of the changes implemented. "Letter from Me" by Anuttama Dasa, the international communications director for ISKCON in 2000, outlined the way the society had responded to the abuse at the gurukula.[36] Anuttama introduced himself as also having served as a board member of the Children of Krishna organization, as well as having been on the task force that established the Office of Child Protection within ISKCON.[37] In this role he lamented that ISKCON's response had sometimes been represented incorrectly or not clearly, and thus demanded that information be as accurate as possible. Anuttama acknowledged the abuse but added that these were acts by individuals in gross violation of the religious teachings, the instructions as well as the personal example of Prabhupada, and the general policies and principles of ISKCON.[38] According to him, the society had reacted by taking steps to assure the children were now safe, to help the young who had suffered, and to investigate fully all allegations of past abuse. In 1990 the GBC had established a series of policies to protect children, requiring abuse-prevention education for all students as well as the immediate reporting of all suspicions of abuse to local government authorities. Six years later the Children of Krishna organization had been established to assist young devotees who had been in gurukulas with support and financial assistance, for counseling, education, and vocational training. In 1998 the Office of Child Protection had been established by ISKCON to investigate and adjudicate the allegations of past abuse. When Anuttama wrote the article in 2000, fifty cases had been decided and more were in process. The Office of Child Protection also provided financial assistance for the abused devotees, with $200,000 having been granted by 2000, and worked with ISKCON to enhance child protection programs.[39]

Anuttama's arguments were countered by former gurukuli Raghunatha Anudasa, who argued that most of these gestures toward the gurukulis were merely superficial operations meant to look good rather than "do good" for the second generation. He asserted that his generation had been neglected and ignored at best. Raghunatha pointed out that the bulk of the second-generation youth were alienated, and made to feel that the problem was with them rather than with the schools. According to him they were branded as disloyal to Prabhupada, spiritually corrupt, and unappreciative of Krishna consciousness. As a result the majority of the second generation had either left or been thrown out.[40] The second generation felt neither part of ISKCON nor karmi, those not of ISKCON. Raghunatha wrote: "ISKCON had eliminated or at least silenced an entire generation of the movements [sic] children."[41] He accused the leadership of not listening to the gurukulis a second time, arguing that the reforms made now were more about the institution's needs than those of the second generation. He alleged that in at least one case much of the money collected through Children of Krishna went to one of its self-appointed directors or for other office expenses. Furthermore, he argued that the GBC's youth minister was "useless" as he was not a representative of the youth: "Never has the [second] generation been asked who they would like to represent them and it is clear that they never will be asked."[42]

There is evidence that the ISKCON leadership structure was, indeed, resistant to change in reverence for their tradition. For example, in 1996, former students from the Vrindavana, India, gurukula confronted Dhanurdara Swami, the former school principal, about the abuse that occurred under his leadership. The meeting was arranged and facilitated by GBC member Badrinarayan. After the confrontation, however, Dhanurdara continued his position as a guru and sannyasi.[43] An appointed guru is not easily deposed. But at the same time, there are many avenues for discussion within and around ISKCON that challenges the leadership, such as chakra. org, a forum for discussing controversial issues within and surrounding ISKCON, vnn.org (Vaisnava News Network), an independent discussion network for Vaisnavas (followers of the Hindu god Vishnu) worldwide, and the forums and newsletters for former gurukulis (the *Gurukuli Youth Veteran Newsletter*, and former member Nori Muster's website, surrealist. org, among others). In 1998, the *ISKCON Communications Journal* published the study of the abuse in the gurukulas written by Rochford and Heinlein, independent scholars. ISKCON Communications issued a press release and outside media covered the story. For the first time, gurukula abuse was widely publicized. Two years later, chakra.org published the results of a gurukula alumni survey sent out by the ISKCON Youth Ministry to 800 people who grew up in ISKCON—115 were returned. The questions focused on sexual, physical, and emotional abuse experienced and witnessed. In summary, 37.4 percent saw or knew of friends being repeatedly hit to the point of having marks on their bodies. Over a third of respondents admitted to a lack of feeling safe and protected from the teachers, and roughly a quarter admitted to being touched with sexual intent by an older person before the age of eighteen at an ISKCON community.[44] The ISKCON gurukulas were meant to be a place where the children of the devotees could be raised in Krishna consciousness, but in reality the juggling of priorities and lack of management and training of gurukula staff meant that the ashram schools were far from the ideal envisaged by devotees.

The Bruderhof's Ausschluss

The Bruderhof's main disciplining method is shunning, which is also used by the Exclusive Brethren, Jehovah's Witnesses (disfellowshipping), Amish (*Meidung*), Hutterites, and Mennonite communities, among others. In the Bruderhof, deviations from doctrine, practice, and the communal norm are believed to threaten the social and spiritual base of the community. Those whose ideas or behavior are believed to threaten unity, and who will not reform from and repent alleged or reported sinful thoughts and conduct, are disciplined. Members who commit minor infractions are prohibited from attending the *Gemeindestunde* (prayer circle). Larger infractions result in the *kleiner Ausschluss* (small exclusion); the member remains within the community, working and eating with fellow members, but is shunned and excluded from the *Gemeindestunde*. At this stage, a member is also deemed unfit to work with children, and is likely to be put to work in the laundry room, kitchen, or field.[45] The *grosser Ausschluss* (great exclusion) involves exclusion from all community activity and complete shunning—in some cases this entails expulsion from the community for an indefinite length of time, although a member might still physically be in or near the community.[46] These punishments transcend blood ties and marriage vows; children, spouse, and other relatives have to shun the offending member, and accept the expulsion if the leadership decides the great exclusion is appropriate (see Rubin 1997: 88).[47]

When parents are put in grosser Ausschluss, children are affected—they are sent to live with another couple or family for the duration of the exclusion. They are usually not told where their parents are, or how long the exclusion will last. Siblings are often separated. One former member, Janet, came home from school one day when she was aged nine to an empty house. A group of parents had disagreed with a minister, and were put in exclusion; the fathers on one farm and the mothers on another. (This was on an English hof, which consisted of three farms.) Her eldest brother, who was twelve at the time, was also in exclusion—he ended up being in exclusion for six months. With her parents gone, she and her other siblings were separated and taken to other families for the duration of the parents' exclusion. At the time she did not know where her parents were, and when she spoke with me she still did not know where her siblings stayed.[48] For another former member, Frank, a similar scenario lasted almost a year.[49]

When children are in the great exclusion, they are separated from family and friends. According to Nadine Pleil (1994: 86), a former member who has published a memoir, young children could be excluded for years; the elders believed that children needed a longer interval to repent and experience a freeing of their sins than adults. Children are seen as points of entry for demonic attack, and they can be tools of Satan. Parents are told that their children are inherently inclined to sin, and the parents must guard against this (Arnold 1996: 77). Hence the children's environment must be filled with purity and love. Children follow the examples of others, and if people around them sin, they will do so as well: "As parents we must always be ready to fight evil in our children, whether it takes the form of lying, stealing, disrespect, or sexual impurity" (Arnold 1996: 79). The issue of sexual impurity in children needs "special sensitivity and discernment," according to Johann Christoph Arnold (Arnold 1996: 80). In the Bruderhof's battle to put Agape over Eros, erotic thought, action, and sexuality are highly regulated. Christoph Arnold wrote:

> Yet just as the area of sensuous experience can bring us close to God, it can mislead us and even bring us into satanic darkness. All too often we tend towards the superficial and miss the might and power of what God could otherwise give us. Too often, in grasping at what we experience with our senses, we forget about God and miss the possibility of experiencing the full depth of his will. (1996:33)

Hence, children and young teenagers who showed an interest in general issues of reproduction could be branded as sinful and be subject to "clearances," interrogations to garner confessions of sexual sin and impurity, and exclusion. After clearances, children were separated from their parents in order to repent for their sins. Yaacov Oved argues that one of the dynamics that led to the Great Crisis was a perception of the moral decline of the younger generation. Schoolchildren had been involved in petty theft and bartered these stolen goods with the hired workers. The leadership's greatest worry was not the stealing, but the relations with the Paraguayan workers, which, they feared, put the children's puritanical sex education in jeopardy. The boys involved were brought before the entire community and those found guilty were punished by exclusion (Oved 1996: chapter 8).

Clearances appear to have been a part of life in the Bruderhof for a number of people. Former member Elizabeth Bohlken-Zumpe describes in her memoir how she went through a clearance without knowing what she had done wrong. She had to spend the night outside, away from her family. When her friend told her to tell the elders that they had been "looking at each other's bottoms" (although they had not) in order to force the ordeal to an end, Elizabeth was relieved to be able to tell the elders something they might accept as a truthful answer—and then the questioning would be over. She and her friend were excluded from the other children for ten days and were put to work in the laundry (Bohlken-Zumpe 1993: 58). Julius Rubin (1997) describes the "struggle for the soul of Faith," who was suspected of harboring impure thoughts after reading sections of *The Catcher in the Rye* by J. D. Salinger. Intense interrogations followed, as well as grosser Ausschluss, leaving her clinically depressed. She was eventually expelled after attempting suicide. Another young woman, reportedly thought by Heini to be possessed by evil demons, was never fully "cleared," and eventually institutionalized (Rubin 1997). The three former members I have interviewed had their own accounts of clearances as well as accounts of those of siblings and friends, and the corporal punishment that occasionally followed.[50] Between clearances of children and perceived wrongdoings by adults, many childhoods in the Bruderhof have been marked by disruptions when one or both parents or siblings were excluded.

The height of clearances came with the leadership schism, when the American brothers and Heini visited hofs in Paraguay, England, and Germany, demanding self-examination and repentance for alleged coldheartedness. Those deemed spiritually weak were shunned and disfellowshipped. One former member in Paraguay, Anna, was fourteen at the time of the Great Crisis, and her parents were sent away. She was asked whether she wanted to stay, but she chose to go to a hof in England with her parents, who were in disgrace. Several years later, the English hof closed down, and with her parents she moved to a hof in the United States. But, being still in disgrace, they had to live on the outskirts of the hof. In her own words: "To live near a community has huge stuff around it. It's a position of disgrace, of punishment, of being totally beholden. Writing endless letters and definitely not putting a foot wrong, hanging on every invitation to come to some special meal." She wrote letters for years asking to be allowed in, harboring feelings of shame, as well as anger toward her parents for being in exclusion—and, she argued, never able to respect her father because of the shame as a teenager. For five years she lived on the outskirts of the hof. "[I] felt depressed all that time, a failure before God and the community—just for not being allowed in." She did, however, go to college with "the girls from the inner circle," but at the end of the day was dropped off at the bottom of the hill, outside the hof. "And you can't be quite out because you're not feeling out inside," she said. "You're still a Bruderhof person. And you dress like a Bruderhof person and you want to go back to the Bruderhof so you don't do anything to damage that." Eventually she began a cycle of confessing to sexual thoughts and masturbation, thinking that would enable her to join the brotherhood.[51]

Another former member, Janet, was twenty years old and living in Paraguay when her parents were sent to England, but she was asked to stay. A year later she was in exclusion without knowing why. Frank, who did not know exactly why he was in exclusion, spent sixteen years in kleiner Ausschluss, after which he was sent to another hof to make a new beginning.[52] Most of these people were sabra youth, thought to have the advantage of being raised in community. They generally "survived" the Great Crisis and were moved to the new communities. The leadership schism and enforcement of so-called warm-hearted spirituality resulted in the expulsion of hundreds of members who had considered the Bruderhof their family and their home. Rubin describes the effect: "Those shunned in 'disfellowship' experienced traumatic loss and disorientation, at first blaming their fate on their own spiritual inadequacies. Later, when confirmed as apostates with no way back, they came to view exclusion as a callous act of unloving, unbrotherly cruelty" (2000: 106). The Bruderhof leadership remained rigid in its preservation of a certain tradition, and dissenters had a choice; they could conform or they would be shunned and possibly excluded.

Leadership, Stasis, and Change

The Family, through Victor Programs, attempted to make the children conform to the vision the leaders had for them in the spirit of "the end justifies the means." Kent (1997) argues that the Family's Victor Program was an exercise in "brainwashing" and an attempt to mold the children to the image held by Family leadership and parents. According to Ward, the means employed had significant costs: "The cost to the children was to rob them of their personal identity. It was an invasion of personal freedom" (1995: 157). Similarly, gurukulas could be seen as a way to raise the children to conform to the practice and lifestyle of Krishna devotees, in the same spirit of "the end justifies the means." It is equally important, however, to look at the overall structure of the movement and the changes made over time. In both cases, the communal structure, allocation of resources, and division of labor made it sensible to have organized education and camps for children; the parents could continue their tasks while the children were cared for and educated. This is not an unusual lifestyle, and can be found in many other situations where neglect and abuse have not been institutionalized.

Similarly, disciplining is part of socialization, and not necessarily problematic or harmful. Yet in certain settings abuse is more likely to occur, and in certain structures abuse can be institutionalized.[53] The Family and ISKCON separated children from their parents, and appointed teachers who were not appropriately trained. And in both cases the aims were neither flexible nor under frequent review. In the Bruderhof and the Family disciplining was also used in the context of beliefs in evil spirits and possession, a condition that can be, in certain mindsets, easy to "prove" and impossible to refute. Neither corporal punishment nor exorcisms (more commonly referred to as deliverance) are unusual among religious populations (although of course both include a wide possible range of ways to practice them). Yet some social structures and hierarchies can create an environment where harmful practices can occur and possibly continue unchecked and unchallenged. Challenging authority in the Bruderhof was likely to lead to exclusion, after which a member could no longer communicate his or her complaints. In the Family and ISKCON, extreme disciplining of the children could go unchecked; the Victor Programs and gurukulas were not easily accessed by outsiders, and were practically unscrutinized for several years. The disciplining practices were not visible to the relevant authorities. These were decisions related to the chosen modes of insertion into the wider society.

What I have described as attempts to reinvent the wheel, ignoring existing customs and regulations in favor of new ways and methods, occasionally through a process that may seem like trial and error, appears to be more characteristic of charismatic communities. Yet communities with strong ties to tradition can equally have a doctrine and practices that are experimental (such as instituting a new governing board of gurus), and because of the reverence for traditional ties, even such new developments can become difficult to overturn. Thus the Family, a charismatic community, eventually managed to put safeguards around its Law of Love that, to some extent, protects the children. At the time of the raids, changes had already begun, and no evidence of abuse was found. ISKCON's gurukulas, however, continued despite complaints from children and some parents—the authority structure was steeped in Vaisnava tradition. Furthermore, devotees were reluctant to change a structure created by their founding guru. Changes were eventually initiated when the former gurukulis organized and put pressure on the leadership. The practice of shunning in the Bruderhof has not been overturned. Although there has never again been the number of exclusions there were following the Great Crisis, there have been smaller crises since. The Arnold leadership held on to certain traditions, and in the process shut its ears to the former members, most of them sabras who have organized themselves against the sect and lobbied for change.

New Challenges

The authority structure, flexibility, modes of insertion and recovery from trial and error are important factors in establishing the extent of a community's accommodation over time. The moment a new generation is born into the community, new pressures crop up. Tensions arise between the demands of the second generation and the demands of the founding members. The journey toward accommodation can be fraught with battles and back-and-forth maneuvering as the leadership tries to please several parties at once. The leadership can steer a straight and narrow path, pushing away those who demand accommodation, or adjust and accommodate at the risk of alienating some of the founding members. How exactly are the tensions resolved that arise from the differing demands of the first generation and the second generation? Initial questions that arose with the birth of the second generation were: To what extent can the religious groups shift the priorities? Is it acceptable to send the children to a regular school? Can members afford to spend less time witnessing? Under what circumstances can members take on an outside job? Over time, other questions arise: Is it appropriate to change the rituals for the children? To what extent do we change the rules of engagement within the community? Can children be members according to different standards? Can we "sell out" for our children by adjusting the modes of insertion into society? These questions can lead to long and heated discussions regarding the founding principles and the direction the group should take.

The Family adapted as a result of outside scrutiny by opening itself up to investigation and changing its behavior. In a controversial and unusual move, the Family leadership allowed academics to approach certain communities and interview certain members.[54] Consequently, there was some degree of dialogue between Family leadership and outsiders. The leadership reinterpreted rules within the Law of Love to increase safeguards for the children, and although several of their practices were still highly controversial, there was, within the movement, more reflection regarding how society would perceive certain teachings.[55] ISKCON adapted by opening up to inside scrutiny and discussion as well as outside scrutiny. The leadership set up structures within the movement to look after children, giving them a forum for discussion and complaints. Leaders also made room for the initiatives of the second generation, who in turn put pressure on them to implement many of these changes. The Bruderhof, rather than adapting, increased its separation from "outside" relatives and former members. Although visitors were generally welcomed to the communities, this invitation did not stand for those who have an erstwhile connection to the community and who were critical of the leadership.

The conclusion of whether a sect's attitude toward change is "rigid" (because the leadership aims to adhere to a particular tradition) or "relatively flexible" (because the charismatic leader may decide on particular changes and implement them) should involve analysis of a multitude of factors.[56] Important factors include leadership, social structure, importance of certain key teachings, and attitude to accommodation. Change is inevitable, but the attitude to change and the measures taken to either facilitate or fight certain processes are important to the social dynamics both within the sect and between the sect and society; changes tend to affect a group's modes of insertion into society. Hence, before embarking on the next chapter, it may be useful to generalize and create a working framework of a sect's general predisposition toward change. The sects with traditional leadership or a strongly established bureaucratic structure were generally more resistant to change. As a result of the tradition or hierarchical structure, matters of doctrine and practice were not up for bottom-up debate. There was little flexibility regarding experimentation and trial and error, as practices tended to be entrenched and nonnegotiable. There was relatively more flexibility toward change in groups with charismatic leaders, who could change their mind and quickly implement the changes (as it would be with groups where leadership is according to democratic decision and doctrine and practice are up for discussion).[57] There is room for trial and error, as experiments that do not work out as planned can be changed relatively quickly (for better or worse).

However, resistance or surrender to change strongly depends on whose idea it is. Parts of the leadership or membership suggesting changes is significantly different from outside agents or authorities suggesting, or even enforcing, changes. Throughout their history, groups engage in boundary maintenance and tend to increase and decrease their modes of insertion into society as a result of internal and external events, pressures, and changes. Hence it is important to analyze changing dynamics within and surrounding sectarian communities. And in analyzing changing dynamics, it is important to identify which changes are in response to external demands. This is the subject of the following chapter.

3

Points of Conflict

THE CHILDREN OF GOD AND THE STATE

THIS CHAPTER FOCUSES on a controversial part of the history of the Family International (then known as the Children of God, among other names). This case illustrates the difficulties involved in balancing the rights of parents and children, as well as the difficulties faced by statutory bodies when dealing with sectarian communities. The way in which the group faced up to its problems, dealt with them, and reinvigorated its members is a fascinating, but disconcerting, account.

Boundary Dynamics

No sect operates in a vacuum; no matter how much a group tries to remove itself from the surrounding society, it remains a part of society—although some are deeply inserted while others are only loosely coupled. Sects work on boundary maintenance while being embedded in the society they are critical of, if not opposed to.[1] I refer to this process of boundary maintenance in light of interaction and exchange with members of the surrounding society as "boundary dynamics." Boundary dynamics are much influenced by a society's history of diversity and attitude to minority religions.[2] Depending on the existing diversity and laws regarding religious freedom, a group might be illegal and operating underground rather than as an accepted minority religion. Yet a "legal" minority religion, if it perceives the wider society as being against its objectives, may portray itself as a world-rejecting and revolutionary entity that *ought to* operate underground for the safety of its members. This is in contrast to more world-accommodating and world-affirming groups that are overtly part of the religious landscape and consider themselves, by and large, to be beneficial to society as a whole.[3] Consequently, different religious groups negotiate different modes of insertion into society depending on their aims, objectives, and worldviews, and contribute to different boundary dynamics. Of course this dynamic works both ways as society, in turn, can alienate minority groups as well. Social boundaries are constructed from two sides, internally as well as externally, and the strength or weakness of negotiations between the two sides varies according to action and reaction on both sides to the issues that are deemed important. This can lead to a deviance-amplification spiral, an escalating negative relationship between small social enclaves, on the one hand, and authorities on the other (Cohen 1972; Wessinger 2000).[4] There are, of course, other variables involved, and there can be different types of authorities.[5] The social dynamics surrounding sects depend on the relationship between sects and authorities (the state, government bodies, any organization in civil society perceived as an authority on the issues, the media, and so forth), but also on the relationship between sects and their surrounding society, which consists of the general public as well as relatives of members of the sects and former members of the sects. The latter groups can have a great impact on the perceptions of the general public and the state toward the sect, and on the sects' perceived need for boundary maintenance. For example, relatives and former members can have a significant impact through the provision of information if a group is isolated or underground (as it is then often difficult to gather information). Former members and relatives of members can also tell others about their experiences, which, although subjective, may be the only information available. They then become de-facto authorities on the subject.

The nature of disputes surrounding a sect can sometimes be identified by reviewing the literature that is available about the sect. It is often challenging to find balanced information about religious communities, as this material is not always available in bookshops and libraries, and when it is, it is often from a particular perspective, and the media (especially the Internet) are overloaded with polarized and partisan accounts describing, selectively, either the best or the worst aspects of particular religious communities. The consequences of qualitatively questionable information can be significant. And when government bodies need to rely on information, more questions arise: who are the information providers, and what is the government's objective? While reliable information is of vital importance, it is neither always available nor always desired or sought. Academic research is often criticized by nonacademics for being out of touch, removed from reality, and not understanding the religious dimension, while information from former members and critics often has a bias that makes it unsuitable as a representative reflection of the religious community in question (Beckford 1985; Barker 1995b).[6] Furthermore, the latter do not always report the changes that invariably occur over time within sectarian movements (which is often inevitable, as former members have lost their access when they left).

As I have described in the previous chapter, the history of a sect can take the form of periods of revolutionary social experiments, or trial and error, according to the whims of a charismatic leader. Hence, former member accounts of a tumultuous and problematic period are not necessarily representative of how the sect is several years, or even a decade, after they have left. However, there may not be balanced and up-to-date information available, and as a result, much decision making (be it private or public, for policymaking) is based on the old information—which is usually freely available in the media. The media tend to prefer the type of information that is more likely to sell, that is, "atrocity tales" rather than balanced accounts (Beckford 1985). Such discrepancies are likely to create a larger chasm between a sect and the surrounding society. Social isolation is acceptable when the sect consists of consenting adults who abide by the law of the land. But when minors are involved, the state, as well as local authorities such as social services, has a responsibility over the well-being of the child.[7] Such institutions may seek to impose limits on a sect's social isolation. Any imposition will elicit a response from the sect, which might either choose to accommodate or attempt to remove itself further from social scrutiny and possible external interference. Famously, the Branch Davidians did not accept external interference from the American FBI and the Bureau of Alcohol, Tobacco, and Firearms, which sought to impose limits on the group. The leader had no faith in these earthly authorities, and the clashes resulted in many deaths.[8]

UN member states and their relevant institutions have a responsibility toward their minors according to the United Nations convention; but so do parents. This is an ambiguous balance, and there are ongoing discussions about whether children are, or ought to be, under the jurisdiction of the state over and above the rights of the parents, or vice versa.[9] The 1989 UN Convention on the Rights of the Child lays out the responsibilities, rights, and duties of parents to raise their children, which they can exercise according to their religion, within the constraints of the law of the land (Art. 5). This is especially important in the context of the right to freedom of thought, conscience, and religion, which is subject only to limitations prescribed by law—in the interest of public safety and the protection of the rights and freedoms of others (Art. 9). The last point creates another ambiguity as it can put the parents' right to freedom against the protection of the rights and freedoms of a child, another variable in what is now a precarious balance between state, parent, and child. One example of such a precarious balance, and where the rights of the parents clash with local authority, or in this case the family court, is the request by the Exclusive Brethren to have full custody of the children in cases of divorce where one parent has left or is leaving the religious community. The Exclusive Brethren have put pressure on family courts in New Zealand to allow them full custody of their children, and deny custody and visitation rights to the outside parent, in order to safeguard the children from non-Brethren influences. In one case a judge ordered shared custody, and when the mother (and community members) ignored the court order and refused to comply, the judge warned of the imposition of hefty fines or imprisonment if the mother contravened court orders, but eventually, two years later, the father was banned from seeing his children.[10]

The law of the land is not always free from ambiguity and leaves ample room for gaps and clashes between adult and child human rights and parent and state responsibilities, and consequently cases regarding children's rights frequently have to be dealt with in family courts. In other cases, however, family courts are bypassed and the state becomes directly involved. For example, medical issues (i.e., Jehovah's Witnesses, whose parents of minors or minors refuse vital blood transfusions, versus the state's responsibility for the well-being of children) and education issues (i.e., a sectarian group's refusal to follow the state's educational curriculum) occasionally warrant higher-level legal intervention (van Eck Duymaer van Twist 2010). These issues have repeatedly uncovered the gray area where the different parties' rights, freedoms, and responsibilities overlap. These gray areas also frequently involve topics closely tied in with religious doctrine and ideals, and which elicit strong opinions. Consequently, they can be strong catalysts of disputes and conflict between the sect and the state. Another situation where a sect's right to seclusion and self-governance is severely tested, and when the state has to intervene, is when there are suspicions of child abuse or child sexual abuse. In such cases there tends to be little ambiguity, as child abuse is an infringement in most countries (although there are different opinions as to what constitutes "child" and "abuse").

In the following section I provide an extended example of the Family International, where the leader's teachings on the topic of sexuality led to extensive outside scrutiny over the well-being of the members' children. The Family is a good illustration for this chapter as there have been numerous points of conflict, and the followers' attitudes to society, as well as society's attitude towards them, have changed significantly over time. The clashes have been very intense as authorities have interfered and taken some of their children into custody on several occasions (although not found evidence of abuse), and subsequently somewhat relaxed as the group has adapted and changed in order to align itself more with society's standards. The sectarian group has renegotiated its modes of insertion into society as the leadership struggled to retain the group's revolutionary stance while also offering a wider range of options for members.

The Family and the State

To the pure all things are pure.
—TIT.1:15
All things are lawful unto me (1Cor. 10:23). But... [a]ll things are not expedient.
—BERG 1992

History

The Family International is a sectarian community, historically frequently unpopular with the state and the general public, who tend to classify it as a cult (Bromley and Shupe 1981; Beckford 1985).[11] Academics have identified several stages in the history of the group in which members either shunned society or more or less interacted with it (van Zandt 1991; Introvigne 1994). The group was founded around the time of the Jesus Revolution, and although this was before the development of the sexually free, experimental, and explicit behavior the group is known for, the US media were already discussing it, and gave it the name Children of God, a name the group later adopted. The members were social and religious revolutionaries and they stood out. In 1969 members started travelling around the United States in several mission teams before regrouping in Canada. There, Berg met Karen Zerby. At this time Berg wrote that the old church was corrupt and needed replacing with the new church (Berg 1969). Berg left his first wife in favor of Karen, subsequently known within the movement as (Mother) Maria, and together they formed the new church.

In 1970 and 1971 the group lived a disciplinary life in Texas at the Soul Clinic Ranch, where the members continued building the new church. Here the Children of God grew from less than one hundred to fifteen hundred members (Bromley and Newton 1994). This is where the movement developed a strong separation from the outside world. Joining the group meant forsaking all and severing world ties. In reaction to this stance, the group Free Our Children from the Children of God was formed by relatives of members. This was one of the first of the so-called anticult groups in the United States. In 1971 Berg and Maria moved to Europe, and members soon followed. A hierarchy developed as the group spread out. Overall control was in the hands of the "royal family" (Berg's family), and local control with "shepherds" (senior members elected for local leadership positions).

Within several years Berg changed this structure; in 1978 he initiated the reorganization and nationalization revolution (RNR). The RNR entailed the elimination of all the intermediate leadership between Berg and the membership, and the downsizing of communities. The smaller communities were now largely independent, isolated from each other. Witnessing and outreach increased during this time, and as a result the strong boundaries between members and the outside world diminished as they inserted themselves more into the surrounding community. Also, many children were born into the movement during this time, adding responsibilities and changing the dynamic drastically. Some members moved back to the more familiar territory of the United States, but kept a low profile.[12] Some even took "regular" employment and sent their children to mainstream schools. The Children of God had developed into a different group, and it was operating under a new name: the Family of Love.

In 1981 there was an attempt to reverse the chaos and diffusion of the RNR and encourage members to establish new fellowship links with one another—this was called the local area fellowship mission, or the fellowship revolution. Communities, called "homes," were encouraged to meet up with other Family of Love homes in the area. A new hierarchy developed, although this time more democratically; leaders were appointed by members in the individual areas. This new leadership brought a newfound organization, and soon these leaders recognized a problem arising from the many fellowship meetings between homes coupled with the teachings regarding free love that had been widely instituted by then. In 1983 a publication called *Ban the Bomb* drew attention to the spread of venereal diseases within the group, and brought about a new rule: "sexual sharing" was to be limited to the home fellowship only. This new rule was followed by the initiation of a six-month period during which new members were not to participate in "sharing," and marked the beginning of a policy on sex. The renewed fellowship between members and the system of leadership led to the solidifying of social boundaries and relative isolation from society again as the group focused inward. Around 1987 the group changed its name from the Family of Love to the Family.

Throughout the 1990s, Family communities were subject to investigations by authorities. These events led to a significant turnaround as the group decided to emerge from seclusion and interact with authorities and academics in an attempt to control the damage to its image and, crucially, keep members' children. This accommodation did involve some sacrifices, mainly to the doctrine and legacy of their late leader (who had died in 1994).[13] In this case study I will elaborate on Berg's interpretation of the Law of Love and how this has affected the Family doctrine and practices. This was important because of the impact that some of the teachings, especially the more controversial ones, had on the children and the relationship between the group and its detractors, and how in turn this dynamic affected the minors within the community. I will chart the extent to which some teachings changed over time with the maturation of the children, and as a result of interference from outside authorities.

The Law of Love

For Berg and devoted members of the Family, the Law of Love is the most important commandment. The Law of Love can be traced to Matthew 22:36, which describes when Jesus was asked about the greatest commandment in the law. He reportedly gave two: "Love the Lord your God with all your heart and with all your soul and with all your mind [and] love your neighbor as yourself"—and continued to say that "all the law and the prophets hang on these two commandments." The Family regarded the teachings of Jesus to be crucial in establishing the supremacy of love—selfless and unconditional love should guide all behavior (Millikan 1994: 232). Berg considered Jesus's commandments ("God's only law is Love") and Jesus's and Paul's teachings (the New Testament gospel of grace) more important than the Ten Commandments and other teachings considered "old law" (Amsterdam and Apollos 1993). Hence, for the Family, love is the primary moral arbiter; love guides the group's decisions rather than law, regulation, or tradition. This extended to the Family's everyday behavior, as well as its ministry. In the mid-1970s Berg and Maria experimented with a new ministry, which was communicated to the followers in the late 1970s: the Flirty Fishing ministry (described in their publications as "FFing"). This was to be the most controversial time in the history of the Family.

Flirty Fishing

Berg, Maria, and their immediate circle had been experimenting with new ways of witnessing since the early to mid-1970s, processes they described in the publication entitled *The One That Got Away*, published in two parts (Berg and Maria 1974a, b).[14] This letter described how Maria aimed to witness to a man through a sexual relationship, but this man rejected going "all the way" with Maria. His rejection of Maria's sexual advances was described as equivalent to a person rejecting Jesus, and in part 2 of the publication the man was portrayed as the "stubborn wilful sinner," in tune with the devil. In contrast, another man, named Arthur, was very willing to receive this "gift" from Maria, and he was described as being in tune with the Lord. "*We are actually going through an experiment*, an amazing and most remarkable experiment—almost like a *clinical* experiment in this thing! Here is the actual illustration of the love of God! It's just like a clinical experiment in illustrating the love of God in terms the world should understand, right?" (1974a: 7 par. 53; emphasis in the original). The two-part letter ended with: "Hook 'em for Jesus!" (1974b: 8).

In 1976 a series of widely distributed Mo letters, entitled *King Arthur's Nights*, began to describe in more detail this new form of witnessing in which Berg, Maria, and other members of the leadership had been involved—mostly in London dance clubs and in Tenerife. The experiment had moved on from Maria to other senior members, and now it was to become a ministry available to all members of the Family community. Over the next series of letters discussions developed about the sacrificial nature of Flirty Fishing and the importance of using sexuality as a tool in witnessing to establish contact with outsiders. Sexual intercourse was an acceptable outcome, and even encouraged. There were theological justifications. Because of the belief in the imminence of the end (the return of Jesus and the start of the events leading to the millennium), there was a sense of urgency and insistence on witnessing. Family teachings paved the way for this new development. Sexual intercourse outside marriage was not considered adultery, but an outpouring of sacrificial love. Flirty Fishing, it was argued, was not driven by lustful motives—it was a ministry of love. And, crucially, it was a ministry of sacrifice. Women were giving themselves to the sexual needs of their fish (a person who is witnessed to) for the sake of the latter's salvation. The atmosphere was one of personal sacrifice for the salvation of others, a ministry of selflessness. The following quotes are from the start of the Flirty Fishing era, and give a good picture of the excitement and fervor of the time. They describe "[t]he real meaning of 'The Lord's Supper:'—Do *You* have *Come-union?*" (Berg 1978b):

> *DO WE HAVE COMPLETE FULL COMMUNION?*—*Come-union? Common-union? 'All* things *common'?* (Ac.2:44.) Communion in the *flesh* as well as the *spirit?* How long has it been since *you've* given *your* body to someone, a brother or sister or even a fish? *JESUS GAVE HIS BODY EVEN FOR THE UNSAVED!* Have *you?* Surely you should be willing to give yourself at least to <u>each other</u>! Have you been withholding yourself, *your* flesh, from a brother or sister or a fish?—Or even from your own *mate?*—Such selfishness is absolutely unscriptural! (See Acts 2:44, 4:32, 1Cor.7:5, Jas. 2:15, 16 etc)[.] *Love* sacrifices the *flesh* for *others*! (emphasis in the original)

Berg argues that the Holy Spirit is the female aspect of God—in many of the drawings that accompany the literature she is portrayed as the third person in the Trinity, a young, beautiful, and sexual woman:[15] "We talk about the Holy Spirit wooing us, so that means the Holy Spirit makes love to us. Let's face it!—she stoops to make love to all of us just like Jesus did and like God does!" (Berg 1982). Throughout the time of the Flirty Fishing ministry, the literature was full of statements regarding this ministry as a test of loyalty.[16] Although some men were involved in the Flirty Fishing ministry, they were not as popular as the women. Hence, Flirty Fishing was essentially a women's issue: the burden was on women, yet, at the same time, the women were considered the real heroines. Flirty Fishing was considered the ultimate gift, and women were the front-line troops in the battle against Satan. The women were in charge of the most important mission; they were the ultimate witnesses. David Millikan, a theologian and expert on the Family, argues that during that time, women moved from a subservient role to an equal role, as did Maria, who had more power after the Flirty Fishing era than she did before (1994: 216).[17]

Sharing

Flirty Fishing was mostly practiced during the RNR, when the Family communities were independent and diffused. The fellowship revolution brought many changes, including renewed contact among members and regional leadership. The Flirty Fishing ministry involved meeting the sexual needs of outsiders, but the philosophy also included the needs of

Family members. Hence within the homes there was a permissive sexual atmosphere that involved the sharing of partners and spouses according to "need" (which was self-defined). The Law of Love was applied to Family members as much as it was to outsiders. When in 1987 the Flirty Fishing ministry was discontinued, mainly as a result of AIDS, the focus of the Law of Love was turned inward to focus on "sexual sharing" among members rather than Flirty Fishing with outsiders.

Sharing is based on the standpoint that there is no evil in any sexual act (except sodomy) provided that it is done as an expression of love, and that the expressions of love are confined within the behavioral code developed by the group (Millikan 1994: 233). The primary responsibility of all members is to the larger community of the Family. The needs of a brother or sister cannot be neglected or ignored because of a prior relationship to a spouse or partner, and the relationship between a husband and wife is secondary to the love that all members should have for one another within the Family. Finally, the needs created by sexuality are given a certain moral weight. The sexual need in one person creates an obligation in others (233). Hence, sharing should always be in the spirit of the Law of Love, and a decision to share should be preceded by several questions. Is it something that is motivated by love? Do all parties involved approve and recognize the love in this act? Is anyone being hurt? Has it been talked through and submitted to counseling? Does this have the Lord's blessing (235)?

Yet there was no regulation or notion of limitation outside of these principles. And although the Law of Love stipulated that all acts should be motivated by love and that nobody should get hurt, this was not necessarily how it always manifested. Between the RNR and the beginning of the fellowship revolution, Family homes were often unregulated, and there were times during the Family of Love era when there were more experimental and unfettered forms of free love. At certain times during the history of the Law of Love, the motivation shifted toward the fulfillment of unmet needs rather than extending the sexual possibilities of all individuals—married and single (Millikan 1994: 235). Flirty Fishing had been the ultimate sacrifice, and hence the ultimate moral good. This attitude extended to sharing—denying the sexual needs of another meant selfishness, a grave sin within the context of the Law of Love. According to Millikan, "By elevating sex to make it a moral good, they have created the obverse, namely that the denial of sex to another in need is a moral evil" (234).

An example of this is described in *The Girl Who Wouldn't* (Berg 1978a). As related by former members, a leader working in the field, Lori, a gay woman, requested a mate and helper to join her on her mission.[18] Berg sent out a female member named Toni to help Lori, and, also, to be her mate. Toni helped with the missionary work, but would not share with Lori, despite Lori's requests. Both sent letters to Berg stating their feelings, and Berg published these as part of a Mo letter, a response to Lori and Toni, in which he was critical of Toni and her refusal to be intimate with Lori. I quote at length from this publication:

> [W]e're greatly disappointed in Toni, sorry to say, that she could have withheld herself from you when you had need, and she was your travelling mate. She withheld herself from her sister in need.... She should have supplied the love and affection and the sex you needed, but she denied it selfishly, independently, wilfully, in spite of all our Letters on love and sharing and mutual supplying of each other's needs. As far as we are concerned, she is without excuse, and we're both highly disappointed in her that she denied herself to you, even if she didn't like it, even if she didn't particularly care for it herself. (Berg 1978a pars. 3–5)

Berg used this as an excuse to criticize attitudes that he considered to be out of line with the Law of Love. He emphasized that Toni should at least have tried to be intimate with Lori, and criticized her for using the same excuse he claimed others gave in the past for not engaging in Flirty Fishing. Berg used himself as an example of how the Law of Love should be practiced. Sharing, according to him, should be practiced with the aim of pleasing others; it is about sacrifice, and should be done sacrificially (par. 14). Pleasing another should make one happy, he argued. But compromisers and halfhearted people, whom he considered selfish, were, according to Berg, worse than honest sinners (par. 17): "Even if it rubbed her the wrong way and she didn't like it at all, she should have gritted her teeth and borne it, just like any husband or any wife or any mate or any FFer has to do sometimes, even if she hated it! She should have done it for your sake and out of love, compassion, sacrifice, unselfishness and sharing!" (par. 23). Berg then advised Lori that she could either keep Toni or send her away, but that he, himself, wouldn't want her to work in his area: "As far as I'm concerned, she doesn't believe what I write because she doesn't obey what I write" (par. 22). Hence, Berg argued, she failed God by failing Lori, and she was a disappointment to God. And after failing this test of God, after failing the Family and Lori, what task could she be trusted to do? Berg wrote that he did not want her on his team, and after such a statement, one wonders who in the Family would have wanted her on their team? Toni was likely to have felt strongly reprimanded and rejected. And for others within the Family, this publication stressed the importance of sharing, whether one wanted to or not, and is likely to have put pressure on some members to take part in this ministry. Sharing is an integral aspect of the Law of Love. Although this law was meant to encourage respect and equality, it was also open to abuse (especially at times when there was no official charter). Many in the Family argue that there are ways in which they were protected from sharing against their will.[19] But at times homes were spread out and there was no central leadership, and consequently many members had to rely on Mo letters and personal interpretation—and Law of Love concepts such as respect and equality were competing with sacrifice and the sin of selfishness. Over time official safety measures had to be put in place in order to protect members, especially the younger members in the Family.

Children

When sharing results in pregnancy, the spouse or partner is expected to welcome the child within the union—and raise it as his own. The biological father is not excluded, but the spouse or partner virtually adopts the child. The years following the start of the Flirty Fishing ministry were ones of considerable sexual freedom within the group, and this was manifested in the number of children born within the Family. This decade of the Family's history, however, is also the one that has raised most concerns among child welfare authorities. At a time when all forms of sexual interchange outside male homosexuality were allowed, and when individuals were experimenting with the boundaries of the Law of Love, the presence of children raised further questions about what was possible within the Law of Love.

Millikan wrote: "it is clear from the literature and the history of The Family that there were occasions when the sexual division between adults and children were blurred. I am aware of a number of instances where the literature led some Family members to explore the fullest dimensions of sexual freedom, even with children" (1994: 241). According to Berg, children should be given the greatest freedom possible. He taught that our bodies are natural, and that sex is a natural need and God-given expression. He also taught that children should be raised without inhibitions to their own God-given bodies and urges. Berg argued that if children can already enjoy sexual feelings at such a young age, then what is wrong with sexual experimentation happening in a loving way (Berg 1977a, 1980, 1987)?

It was around this time in the group's doctrinal history that the Davidito Letters were written (these letters circulated from about 1975 until 1981) in which instances of sexual contact, including oral sex between Maria's three-year old son and his young nanny, Sara, were related. *The Story of Davidito* is a 750-page book published in 1982 and consists of a compilation of these letters; it covers the birth and rearing of Davidito, and includes twenty pages that deal with the Family's attitudes to Davidito's sexual development.[20] It is the most contentious of the Family's publications. According to Millikan, the book includes descriptions of Davidito being involved in a wide range of sexual behaviors with adults, watching couples having sexual intercourse on various occasions, and being allowed sexual contact with the women around him.[21] The book was removed from circulation in 1987, and, according to Millikan, prior to this it was not read by the majority of the group (1994: 245).[22] The book was reportedly written by Sara, who had primary responsibility for Davidito's care. It allegedly never carried the same authority as Mo letters and other direct communications from Berg.

Millikan met Davidito in 1994 and quotes him saying he was a test tube, an experiment, but that it didn't harm him in any way, and that it was not like "he was having sex all the time.... I really don't think it hurt me in any way. I never felt uncomfortable with it" (1994: 247). This is in contrast, however, with comments Davidito wrote in 2002, after leaving the Family, on movingon.org, a website of former second-generation members, using the name Ricky.[23] There he wrote about Mene (Berg's granddaughter; see chapter 2) and what life was like for the children who lived with Berg when he, Ricky, was growing up: "Maria and Sara were obsessed with their image and the reflection we cast on it. We not only had to be 'good kids', but we had to be the best! After all, we were 'Grandpa and Maria's kids'. We were supposed to be super-kids, commissioned with taking over the Family when Berg died, and leading God's Endtime Army through the Great Tribulation!" (Rodriguez 2002). This story includes strong criticism of the overly sexualized atmosphere, and how this affected some of the young girls. Ricky elaborates on the sexual abuse of Deborah (Berg's daughter, who eventually left the movement and wrote a book detailing her experiences) and Mene, among others. He described the atmosphere at their community in the Philippines as sexualized; as a child he frequently observed adults engaging in sexual intercourse, and said he was supposed to engage in similar behavior himself (Rodriguez 2002). Posting again on movingon.org, he described the experiences in more detail:[24]

> Berg also came up with the bright idea that the teen girls and I should have regular sex together on a rotating schedule.... Of course, I didn't have to have my arm twisted for that, but I must say, it was a little awkward—especially since I was much younger than most of them were, and I could tell that a couple of them were uncomfortable with it. I hoped that after some of the teen girls left, and we moved to a new compound christened the "Hilltop", that Teen Training would end, and things would be a little easier. How wrong I was! Round one of Teen Training looked like a Sunday School Picnic compared to round two, and we were miserable! (Rodriguez 2002)

Several family members I have interviewed have argued that this kind of sexual experimentation happened at a time when the organization of the Family was looser and more diverse than before, or than it has been since. They argue that there was a fluid membership and less cohesion between the households. Hence there was diversity between households, and some households embraced this greater freedom, whereas others did not do so to the same extent. This appears to be a well-accepted explanation, as the same argument has been made by a number of scholars.[25]

History of Investigations

The first wave of people leaving the Family had brought internal literature into the wider society, as well as stories of their experiences. With the help and support of anticult organizations, authorities were made aware of the concerns surrounding children. Between 1989 and 1994, Family communities were investigated in Venezuela, Italy, Argentina, Spain, the United Kingdom, Norway, Peru, Australia, France, the United States, Belgium, and Sweden by the relevant child-welfare authorities—although in most cases the communities were entered by local police, after which the children were handed over to social services and the courts. In some cases the parents were held in prison while their children were taken into state custody. This was to become a lengthy battle for Family communities.

In 1989 police raided two Family communities in Argentina.[26] Adults were arrested and held for two weeks, while 18 children were placed in state custody, and returned a little over six weeks later. In 1993 police raided five Family residences in Buenos Aires, arresting and imprisoning 21 adults and holding 137 children in state custody, both groups remaining in custody for three and a half months. By 1993, Argentine authorities had examined over 230 children of Family members; they found no evidence of physical, sexual, or psychological abuse. In Spain, authorities took 21 children into state custody for nearly twelve months in 1990. In 1992, after predawn raids on a community in Sydney, Australia, 65 children were taken into state custody. There was a simultaneous raid in Melbourne in which 56 children were taken into custody. In both cases the children were returned a week later. In 1993 in France 22 adults were arrested and 80 children taken into state custody. The adults were released after forty-eight hours for lack of evidence, and 33 children were released after one week, the others after 51 days.[27]

In all cases where whole communities were investigated the charges included sexual, physical, or psychological abuse of children. In the United Kingdom, this included the charge of ownership of pornographic material. In France the charges also included child prostitution and lack of medical and physical care for the children. In Argentina the charges also included kidnapping, child trafficking, prostitution, and slavery (*Family Vindicated* 1997). The Family estimates that court-appointed and independent authorities around the world have examined approximately 600 children from Family communities (*Family Vindicated* 1997). In no instances were cases of abuse found. The Family has acknowledged that there had been cases of abuse, but argued that there were very few cases, and that changes had already been instituted by the time authorities intervened; critics argue that children had been taught to lie to authorities.[28]

There has been a debate since about who actually committed child abuse, the Family or the authorities who raided the communities and took the children away from the parents, in some cases for extended periods of time, but found no evidence for abuse.[29] The authorities generally relied on information offered to them that portrayed a singularly negative picture of a "sex cult" run by a pedophile, and were rightly concerned. The information was one-sided and portrayed a stereotypically negative view. However, any scrutiny by authorities was likely to have been met with reluctance and cynicism by members, and with fear by the children. The latter had been socialized in a culture of millennialism where the world is seen as corrupt and ruled by evil, and in the belief that the Law of Love superseded all else. An important part of the worldview was that the children were part of a revolutionary group that was working against the system, and were to prepare themselves for the return of Jesus. The system as a concept described society outside the Family and was associated with ungodliness, worldliness, capitalism, and other perceived evils. This vilifying of the outside while teaching that Family members were true followers of God and were to be Jesus's army upon his return created an "us versus them" attitude among members, which was inculcated into the children. The children in the Family considered themselves part of the end-time army, but who were temporarily held captive by the system.

A persistent theme throughout the history of the Family is the adherence to Berg's call of total commitment and renunciation of the world—the system. This could be compared to monastic life, where a person turns from all worldly ties, takes no secular job, and recognizes no allegiance either to family, friends, lovers, or financial security that will threaten the primacy of one's total commitment to Christ (Millikan 1994: 231). Although the level of world renunciation has been flexible and adaptable over time, with some members working outside when necessary or appropriate, it is an aspect of the doctrine that has been strongly present throughout the history of the Family. And this rejection is mutual, as the majority of society regarded the group (and in many cases still regards it) as an aberrant cult. Family members understood this as part of the process, since they took it as their task to unveil what they perceived as the evils of society and to uncover what they recognize as the work of Satan. Hence the Family rejected society, but members also felt persecuted by society, both in a good way (as if they were revolutionaries who were being rebuked by those on the side of Satan) and in a bad way (discrimination and persecution). This feeling of persecution led to the leadership, and at times the movement, going underground. The Family has had a history of responding to difficult situations with local authorities by fleeing, citing Jesus's advice that "when they persecute you in one city, flee ye to another" (Millikan 1994: 224). Many of the first members of the second generation were raised with "flee bags" under their beds, so that they were ready to flee when necessary. This background provides some context to the polarized and hardhanded approach chosen by authorities, whether one deems it appropriate or not. There was simply no history of cooperation with outsiders, and quite a few anecdotes of lack of cooperation.

Accommodation

No evidence of sexual abuse was found during the investigations; the Family had already undergone some changes by the time authorities stepped in.

During the late 1980s several significant changes were initiated in the Family. Flirty Fishing or FFing became DFing (the Daily Food ministry, developed through the publication and distribution of a series of booklets entitled Daily Food), sex between adults and minors was prohibited, and sex among teenagers was restricted.[30] But was this because of internal decisions, or a result of external pressures and events? Although the Family leadership argues that it had initiated many changes before the peak of outside scrutiny, many of the leaders' writings from that time appear to be in response to outside criticism. From the late 1980s there appears to be an important and ongoing interaction between the group and society, which is illustrated in the publications of that time, and it shows that outside pressure certainly had a significant influence on their decisions.

In these publications, the leaders strongly insisted that these changes did not mean that the previous practices had been wrong. Members were encouraged to be proud of their Flirty Fishing history. But AIDS had forced a different approach, and, reportedly, the Lord had intimated to Berg and Maria that it was time to switch to DFing—the Daily Food ministry. Similarly, sex among teenagers had been restricted, not, reportedly, because it was deemed to be wrong, but because sexual and romantic involvement often wound up complicating the lives of the young members and distracting them from the service for the Lord. The leadership asserted that teenagers lack the spiritual maturity and foundation in the Word. Yet leaders also mentioned that in many countries such behavior is either prohibited or frowned on by the authorities (Amsterdam and Apollos 1993).

The push and pull that resulted from outside scrutiny and criticism versus the doctrinal priorities of the group is clearly illustrated in two publications written after the height of the investigations, *Why Do Ye Stone Us?* (Berg 1992) and the following General Newsletter (referred to as GN), *Our Beliefs concerning the Lord's Law of Love*, written by Peter Amsterdam and Apollos (1993), members of the leadership. The publications are ambiguous—they show an awareness of mainstream concepts of harm and abuse and a willingness to conform, while also rebuking these mainstream concepts and insisting that these do not parallel the Law of Love. *Why Do Ye Stone Us?* asserts (throughout, emphasis in original):

> *Of course, we have never allowed actual child abuse of any kind, as we would never think of harming our children!* We are completely against any kind of child abuse, not only because of the System, but because we *love* our children & to harm them in any way would be

completely against our principles of love. We cannot even allow *any* kind of sexual affection between minors & adults whatsoever, even though the Bible says that 'to the pure, *all* things are pure.'—Tit. 1:15. We have found that even though 'all things are *lawful* unto us, all things are not *expedient*' (1 Cor. 10:23), which means that even though some things may be perfectly *lawful* & all right in the eyes of *God*, they may not be helpful or profitable for us.

We certainly do not condone nor approve of child sexual molestation, exploitation or abuse. In fact, we have very stringently condemned it & have made it very clear that not only is any kind of actual child abuse absolutely *illegal* in our Homes & that anyone guilty of any such practices must be excommunicated & ostracised & cast out of our Homes & our fellowship, but we've also had to go as far as to ban any *non*-abusive contact with minors which could be construed as 'abuse' by the System! (Berg 1992 pars. 62–63)

In this publication, Berg continues to argue that the system is full of sins and false rules, and were the Bible used as a standard, then society would not be able to argue that the Family had sinned. The Family and the system, including established religion, are worlds apart regarding their policies on sexuality, and Berg describes this as the same difference between God's opinion and the devil's opinion—a divide so great that it cannot be bridged. It is the difference between the doctrine that "sex is a sin" and the doctrine that "sex as a manifestation of Love is pure." Berg argues that now, in some cases, the laws of society are completely contrary to the laws of God: "So you who rebuke me, I in turn rebuke you as the sinners" (1992: par. 68).

The Family's doctrine maintained this distinction, and continued to give priority to the Law of Love. This is clear from the publication *Our Beliefs concerning the Lord's Law of Love*, which acted as a reminder of what exactly the Law of Love is, in light of the changes to sexual freedoms within the Family. This publication explained the current restrictions placed on sexual policies and why they have been instituted and argued that they do not alter the Law of Love:

The main reason we don't have as many freedoms along those lines today as we once had is because many of us *misused* them. The Lord gave us those freedoms so we could *sacrificially* & *unselfishly* help *others*. But many of us simply weren't *mature* enough to handle them wisely & responsibly, thus we wound up using—or *misusing*—them *selfishly* & getting way off the track. So for our *own* well-being & for His *Work's* sake, the Lord had to restrict or severely limit many of those freedoms. (Amsterdam and Apollos 1993: 2)

But Amsterdam and Apollos also admitted that there have been some wider "*misinterpretations*":

Unfortunately, the teachings of the Letters & the principles of the Law of Love were not always carried out perfectly by every Family Member. Many of us were young & immature when we were first learning to apply the Law of Love, so there were cases where the Word was misinterpreted or misunderstood, & these freedoms were used 'as an occasion to the flesh' (Gal. 5:13) & not applied lovingly & unselfishly as the Lord and Dad [Berg] had intended. When Dad wrote those letters, he expected us to be *Loving, unselfish, considerate & mature* enough in spirit that we wouldn't do anything that would hurt anyone else. (3)

Overall, our past practice of the Law of Love bore good fruit & had wonderful results. But because some of us were not as mature & loving & yielded to the Lord as we should have been, there were some problems & some mistakes were made. But the Lord even used our mistakes to teach us some valuable lessons, & we have since learned that it's better to wisely curb some of our sexual freedoms because they're not all necessary or helpful. We've also learned that by putting less emphasis on sexual freedoms & relationships, we can thereby devote ourselves more fully to the Lord's Work. (3)

Peter Amsterdam and Apollos continuously reinforced the argument that the different rules and restrictions regarding sexual activities that were incorporated did not signify a departure from the principles of the Law of Love, but an affirmation of it. Essentially, they argued that the Law of Love worked, and problems were blamed on the proverbial "bad apples" and misinterpretations. The new rules and restrictions, they argued, act as a safeguard to help ensure that everyone is indeed acting in accordance with the Law of Love—by removing some potential problems these new rules ensure that no one is "hurt" or "harmed" (3). Hence there is an affirmation that these freedoms are biblical and according to principles. But according to the authors, the system does not understand, and hence they have decided to curb some of these freedoms.

> We've also learned that some of our past freedoms were difficult for a lot of weak & unenlightened outsiders to comprehend.... We have chosen to discontinue some of the freedoms we practiced [sic] in the past, even though 'all things indeed are pure.'... But according to God's Word there is absolutely nothing wrong with the freedom of Love & the principles of the Law of Love.... (3)
>
> *Yet another area in which we've changed over the years* is regarding any kind of intimate relationships between adults (those over 21 years of age) & minors (those under 21 years of age).... *As you are probably aware, in recent years, the System has been on an absolute rampage against child abuse*, & we totally agree with them that there is a lot of genuine abuse out there... However, if someone were to specifically ask us if any intimate contact between an adult and a minor is inherently wrong, abusive & bound to cause psychological harm, we would have to honestly answer 'no.' (4–5)

Seemingly in contradiction with the above, the authors also claimed that these freedoms were not curbed because of the system's demands, but rather, and more importantly, as a result of a teen training camp meeting in Mexico, the first large gathering of teenagers. Berg and Maria became aware that there had been sexual interaction between adults and minors, and that this was not in the best interest of the teenagers—it hindered their interaction with the Lord. Reportedly, Berg and Maria were worried about the emotional and spiritual well-being of the teenagers, and also curbed the relationships between the teenagers with new rules in 1986. Hence they argued that the changes were made as a result of internal demands rather than external pressures.

The publications at this time presented an ambiguous message; some problematic practices were described as "fine" and "Godly," but not "expedient" (Berg 1992). There was neither outright condemnation of sexual relations with minors, nor approval. Changes at this time appeared to be part of a transitional era in the Family; the leaders were beginning to listen and react to outside scrutiny. But there were not, at this point, many sacrifices regarding Family doctrine and tradition. Ward argued that the line of reasoning in publication GN 555 (Amsterdam and Apollos 1993) was that neither Berg nor Maria nor the Law of Love was to blame for any of the "excesses of the flesh." Instead, these were blamed on the weak members (Ward 1995). James Penn (2000: 8), a former member who published a memoir, refers to these alleged weak members (or "bad apples," as I have referred to them above) as the "usual suspects"—the ones consistently blamed by the leadership for any wrongdoings. Ward also described the publication as ambiguous and confusing in the sense that it states that adult-child sex is not wrong, it is right for members of the Family, but they should not do it because "the System does not understand," and as a result they could get into trouble (1995). And they did, so this message would have resonated with followers. A later publication, GN 653, written by Maria, includes Amsterdam's letter to Ward (in response to the latter's request that the Family denounce some of Berg's teachings), in which he did accept and acknowledge that Berg bears responsibility for what arose as a result of some of his teachings, namely the overly sexualized atmosphere in a number of Family communities, which in some cases led to a number of children being subjected to sexually inappropriate behavior (Maria 1995). Maria, too, acknowledged that in hindsight, some of that material should not have been published (1995). (This was a big move away from GN 555, and I elaborate on these developments later in this chapter.) Penn (2000: 10) argues that it took Maria and Peter seven years to admit that sexual abuse of minors had occurred in the Family, and that Berg, through his writings, had to bear a responsibility for this. According to Penn (2000: 11), "They published GN 555 because they *wanted* to; they published GN 653 because they were *forced* to." Thus, Penn suggests, the Family changed as a result of outside pressure.

The Reliability of Literature

Despite the apologetics in the literature, the Family adapted as a result of external pressure. Yet analysis of the literature shows a great reluctance to change, which raises questions about the unwritten culture within the group, and the extent to which we can rely on the literature being representative of the mood in the movement as a whole. Millikan argues that it was not uncommon for literature, which was considered normative, to be discarded on the basis of a further revelation from Berg (1994: 183). This is, of course, intrinsic to charismatic leadership, which is generally not governed by rules or traditions and is consequently susceptible to changes following new revelations or realizations. This flexibility, for example, affected the status assigned to *The Story of Davidito*, which followers were urged to destroy once the leadership realized the contents could cause problems.[31]

> As you know, some years ago we instructed all of our Homes worldwide to dispose of any copies they may still have had of the "Dito"

book, as well as the "Adults Only" TK volume. We explained then that because of society's increasing hyper-sensitivity to any publications for or about children that could even be remotely construed as having any sexual overtones to them, the modern-day inquisitors and witch-hunters who are bent on destroying our Family and our work for the Lord are declaring that many of our Family pubs appear "evil" to them. (1Thes. 5:22)

To our ungodly enemies and vengeful false accusers, some of our perfectly pure doctrines and views regarding God's Own natural and beautiful sinless creation are very "defiled" and "impure" in their soiled minds! (See Titus 1:15) In fact, they're so offended by some of our views (or their interpretations and misinterpretations of what they think are our views) and publications and pictures, that they seem bent on using (misusing) them to try to substantiate their very false and malicious accusations against us that we abuse our own dear children! So for this reason, we are now initiating an extensive "purge" of our publications. Thank the Lord, most of our publications will come through this purge with only a few pages missing. (*Pubs Purge Advisory* 1991)

Although here the concerns appear to be more about destroying past literature than explaining that the past teachings are no longer appropriate, the result is nonetheless that contentious literature was then no longer widely accessible. At the same time, other measures were taken to ensure the system would not be able to "destroy" the Family. For instance, the creation of the Charter ensured the organization could show it had formalized and institutionalized rules, and the result was seemingly a more responsible group. Hence, questions must be asked before deciding on the validity of literature, for example, the date (the most recent publications must take precedence, especially when it covers contentious topics) and the author.

Throughout the history of the Family, the literature relating to issues of doctrine has come from a number of sources: Berg himself, Maria, Peter Amsterdam, Apollos and others in the leadership, and many other voices have been added through prophecy, including those of Berg after his death and Jesus.[32] The Family's revelations have changed with time as well—they are dynamic, following the idea of "progressive revelation," that is, the belief that God did not reveal his mind once and for all, but in parts according to the demands of the situation (Millikan 1994: 184). Hence some things in the past can be superseded or "explained" by new insights. This means that Mo letters are subject to the limitations of history. And members are, apparently, expected to judge the truth of the literature sent to them on the basis of their own understanding and their own contact with the Bible (Millikan 1994: 185–186). More recently, members were also encouraged to rely on their own prophecies when making judgments (Bainbridge 2002). The Family publication *Our Replies to Allegations of Child Abuse* (1992) asserts that the fact that certain ideas are openly discussed in literature does not mean that they become, or are even supposed to become, standard practice.

Millikan argues that within the Family there is room for questioning, and that there have been occasions where authority in the Family was challenged successfully. He interviewed a member who argued that Berg was a man who was iconoclastic by inclination and that his letters should not be read as literal statements of what must be (Millikan 1994: 187). This is, however, a much-challenged position. There are also accounts of members being ridiculed and publicly ostracized for challenging, or even questioning, authority or the status quo. Former member Miriam Williams (1998), in her account of her life in the Family, describes being publicly ostracized and ridiculed after writing a children's story that had not impressed Berg. Toni in *The Girl Who Wouldn't* (Berg 1978a) was also publicly criticized, in this case for not sexually sharing with another woman—as described above. More recently, in April 2002, a disillusioned second-generation adult sent a letter to friends to be forwarded as a chain among other young adults. The young man was upset over the fact that many of his friends within his cohort were leaving. He commented that the group had a majority of young people, yet was still run by the first generation, whom he regarded as stiff and inflexible, and who came down very hard on the small mistakes of the younger generation. When Amsterdam and Maria were sent a copy by another member, they published the letter, with their disparaging response, in a general publication entitled *The Professionals*. On the one hand this can be seen as management of a potentially damaging situation, as the letter was in parts critical of aspects of life in the Family, and was being distributed informally. On the other hand, Amsterdam (2002), in his answer, mentioned on several occasions that the author of the letter had an "attitude issue," was immature, and suffered from negativity.[33] The author had been labeled in such a way that Family members could ignore his views as coming from a young man who had so-called personal problems. *The Professionals* was followed by *Speak for Yourself!* (2002), devoted to thoughts, reactions, and replies to the young member's critical letter, and which consisted almost entirely of praise for the Family and scathing criticism of the young member's letter, including comments about him being a "loser" and a "coward." These two publications read like a warning to all second-generation adults—this was not an appropriate criticism, and the bearer of this criticism was widely ridiculed. There may be room for questioning and interpretation, but within boundaries.

In every religious tradition there is a gap between what the leadership and the literature call for and the way in which the followers respond. Maria has written at the end of the publication by Amsterdam and Apollos (emphasis in original):

> We also need to understand that The Family's teachings & principles are not necessarily always carried out perfectly by all of our members. In other words, the actions of one person or Home do not always accurately reflect the policies & principles of The Family. Unfortunately, some of our Homes or followers have fallen far short of that standard. (1993 par. 67)

With regard to the Family it is important to establish to what extent literature was considered normative, and to what extent there was freedom to not accept it. Millikan (1994: 186), for example, argues that Flirty Fishing was never universally accepted, and that there were acceptable reasons within communities not to practice Flirty Fishing. Yet this also depended on the communities—some were reported to be more bohemian and experimental than others.[34] This lack of uniformity is a theme throughout the history of the Family; teachings have always been fluid. Before 1978, sexual activities outside marriage needed approval from the home leadership. In 1978, the RNR brought chaos as the communities became independent, spread globally, and were out of touch with the leadership. Poor communication between communities intensified the isolation, and homes were free to interpret literature as they thought appropriate—they no longer needed leadership permission. After 1978 all members were free to exercise their faith in regard to sexual sharing (Maria 1995). The publication of Berg's *The Devil Hates Sex* in 1980 opened the door to the possibilities of sexual relations with minors, and the Fellowship Revolution initiated a rise in sexual contacts between adults within the communities.[35] Gordon Melton wrote:

> Without a doubt 1981 and 1982 were the years in which most of the events for which The Family has been criticised occurred. It was the

era of the first dance videos, it was a time in which adult-teenage sex was allowed (though it was never the norm), and it was the period in which the widest range and the most sensitive issues of sexual conduct was [sic] discussed by Father David in the literature. (1994b: 88)[36]

Yet through a process one could call trial and error, the Family has, over time, moved away from some of its teachings and adapted, to a considerable extent, some of its practices. (One could argue that, since the 2012 reboot, the sect has transformed itself beyond recognition, choosing biblical authority over the old authority structures and teachings of Berg.)

Bending versus Breaking

In the United Kingdom, what the Family has referred to as persecution came in the form of a custody dispute, generally referred to as the Ward case (in reference to the judge overseeing the case, Lord Justice Ward), in which a grandmother sought custody of her grandson who was born within the Family.[37] This court case initiated some of the most significant changes within the Family, which included a letter to Ward in which one of the leaders, Peter Amsterdam, distanced himself and the Family from some of Berg's writings, as Ward had demanded.[38] In a Family publication distributed after the court case, which also included the text of the letter to Ward, Amsterdam admitted that some of the resentful former members have legitimate grievances (Maria 1995: 1). He also, however, again put the blame on the proverbial bad apples who did not adhere to the "Golden Rule" of the Law of Love, despite Berg's writings not being very clear on the limitations of this "law" (1, 6, 8). But there was, nonetheless, an admission of past mistakes. This change in tone had, apparently, been approved from above. Through prophecy, Maria and Peter had received messages from Berg allegedly telling them that it was acceptable to blame Berg, since he was the leader and "the buck stops with the leader." Berg's message, through prophecy, explained that he had not meant to hurt anyone, but in hindsight he realized that some people had been hurt nonetheless. He reportedly urged Peter and Maria to go ahead and say that he, Berg, should have been wiser (2–3). There were other messages. The Lord allegedly, through prophecy, urged them to "bend, but not break" (2–3). This was reinforced by another prophecy from Berg who specified that "bending" means "putting the blame on him" while breaking would be to "deny the Law of Love" (4). "*Don't deny the Truth, don't deny the Truth-Giver, and don't deny the messenger*. But if you have to poke a little at the messenger, some of the faults and failings, and point some blame here and there, don't worry about it! There are lots of things I could've done better, and boy, if I had known then what I know now, there are things I would've done differently" (4–5). Amsterdam and Maria, with alleged permission from Berg, described how the Law of Love was handled and mishandled: through lack of leadership during the RNR combined with Berg exploring the boundaries and possibilities of the Law of Love in reality and in the disseminated literature.

In the letter to Ward, the authors, Amsterdam and Apollos, claim they were given "skill and power from on High" as well (Maria 1995: 11). The letter details the changes they have undertaken regarding child discipline rules, education (the establishment of an educational steering committee), and reconciliation with former members (attached was a report with the progress of the Ministry of Reconciliation). But the most significant change was an acknowledgment of David Berg's responsibility regarding inappropriate sexual activity with children in the Family. The authors acknowledged that the Family had, in certain places and at certain times, not been as safe an environment for children as it should have been. In the letter to Ward they respond to his crucial demand:

> Your Lordship has asked us to acknowledge that Father David, through his writings, was personally responsible for children in The Family being sexually abused. Father David wrote a series of Letters concerning sexual behaviour. The Judgement refers in particular to 'The Law of Love' and 'The Devil Hates Sex', and we accept that as the author of ideas upon which some members acted to the harm of minors in The Family, he must bear responsibility for that harm. (Maria 1995: 14)

Amsterdam and Apollos added that Maria and World Services leadership also felt the burden of responsibility. This statement was followed by the argument that the global spread of independent communities during this time of their history left them out of touch with World Services, the central administrative wing of the organization. Hence there was no direct guidance accompanying the literature, and World Services did not have the connection necessary to function as effective "leaders" (15). Wherever the bulk of responsibility was placed—Berg's exploring of boundaries, a time of lawlessness, a few bad apples, or a combination of these—the Family leaders distanced themselves from some of the key doctrinal aspects of their past.[39] They accommodated to Ward's demands and, consequently, the mother retained custody of the child.

The Changes after the Ward Case

The recantations in response to the Ward case, however, do not necessarily mean that the Family denominationalized in a process to blend with the mainstream.[40] The years following the Ward case saw several missions aimed at reinforcing the importance of the Law of Love, recapturing the Family's tenuous level of insertion into society—reclaiming their space as revolutionaries. In 1997 a mission to bridge the generation gap was initiated, where members were encouraged to bring the entire Family community, young and old, closer together in the spirit of "loving Jesus," which included intergenerational sexual sharing according to age guidelines stipulated in the Charter (Maria 1997). This mission had followed closely on a previous one, in 1996, which was an effort to bring the entire Family community closer to Jesus, through the *Loving Jesus Revelation* (Apollos 1996). This was a revelation that encouraged members to think of Jesus and communicate with him not only when praying but also when being intimate with a partner and when masturbating. Followers were encouraged to imagine themselves having an intimate relationship with Jesus. This was a controversial practice, and several members, especially young members, left the movement as a result (Apollos 1996; Maria 1996a). Men, especially, found it difficult to imagine themselves in an intimate relationship with someone they considered to be another man, Jesus. But it was explained that, in the spirit, you can be anything you want, hence a man could have characteristics traditionally regarded as "female," and men were to think of themselves as "spiritually receptive" in their relationship with Jesus (Maria 1996a). This particular practice was claimed to be optional, but Penn (2000: 26), the former member, argues that this statement was later followed by warnings that God would withhold his blessing from anyone who did not love Jesus in this intimate new way. Members could be reclassified to the marginal status of "turf supporter" status (members who no longer live in a Family home but still tithe) if they did not join in what the *Loving Jesus Revelation* called for (Penn 2000: 26). The "junior end time teens" received an edited version of the *Loving Jesus Revelation*, as did turf supporters. The unedited version only went to the committed members—the disciples. Through reported prophecy, Jesus had allegedly warned it was preferable to give teens and turf supporters the version without the intimate sexual revelation. Berg had added, through prophecy, that this revelation is "not for the weak" (Maria 1996a).

One young mother was worried about the effects the *Loving Jesus Revelation* might have, and asked, in a letter to Maria, why it was not published as a "burn after reading" publication. She was worried that if these publications fell into the wrong hands, her children might be at risk of being taken away by authorities (Maria 1996b). Maria responded that describing a publication as "burn after reading" material does not guarantee that it will not fall into the hands of the group's detractors, and that, through prophecy, Berg had revealed that this was a call from Jesus for Family members to "lift up the standard" and conquer, knowing they have the truth with them. Through alleged prophecy, Jesus told the Family that this teaching would be misunderstood, but that he would protect them (Maria 1996b). However, former members and critics of the group interpreted this new development as evidence that the Family had not actually changed: "It is now very easy to see that there has not been a dime's worth of real and fundamental change in the COG [Children of God]. Their recent trying to be perceived as more mainstream may have made some of us wonder if in fact there is some sincerity and honesty in all this. Then the Loving Jesus sacrilege came and shattered all hopes" (*More Madness* 1997: 1).

Shakeup 2000

The upcoming new millennium saw a purge to strengthen and cleanse the Family from the alleged external influences of the system. According to Maria, many people in the then "charter member" Family had settled down to the point where they were ineffective and without the vision needed to be a revolutionary.[41] She wrote that quite a few of the young adults and second-generation adults did not seem to want to be in the Family, yet did not take steps to leave. She accused these members of "putting up with The Family" and living in the security of community living, which, for Family members, is safer than the system. But in her opinion, these members did not deserve that privilege (Maria 1999b). Maria put forward an ultimatum: if members do not want to live the charter member standard, then they should not be in the charter member Family. The Family had to go back to its roots and purge itself of system influences. As had become common practice in the Family, these new teachings were reportedly received through prophecy, mainly from Jesus and Berg. According to Maria, Jesus said:

> Now as you and your children near the End, you must go back to the beginning, back to the freshness, the freedom of spirit, the total break with the world as there was in the beginning. There must be a purging, because the children of David must be kept free from the System and the influences of the world, which, if left unchecked, if allowed to continue as they now are, would destroy The Family. (7)

"Back to the beginning," according to Maria, refers to a move back to the spirit of dedication and commitment that the first disciples in the Family had. There was strong criticism of the young members who were thought to be too infatuated with the system and its music, films, Internet, clothes, people, and so on. These members were accused of being bad apples that ruined the batch by allowing poison to seep into the Family communities.[42]

> As Dad [Berg] explains, some of you are also weakening because of the ungodly and unedifying influence of your System jobs or your contact with System relatives or from having your kids in System school. These too can become inroads for the poison of the System in the form of compromise and wrong attitudes, and getting away from not having time for the Lord and His Word.... (7)
>
> What each of you Charter Members need to realise is that the level of ungodly and unedifying influence in your life and Home that was tolerated *before* the publishing of 'The Shakeup 2000!' will no longer be tolerated. It cannot be allowed if we are to strengthen The Family, and to do so, things must change in this area, and change drastically!... (7)
>
> When you have total incorrigibles who are causing no end of trouble and really poisoning the flock, you want to get them out as quickly as you can, before they contaminate others further, but you can still be loving. (17)

This poisoning of the communities, according to Jesus (through prophecy) would weaken the communities and, eventually, lead to persecution (Maria 1999b). Hence, Maria argued, the Family needed to go back to the basics: total commitment and rejection of the system. *Shakeup 2000* (Maria 1999b) was a criticism of anyone who was not a full-time, devoted, and committed revolutionary for the Family—those not showing the dedication expected of a devoted member were urged either to change their attitude or to leave the charter membership. Charter members were given a six-month probation period to give Jesus and the Family their full devotion, after which they had to decide whether or not they wanted to continue as charter members. Senior teens (age sixteen and up), as voting members of the Family, were given the same ultimatum, but the commitment required of them was different: they were to sign a provisional charter member contract.[43]

Homes, in order to resist ungodly and unedifying influences, were required to vote on whether individuals could watch certain movies, read certain novels, play certain computer games, take a system job, send kids to a system school, and more. And these decisions were to be made using a new standard: the *Shakeup 2000* standard, which was stricter than the Family had been in recent history. Members were urged to consult God in these matters and wait for a prophecy before deciding. They were called on to strictly follow the Charter. Charter members could be disciplined for spiritual infractions of the Charter (when people sow division, mock or talk against the word, are a destructive influence or lead others astray, do not minimize ungodly or unedifying influences, and so forth). Such infractions are not easily proven, but the continental reporting offices and visiting shepherds had the freedom to judge situations for themselves and discipline accordingly (Maria 1999b: 8–9).[44] Teenagers were allowed their teenage moods and attitude, as long as this did not point to "wrong attitude," "bad spirit," or an infatuation with aspects of the system—for which they could be disfellowshipped (14–15).[45] As Jesus allegedly said, through prophecy: "So I don't want to hear of troublemakers and dividers and poison-injectors and System-lovers being tolerated in this Family anymore. We're a revolutionary Gideon's band, and I don't care if we lose one-third of our CM membership, if that's what it takes to keep us pure and separate from the world!" (23).[46] In contrast to the days of the Victor Program, there was an emphasis on being gentle and loving throughout the process of disciplining. There was also an emphasis on disengaged members being allowed to continue membership as "fellow members" rather than charter members, as opposed to earlier times when there were no such membership options, and members had to leave and were consequently alienated.

Yet Berg, through prophecy, had advised that even though not all fellow members and former members were a bad influence, some were. And although the leadership had developed a policy of greater unity with former members, to stem some of the division and bitterness between the two camps, Family disciples also had to protect their children from the possible bad influence of fellow member children and teenagers—as well as those who were no longer associated with the Family. This was a change from what Amsterdam wrote in response to the Ward case, which was that Family children would have regular contact with relatives who were not in the Family, and that young members who left would still have "loving contact" with their parents who remained members, despite having left (Maria 1995).[47] The Family wanted a clean break with the system on the one hand, yet it did not want to appear callous and cold to noncharter members. This is a contradiction, and the leaders appeared to be acutely aware of this:

> It was Dad's prerogative as God's End-time prophet to deliver some fiery messages and really sock it to some people. He was led of the Lord to do this, but I don't think the Lord is going to lead any of *you* to do the same thing. Dad *had* to be very strong for the sake of the Revolution, to get people moving and doing what they were supposed to do.
>
> But now, for us, this is not permissible, and we should not blast people. It's just not done!...
>
> So many of our past leaders got so harsh because they *misinterpreted* how they were supposed to handle people because of Dad's blasts. They did the same thing as Dad, but without the love and mercy that Dad showed, and without the justification that Dad had for doing it, because he was led of the Lord to do it and to be that way. (19–20)

These statements are followed by an alleged prophecy from Jesus, detailing that Berg's leadership is akin to a double act, as part of Berg's ministry was to be a fiery prophet while also being a gentle leader; when Berg gave a "hot" talk, it was claimed, this was Jesus's spirit coming through, not Berg's. But, Jesus declared, this attitude was only permissible to Berg, not to any other leaders currently within the Family (Maria 1995: 20). Hence the times of fiery and iconoclastic talk were to be a thing of the past, not permissible to current leadership. And although the Family had gone "back to the beginning," a time marked by full commitment and rejection of society, the sect was more sophisticated about its level of insertion into society. The Family embraced its roots again, which includes a move toward larger communities, but at the same time members realized the importance of having good relations with outsiders, and since the UK court case the Family has worked hard on maintaining good public relations. Family representatives can be relatively easily contacted by the media, academics, cult-watching groups, and government institutions in the United Kingdom as well as in many other countries. They also have sought contact with other religions in interfaith efforts as well as with nongovernmental organizations and charities working toward similar goals. The Family has, over time, developed more complex and ambiguous modes of insertion whereby parts of the organization reach out and engage in significant interactions with outside institutions, while many followers still aim to be revolutionary missionaries who reject the "system" and what it stands for. Since 2012 the range of insertion has become more varied as the authoritarian structure of the group has been dismantled.

Denial

The Family has had a history of constant change—one could interpret this as trial and error on the path to maturation into a community with a second- and third-generation membership.[48] Berg was an iconoclastic and experimental leader, and tried out a large range of ministries. In fact, it is part of the Family's theology to expect constant change (Bromley and Newton 1994; Melton 1994; Millikan 1994). As a result, one cannot ascertain the behavior of the Family on the basis of old literature; one can only use old literature to illustrate the Family's history and to chart the extent to which the sect has changed over time. The underlying principles have not changed, but the elaboration of them and the way the group is called to act on them have changed drastically. The changing circumstances have affected the way principles are lived out in the day-to-day life of the group. One can see this as accommodation to internal and external circumstances. Although the underlying principles remain relatively static, practices have been adapted and levels of insertion to society have fluctuated significantly. Yet this dual approach, accommodating on one level while holding on to underlying principles, or "bending versus breaking," has not been satisfactory to all—critics and former members have accused the Family of covering up its past mistakes and "cleaning up" superficially only for public relations purposes. The process of changes, as well as the discourse surrounding them, are of sociological interest.

Stanley Cohen's work on denial, *States of Denial: Knowing about Atrocities and Suffering* (2001), provides a useful framework for analyzing and understanding such discrepancies in discourses. Cohen (9) distinguishes between different aspects of denial, which include cognition (not acknowledging the facts), emotion (not feeling, not being disturbed), morality (not recognizing wrongness or responsibility), and action (not taking active steps in response to knowledge). Cohen's is a study of reactions to abuse and suffering, the discrepancy between perceptions of what happened, and both the personal and political ways in which uncomfortable realities are avoided and evaded. He distinguishes between literal denial ("this did not happen"), interpretive denial (the facts are given a different meaning from what seems apparent to others), and implicatory denial (psychological, political, or moral implications that follow are denied or minimized) (Cohen: 9). From an outsider's perspective, the Family is in interpretive denial. What outsiders would generally see as promiscuity, immoral behavior, and child sexual abuse was explained in the Family along the lines of the Law of Love and Berg's teachings—such as described in *The Devil Hates Sex* (Berg 1980). According to this doctrine, sex is a natural thing, and children are prone naturally to explore. The children were therefore encouraged to explore their sexuality with one another and, in some situations, with adult members. The young former members believe that the psychological implications and consequences, for them, have been largely denied.[49] According to Cohen's framework this amounts to implicatory denial on the part of the Family. The young former members focus on the issue that has had the single most impact in their lives, while members still in the Family, when admitting that there has been abuse (in the sense that the Law of Love has been ignored or misinterpreted), will argue that this happened for a short while in only a few homes—and usually the "bad apples" are blamed.[50]

Denial is not necessarily a personal and individual reaction, it can be a shared and collective response—consequently it can be organized and institutionalized (Cohen 2001: 9). And denial does not have to be complete; it can be partial, not acknowledging the extent of the problem or mostly blaming the proverbial bad apples. Not having taken immediate active steps in response to knowledge of a problem can be interpreted as a form of denial. ISKCON, as discussed in chapter 2, was also resistant to change. The leadership was slow in acting (reacting) in response to initial signs of problems within the community, and former members were critical of the speed and the ways in which the organization has attempted to rectify the problems. Such events, and the following types of denial, have consequences for the second generation and the way those persons view the communities of their childhood. This is discussed in the following chapters.

PART TWO

What Happened?

The question of what happened to the children goes beyond the dialectic between the sects and society covered in the first three chapters. In the second part of this book I concentrate on the accounts of the childhoods of those I interviewed, and the decisions they made, occasionally in constrained circumstances, as teenagers and young adults. Were these decisions in line with the expectations the parents had for their children? Have these second-generation members been "successfully socialized" into the beliefs and culture of the sectarian communities in which they were raised? The resulting dynamics with the groups in which they were raised often created a culture of blaming, stigma, and labeling that in turn affected their sense of self, and consequent secondary socialization. In the following chapter I focus on the broad issue of socialization insofar as it relates to the topic of the chapter, the integration of the children into their sectarian cultures, and how this has affected them.

4
When Perfect Children Grow Up

WHEN DAVIDITO WAS eighteen, as noted in chapter 3, he reported to an outside scholar that, although he was a test tube, in a sense, an experiment, he never felt uncomfortable with it and didn't think it hurt him in any way (Millikan 1994). Yet a few years later Davidito wrote some posts on a forum for former members under the name Ricky, in which he denounced the way he and in particular Mene (Berg's grandchild) were treated.

> I never felt any desire from my mother or Berg to want me to better myself emotionally, physically or mentally just because they loved me and wanted to help me as a person. Everything they ever did to me or for me was with the ulterior motive of wanting me to be the best little cultist I could be. They had to prove to the world that they were right, what they said really was true, and they were deserving of everybody's love and loyalty and the power they held over people's minds and souls.[1]

What Is Perceived as Successful Socialization?

The term "socialization" refers to an imprecise concept that has been much debated and fine-tuned. Consequently, there are many related concepts with degrees of affect or even power allocated to either structure or agency or both. Especially when the topic of religious sectarianism is part of the discussion, the process of acculturation may be described rather more extremely as indoctrination or even brainwashing depending on the literature—some of which is rather too simplistic and binary in its analysis.[2] I define socialization broadly as a process by which people learn to become members of the society or community in which they live, both by internalising norms and values of that group and by learning to perform the appropriate social roles. Furthermore, socialization also involves learning layers of interpretive rules for reading, ascertaining, and deconstructing norms, roles, and rules, knowing how to recapitulate them, and knowing when they are appropriate and inappropriate (and what to do in cases of breach). Members of a society internalize their complicated surroundings and its layers of meanings and adapt to them—and they internalize values and religious beliefs as well, as much as they are an integral part of their surrounding culture (although this does not mean that people always conform to the explicit and implicit rules, norms, and values).[3]

In the case of this research the children were socialized into a radically alternative culture. This was not socialization into the mainstream—this was socialization into particular sectarian cultures and their norms and values. And in the case of missionary groups, children may be socialized into an alternative culture within one or several foreign countries. Many of the people I have interviewed did not visit their "native country" until they were adults. Conventional socialization theories tend to focus on the process through which children become members of their particular society. Successful socialization, then, would be a child learning and internalizing the appropriate explicit and implicit norms, values, codes of behavior, and social roles and knowing where generally the line is drawn between acceptable and deviant behavior and understanding how to manage these drawn lines.[4] However, deviancy is an arbitrary concept, subject to change and interpretation within and across cultures. And religion can complicate issues further when, as a system of meaning, its "rights" and "wrongs" do not coincide with the laws and conventions laid down by the wider community or the state. Hence socialization in sectarian movements may have different aims and results from surrounding socializations. The Amish, for example, have gone to court in the United States several times to keep their children out of school from the age of twelve, in order to teach them at home (for the girls) or on the land (for the boys), and in the belief that education instills pride (Kraybill 1989; Hostetler 1993). The socialization aims of the Amish in the United States have been significantly divergent from those of the surrounding society, where, by law, minors have to attend school until the age of sixteen.

The question then becomes: what is considered successful socialization in sectarian movements? Of course this depends on the movement and its priorities, who is making the judgement, when and where the socialization occurs, and many other variables. Furthermore, groups who are faced with a second generation for the first time are new to this topic, as well—they have no previous experience. Consequently, expectations are likely to hinge on ideals rather than custom, and on knowledge of what religious groups now respect or reject from socialization within the wider culture.

Measures of successful socialization might include whether the children remain members of the movement as adults, whether they continue to adhere to the beliefs and practices, whether they maintain the norm and values, and so on. Groups have their own expectations. Whereas some might expect the second-generation members, as adults, to reach salvation more or less by the same means as their parents (by following the "one true path"), other movements may teach, akin to New Age traditions, that "many are the ways" (or at least "several are the ways") and individuals have to find their own paths. Sectarianism is generally not open to the "many are the ways" approach; little cadets who leave Scientology behind will most likely be perceived by other Scientologists as having joined the wogs, and as a result will never be clear or operating Thetans unless they reject so-called wog life and return to Scientology.[5]

One crucial factor in concepts of "successful" socialization is the degree of role flexibility available to the children. Can they stay in the sect if they choose to not completely adhere to the beliefs and practices? Is there room for change within? Can they still be saved by adhering to the beliefs and practices outside the geographical or social boundaries of the community? Can the group's norms and values be separated from the beliefs and practices? Can the second-generation members believe without belonging (Davie 1994)? The main question here, of course, is where the parents and members of the established generation in charge of the group draw the line. And, following that, do the young members accept the lines drawn by the first generation? Where do the second-generation members draw the line? Are the lines they draw accepted by the first-generation members? Part of the dialectic of socialization is the negotiation of the boundaries of the community. Social boundaries are a very important aspect of sectarianism, but they are often challenged with the maturation of the second generation. Whereas established religions have a sense of security through their institutionalization, and are not as threatened by nominal membership, sectarian movements rely on total membership. Grace Davie's (1994) concept of "believing without belonging" would destroy the sectarian community, taking away its raison d'être, as it were. In sects, socialization has a dual purpose—the continuation of norms and values as well as the perpetuation of a way of life that largely creates the community's sense of identity. On a social level, the second generation's socialization has an immediate bearing on the continuation of the group's way of life—sectarianism.

Groups change over time, even if they wish to remain the same—they have to change in order to achieve a level of stasis. As I have addressed in chapters 2 and 3, the presence of children brings changes to a group, but the surrounding community and the state also have their influences. Sectarian groups are often caught between their children's demands and external demands and pressures. How do they balance these pressures? Furthermore, there are also pressures from members of the first generation or the current leaders, who may resent changes and wish for the group to continue as it was—they prioritize the founding ethic, the mission, or whatever they consider the raison d'être of the movement. An important question underlying this balancing exercise is: is the sect ready to denominationalize, or does the group want to remain revolutionary and sectarian?[6] The ways in which these tensions are balanced and navigated is crucial for future relations with the second-generation members. If the group prioritizes sectarianism over the demands of the children, then the young members have to adapt. If the group denominationalizes, then the children will have more flexible boundaries within which to accommodate their plans. For these groups, the plans for the children can change over time, for a number of reasons. For example, whereas the gurukulis were initially trained to become monks, now it is acceptable if these young members remain vegetarian and visit the temple once in a while. The plans for the children have changed in adaptation to an undisputable fact—the gurukulas proved disastrous for many of the children there because of institutionalized neglect and abuse. As the groups changed over time and the priorities were reassessed, the boundaries also changed. The second-generation members, as a result, were often reassessed according to the new boundaries. Whereas the children at first had a special significance, such as end-time teens or blessed children, their roles came to be redefined and renegotiated. This adaptation throughout the process of changes also made for different childhoods for the different cohorts of children, and consequently different experiences for the elder members of the second generation than for their younger counterparts.

The Good, the Bad, and the Troubled…

In many cases the second-generation members turned out not to be as perfect as their parents and other established members had expected. For example, the Reverend Moon's children were "blessed," but not necessarily free of misdeeds, their collective transgressions including spousal abuse, drugs, excessive drinking, and extramarital affairs.[7] There were many among the first wave of blessed children who left the movement, most of them unhappy with their childhoods.[8] As mentioned earlier, the gurukulis frequently were not and did not become the disciplined monks their parents and other first generation devotees had envisaged. Many of the children in the Family were thought to be in need of Victor Programs for disciplining or to "get the Victory." The Bruderhof children might have been raised in propitious circumstances, within a community of brethren, but were still suspected of having "impure thoughts"—and thought to be in need of help, through clearances, to overcome these alleged thoughts.[9] Over time the ideas surrounding the children and what they needed to grow up as responsible assets to the sects changed or at least had to be pragmatically adapted.[10] As a result, programs were developed in order to deal with this discrepancy, that is, the Victor Program, disciplining measures in gurukulas, and so on. The Unification Church began to organize workshops to bring about the bonding and sense of community that the first cohort of children had reportedly not developed, in order to reduce the rate of desertion among the children of the second cohort.[11]

The desertion of the young generations is a difficult issue for sectarian groups, but one they need to face eventually. Accommodation to demanding or difficult children can be too much of a cost to bear (sacrificing religious tradition), and keeping the rebellious children around the fringes can also be costly, as they may influence the others. The more rigidly sectarian the group, the stricter are the boundaries, which means that children have to be either in or out. By sitting on the fence, as it were, the so-called bad apples may pollute the bunch (Douglas 1966). Of course, if such boundaries were to be stretched or slackened, then slight deviants could remain, but this would be a level of accommodation that is not always acceptable in light of doctrine or tradition.[12] Hence the "bad apples" are offered two choices, stay and adapt or leave. Depending on their choices, the designations for special children of earlier chapters, such as the blessed children and end-time teens, have over time been changed, or their meanings have changed. The children who have left or been cast out have been given (and have frequently also assumed) a new status and, accordingly, a new designation.

Social scientists are well aware of the politics of naming—the act of labeling and its consequences (e.g. K. Erikson 1966; Becker [1963] 1973). A deviant receives a deviant label considered fitting by those in her or his surroundings—who have defined the action as deviant (and hence have defined the act as well as the person). Deviance is not about the quality of the act committed, but a consequence of the application, by others, of rules and sanctions. The sanctions can be seen as rites of transition with the purpose of transferring the deviant to a special deviant position (K. Erikson 1966: 15). This can be a symbolic marginal position (such as the kleiner Ausschluss) or a more concrete removal from the community (such as excommunication, the grosser Ausschluss). The deviant label, in a way, says at least as much about the surroundings as about the deviant. And the label may become an entrenched part of the person as she or he is redefined as a transgressor or an outsider, an outcast from the community. Although it is important to keep in mind that labeling is more reflective than deterministic (a perspective rather than a theory), it can help create stigma, which in turn may affect behavior (Plummer 1979). The outsiders are treated as such by the insiders, and as a result they are more likely to associate with other outsiders, hence continuing to engage in behavior that the insiders now expect of them (Becker [1963] 1973). Or as Kai Erikson (1966) argues (elaborating on some of Robert Merton's ideas), the deviant label may become a self-fulfilling prophecy—a way for both the community and the deviant to agree on what kind of person she or he is. If one is already considered to be a deviant, then any behavior is more likely to be considered deviant, and one may as well engage in deviant behavior.[13]

The types of labels that arose in my research can be categorized into a few stereotypes of labels assigned, both by parents and sects, to their children. The young members are described as goodies, rebels, or baddies.[14] These generalized stereotypes largely represent the different categories of how the children were defined as they made their own decisions regarding their future.[15] I shall first briefly introduce the generalized stereotypes that I have created to represent the clusters of labels I encountered in my research, then proceed to more in-depth descriptions using the terminology and language I encountered in interviews, participant observation, content analysis of literature, and online discussion groups and on which I have based these generalized stereotypes.

The children and young members who adapt to their surrounding culture and learn to operate within it are quite simply the goodies. They have internalized the culture, roles, explicit and implicit meanings, successfully conformed to the expectations of others, and report to be happy within this context. Then there are those who love and appreciate their childhood culture, but have some questions about the way things are done and extend some challenges to the existing rules. They want improvements.

They are the rebels (in other contexts they could be described more positively as innovators). Some young members decide very clearly during their teenage years or as young adults that they do not want to live within this culture. In some cases there has been an unhappy childhood (sometimes involving abuse or neglect), in other cases it is a matter of values ("I want to earn my own money and keep it," or "I want to go to university"), or disagreement over future plans ("I do not want to go to that school" or "I do not want to marry that person"). These kinds of matters are not easily resolved, and the young member, by then often a young adult, leaves or is cast out. These young members usually have a past of rebellion and transgression within the group, and their exit marks their new status: a seed gone bad, a lost soul, or other equivalent—the baddies. The baddies are the bad apples who either left or were cast out—they are to be kept away from the other children so they do not spoil the bunch. The "badness" reflects on the fact that these were usually rebellious children who transgressed the boundaries of acceptable rebellion. However, the parents, leaders, or other elders of the religious groups do not always explain the existence of baddies in terms of transgressions. Frequently it is explained as a more intrinsic affliction to do with their emotional stability or spirituality (or lack of) rather than with their behavior. In interviews these young former members were frequently described (by parents, some in leadership or public relations positions) as "troubled."[16] The troubled former members are the ones whose absence from the sect, and attitude toward the sect, is explained by spiritual problems (they have lost their way or are being plagued by problems associated with a lack of spirituality—vanity, doubt, pride, material desire, or other such "problems" depending on the religious beliefs) or by emotional issues (they are depressed, down, have lost their way—possibly under the influence of alcohol or drugs).

Goodies display different characteristics depending on the religious group. In the Unification Church it was not enough to just be a blessed child—there was a further informal distinction between those who were "hard-core blessed children" and those who were not. The hard-core blessed children are activists for the movement; they strive for purity according to UC standards, apply peer pressure to their contemporaries to conform, and are the leaders within the UC youth movement.[17] These goodies are also active in the fund-raising endeavors, despite the original teaching that they have relatively little indemnity to pay.[18] They are spiritual activists who value and enforce the group's morals and values while denouncing the immoral and corrupt standards outside. There are strong parallels to goodies within the Family, who were described as revolutionaries and "professionals"—more than mere missionaries and disciples, they are "go-getters." They are akin to the original Gideon's band.[19] In the Bruderhof the goodies were described as pure (and women as modest) and humble. This language is significantly different from Scientology, where goodies were described as being "clear in the head," "in reality," and generally "able people" who were "in control," productive, and "up-stat." A follower's work ethic is important, and goodies are valued for their productivity, values, and ethics.

Keeping in mind these values and priorities, it is interesting to note the language used to describe those who transgress, whom I have termed the rebels, and what values they are perceived to be transgressing. One rebel in the Unification Church repeatedly used the term "negative" when reporting how his attitude and behavior were perceived by his peers and the leaders in the group. He was told he was "sarcastic," "pessimistic," "cynical" (these attributes were disapproved of within the group), suffering from a lack of faith, and at risk of losing his faith. Hence leaders suggested "spiritual cleansing" to counter his perceived wild and negative attitude and lack of discipline. His peers also considered him to be negative, and "on the edge" (as well as "on the line" and "on the borderline"—a spatially marginal position).[20] This rebel was under pressure to conform. In the Family, rebels were described as suffering or giving in to pride or being lazy—and consequently of "not pulling their weight." These criticisms reflect the values that are important in communal living, and what is considered disruptive to the community. Such behavior or attitudes were described as being symptomatic of spiritual trouble: having bad spirits or possibly being demon possessed.[21] In Scientology, those who are "down stat" are considered a liability and "need correcting." Those who are down stat are literally less productive members of the team.

The existence, or rather creation, of these rebels points to an existence of boundaries that can be transgressed, and each group (or culture) creates its own rebels. In some contexts, rules and moral codes are virtually nonnegotiable, and room for rebellion is limited—rebels have to either adapt and integrate or leave. The rebels who did not conform after sanctions, and left, are the baddies. The Bruderhof (and other Anabaptist or Hutterite groups, as well as Jehovah's Witnessses) discipline their rebels ("impure" members in need of "clearing" or those who suffer from pride or selfishness or display other behaviors that point to them having lost their faith or being spiritually confused) by symbolically and temporarily removing them from the inner circle of their community—the brotherhood. Those who do not repent in order to be allowed back in (and those who try but do not succeed) are eventually excommunicated or leave.[22] There was relatively little room for rebellion in the Bruderhof; pride, self-esteem, ambition, and questioning would get one into trouble with the Brotherhood and was likely to lead to some form of exclusion. The baddies are excluded because they are deemed to be polluting influences. They are no longer members, or no longer part of the inner circle, because the presence of these rotten apples may spoil the bunch.[23] Impurity can be behavioral, physical, and spiritual. Those who have lost their faith are spiritually impure. In the Family it was believed that a lack of faith may lead to someone being possessed by bad spirits or demons (as was the case with Mene, described in chapter 2). This may be a dangerous status: former members can be "Vandaris"—demons who have the power to affect the purity and spiritual status of members.[24] In ISKCON lack of faith and straying from the principles could lead to "*karmi*" behavior and status. *Karmi* is a term reserved for outsiders, those who do not adhere to the principles. In Scientology those who criticize the teachings, the founder, or integral aspects of the organization were labeled "suppressives" and followers were recommended to steer clear of them, to avoid their progress being hampered by the "wrong information." In the Unification Church, pollution was seen to be inherent. Whereas blessed children have a "purified" bloodline, those born of UC members who have an unblessed union do not have a purified bloodline ("Jacob's children"). There are also "fallen children"—blessed children who have not retained their purity (who have had sexual relations before marriage). The latter are no longer considered pure and have to undergo cleaning rituals and will have to be matched and blessed before they can have blessed offspring.[25]

It is important to keep in mind however, that these labels are generalized stereotypes that are used here as a framework—they will never be a perfect fit. Rebels and baddies, for example, frequently display very similar attitudes, behaviors, and spiritual struggles. The main difference is that in some groups there is room for their questioning and rebellions, while in other groups this type of behavior is not acceptable. Similarly, baddies are sometimes described as troubled, depending on the speaker and the audience—rather than being demonized, they are then pitied and condescended to. The troubled are described as having problems; they are "having doubts," are struggling spiritually, or are a "troubled person." Anna had been described as a "troubled person" within the Bruderhof, and at the time she felt a failure before God and her community—yet she was treated like a baddie and shunned. She was not "good enough" to be united with the Brotherhood.[26] A youth worker in the Unification Church described how many children from the first cohort left. He blamed the movement for not having created enough of a community spirit among these teenagers, but also the young members for being "confused," "muddled up," and "a bit lost." Teachers within ISKCON described how some gurukulis were "having a hard time" or "going through a phase," momentarily following desire rather than the principles. Interestingly, being troubled was always described as temporary, and could be reversed.

These generalized labels exist in reference to the sects' social boundaries and as part of their boundary maintenance. The goodies fall neatly within the existing framework. The rebels brush up against the fringes, yet do so in an acceptable or at least manageable way. The baddies do not; they fall outside the framework. As do the troubled—they are not in the "right" spiritual framework. Nonsectarian religious groups do not have such a rigid authoritarian framework and social boundaries, hence their labeling tends not to fall within the same ideal types as mentioned above. Any rebellion within nonsectarian religion is easily seen as part of a larger trend, or as challenging larger social issues, rather than the smaller collective.

Another important aspect of labeling is that the children themselves internalize these labels and incorporate them into their self-definition, appropriating the tags. I elaborate on the labels in the next chapter, where I quote at length the goodies, the rebels, the baddies, and the troubled, as well as their parents, teachers, and other caretakers. In quoting at length I aim to give a flavor of the language and the words used to pinpoint someone's position relative to the sectarian group (in, out, or, when possible, on the margins).[27] But first I elaborate on the young members' accounts of their childhoods and why they chose the paths they have chosen—to stay, become revolutionaries, question the status quo, or leave. In light of this discussion, their prescribed (and occasionally internalized) status and roles is part of the narrative throughout the remaining chapters.

5
The Young Members Who Stay

THERE ARE A number of reasons for young members to stay within the community in which they were raised, and a number of factors involved in their decision. Depending on the sect and the extent to which it has adapted to these members, the decision can be a one-way street, where rigid groups demand that the children adapt, or a two-way street, where the groups and the children compromise and meet halfway. The latter is more typical of fluid groups that have adapted to the demands of having children and the demands imposed by society by sacrificing some aspects of their lifestyle for the benefit of the children.

Why Do They Stay?

Choosing to remain a part of a religious group usually involves both positive factors associated with membership and negative factors associated with nonmembership—or the outside world. Sects have created their own communities of meaning, and leaving this community of meaning is undesirable as there is no match elsewhere. One may speak here of a sense of gemeinschaft and its characteristically close social relations between individuals based on close personal and family ties, rather than gesellschaft where social relations are based on impersonal ties (Tönnies [1887] 1965). The stronger the positive associations with the sectarian culture (the pull), the stronger the negative associations with the external culture (the push), because sectarian groups are formed in opposition to the outside.[1] Hence, for the young people making decisions about their futures, the familiarity of the sect is a very important theme that comes up repeatedly.[2] This is in contrast to descriptions of outside as a place where there is not only unfamiliarity but also different priorities, values, and attitudes that are perceived as less beneficial, than the ones inside the community and sometimes even destructive.

The Bruderhof, for example, has been described as an idyllic community in which to grow up, including by former members who have later either left or been excommunicated. Even those who have serious questions about some of the child-rearing practices (as mentioned in chapter 2) admit that there were wonderful aspects to the communal lifestyle. Elizabeth Bohlken Zumpe (1993: 69), in a book describing the hardship she has endured with the Bruderhof and the harm she believes has been done to many members and former members nonetheless also describes how she enjoyed life as a nine-year-old in the Primavera community in Paraguay. This was reflected in interviews with former members, where, for example, Frank described his childhood in Paraguay as "idyllic." He thought it was a beautiful place, wonderful for children, and has fond memories of a large and well-stocked library.[3] In most of the accounts I have come across there were positive accounts of childhoods in the Bruderhof. One of the former members I interviewed, Anna, described her childhood love for the Bruderhof and her desire to be a part of its inner circle.[4] Her story also unearths her fear, as a child and young woman, of "being out" and believing that all the good things in the world were within the Bruderhof. Hence, not being a part of the Bruderhof, to her, felt like being cast to the lions.

Anna describes herself as having been a very happy child. She believed she was called to the Bruderhof and did everything within her powers to stay in the fold. "The thought of not joining the Bruderhof was frightening to me," she said. As a child she had been moved by the Christian teachings of the Bruderhof, and she had also had a religious experience, which made her very sympathetic to the values and practices of the movement. "I was actually ideal material for the Bruderhof," she added. "I felt called to the Bruderhof—always did." As the Paraguayan community was facing difficulties, at the time of the Great Crisis Anna and her family went to England, their original homeland, where they did not live with a community—they were in exclusion. But soon her parents started writing to a local community asking to be allowed back in. Anna was "desperately keen" to return to the community. When asked what she had missed about living in the community, she said, "It was fellowship, the children, [a] sense of justice. What comes to mind [about not living in the community] is an incredible emptiness and nothing would fill it. It was like a hole inside me. I was always hungry because we didn't have a lot, and always trying to fill [the hole] with eating. Incredible emptiness." Anna describes a terrible homesickness for the Bruderhof. The yearning for the Bruderhof grew as she was feeling more and more out of place in school. After Anna finished her general certificates of secondary education, her family was allowed back into the community, but soon her parents were out again, in exclusion. "By parents having been in trouble with the Brotherhood," she said, "that affected the children, in a most damaging, corrosive way. No self-esteem, huge anxieties about making decisions.... They got back into the Brotherhood, and as soon as there was another crisis, Mom and Dad were out again." Anna's parents were in and out a few more times, and eventually moved to a community in the United States. Anna was then twenty-one. In America, the family was still in disgrace. They lived on the outskirts of the community for five years, lobbying to be allowed in. This was, to her, like a manifestation of her disgraced status—being relegated to the physical margins of the community. As a result Anna had issues with low self-esteem, and felt like a failure in several ways. She now believes, in hindsight, that she might have been clinically depressed at the time. Then, she was certainly considered to be problematic—a baddie needing to be kept away from the flock.

> To live near a community has huge stuff around it. It's a position of disgrace, of punishment, of being totally beholden. Writing endless letters and definitely not putting a foot wrong—hanging on every invitation to come to some special meal.... Me, yearning to be part of the community, yearning to be free. Depressed and more and more self-conscious and unfree and tied up in knots about everything.

Despite the disgrace of exclusion, the family, and especially Anna, longed to be a part of the community and its ideals of a perfect life. The teachings of the Bruderhof were a big pull; but there were also pushes. Anna certainly had fears about leaving: "Because it's so scary to come out, because you can't actually stand on your own feet.... You've got the loyalty issue, the whole thing with God and Christ. You're brought up not to trust anyone but the people in the community." Anna believed that those who were not part of the Bruderhof would go to hell.

Although it was, according to her, never quite spelled out like that, it was nonetheless very clear to her.[5] As a result Anna continued to petition the community to allow her back in. This process lasted until she was in her thirties. She eventually stopped trying to get back into the community, assuming she would still be in exclusion when returning. "Being outside meant the fear of losing that connection with God and everything that made life worth living," she said. "Being in the Bruderhof was what made life worth living." In the case of Anna the Bruderhof proved to have a strong pull on her. Despite the difficulties involved in being part of the community, she fought hard to be a part of it.

On a less extreme level, this idea of the "goodness within" versus the "badness outside" is mirrored in the attitude of a young man who was a blessed child in the Unification Church, and whom I will refer to as Sam.[6] For Sam, the most important aspect of being a Unificationist was the values, compared to the lack of values and integrity outside.[7] Sam was in his early twenties, and both his parents were missionaries for the church. As a result, they were not well off, and he had worked outside for a few years in order to save money for college, where he was enrolled when I interviewed him. His childhood was spent mostly in the United States, where he was part of a sizable network of blessed children. They had their own meetings and workshops, and had developed strong gemeinschaft bonds. This unity, or cohesion, was due to the time spent together, but also due to the shared values, which he considered intrinsic to the movement: "On the whole I think people who have grown up in the movement, they're more sincere, they're more honest, I think they're just more well-rounded individuals in terms of just being able to understand people, being more compassionate, kind of. They're not as sarcastic, or pessimistic, or put people down. I think they're just nicer, easier to get along with, in general."[8] According to him these values were passed down to him by his parents and other first-generation church members, not necessarily through (overt) teachings, but (more implicitly) by giving the right example. He believed he has been better off than many of his peers.

> I just think that, [with] families within the church, there is certainly less divorce. On average there are higher standards of morals. I think I grew up with [a] bigger sense of awareness of good moral values or something.... In the US half [of] my friends are living just with their mom or their dad. They're totally rebellious. They didn't like the fact that they just lived with their dad or their mom, and they had a stepmom they hated or a stepdad they thought was a jerk. I think there's just less of that [in the church]. You just grow up in a healthier environment.

And he wants to pass this on to his children.

> I'd like my kids to get some of the values I've learned. I think it's really important to grow up with some moral standards.... Respecting

your parents. Just respecting people in general. Moon has definitely talked about [it], he doesn't judge anybody so I try to do the same. I try to be really open. And the more open you are to people, the more opportunities come your way, I think. And the more you can rub off on people that you are genuine. I think a lot of times that's difficult to find in today's world. A lot of people are too fake, they put up a front to try and get what they want. But I think if someone really comes across someone genuine, I think it's really to your advantage. I think that's helped me in my career as well.

Sam argues that by his setting the right example, "doing right," others will do the same in return. He admires and respects the people within the church, and wants to be a part of it—maybe not as a missionary like his parents (he wants to earn enough money to be able to send his children to university), but certainly in a way that the values and teachings continue to affect on his life. One of the teachings of the church of which Sam thinks very highly centers on sexual purity.[9] For blessed children, the most important thing, according to Moon, is that they remain pure and continue to build on this foundation, so that eventually there is a foundation upon which heaven on earth can be created. Hence, the blessed children, both male and female, have a quest for purity. As Moon put it:

> You should not ruin your purity during your adolescence, which is the precious time when you cleanse and indemnify the purity lost by Adam and Eve during their youth. You should preserve your purity, precious and clean, and you should have the mind and the determination that "even if I have to live a thousand or ten thousand years alone, my love will absolutely never be misused."[10]

Sam has internalized this teaching; he practices it and plans to pass it on:

> Honestly, try and keep yourself pure. That's one of the big things we stress in our movement. No sex before marriage type thing. I think that's really important. So if I can pass these kinds of things down, that would be great.
>
> If I had kids I wouldn't really want my daughter to go around sleeping around with, you know, ten or fifteen guys and then try and find someone to settle down with. I'd rather her just be clean and whatever. I don't know if I can pass down those values to my

kids, that's probably one of the most challenging things. For me, that's one of the best things I've gotten out of it, that's one of the things I wanna do to my children.

It is for this reason that he wants to marry another blessed child.[11] For Sam, part of the reason for wanting to marry someone "within" is that he can then be confident that she would have had a similar upbringing and would share the same values and beliefs regarding purity.[12] Then, he argued, "it would be easier to teach our children the same thing, if both parents are on the same page."

More importantly, there is such a strong feeling of community among some of the blessed children, that an outsider simply does not seem equally approachable or even desirable.[13] Another blessed child, whom I will refer to as Kevin, echoed this point: "What's really positive is that we always feel comfortable and there's a connection there, and I can probably feel closer to some kids who I don't really know so well, but I've seen them around, I know their brothers and sisters. But I can feel more comfortable with them than some people at college, because I just have an understanding that they're of the same faith." This sense of community and connection is an important aspect of what young members see as the good aspects of their involvement (the pull), and it is something that came up repeatedly in interviews with young members—both the goodies and the rebels.[14] It was strongly emphasized by a young member of the Family, whom I will refer to as Sally. Sally's parents separated when she was young, and as a result she was out for three to four years, as she lived with her father, who had left the movement.[15] Sally was not impressed with the system as she experienced it while she was away from the Family as a young teenager. As a child she had loved life in the Family. Her parents and siblings had lived as a nuclear family until she was six, after which they had moved to India as missionaries, where they lived in a large Family community. There were many other children. She had previously been educated at home, but in India she was schooled with the other young children within the community. She liked being a missionaries' child: "I was aware that I was a missionary; my parents were always sure to make sure it didn't get to my pride." She described Family missionaries and members as having something special about them, and was convinced that she can point out a Family member in a crowd, not because of dress or style necessarily, but because of something more ethereal. And, she argued, there immediately would be a feeling of familiarity:

> I guess there is something different about us—can't necessarily put your finger on it. There's something different, and I think its cool. Someone can actually spot you.... I guess there is a little bit more.
>
> I don't say you can tell a person's religion, but you can definitely tell their spirit, whether it's the Christian spirit or not. People's spirit, their outlook, is reflected on their face, [in] their eyes.

When she went to live with her father after her parents' separation, she had in effect left the Family. She had difficulty adjusting to life outside, and did not enjoy it, she said. "I didn't really enjoy myself.... We've grown up trying to save the world—or change the world, or something like that." Instead she found herself among her cousins, who were into makeup, clothes, and Tom Cruise. Sally said: "[Inside the Family there are] a lot of people like me, [with the] same vision.... [There is] a feeling of being at home. Outside, I was not the oddball, I felt they were the weirdos."

Sally wanted to rejoin the Family as soon as possible, and asked special permission to stay with "foster parents" within the Family while she was still a minor, at the age of sixteen, and while her mother was in the mission field. She received the necessary written permission from her mother and eventually moved to the United States and took a secretarial job within the movement. She felt at home, and she felt a sense of purpose in her life: "Knowing they were there, that there was actually a goal ... you're part of the world. If you can make a little difference, a change, you can do something. It might not be big, but it's something. It's an accomplishment which goes further than yourself. It's not just for yourself. It's not just material." Sally also described a feeling of appreciation that others have toward the Family. According to her, other missionaries appreciate Family missionaries and look up to them.[16] Her work was important to Sally, and it provided meaning to her life. This meaning, as well as the sense of community, was something she would not jeopardize. They were things she respected and valued, and they were benefits to her life.

Nadine (not her real name) had similar feelings toward the religious group she chose to formally join as a teenager.[17] Her parents were both involved with Scientology throughout her childhood, and although they lived as a nuclear family and she went to mainstream schools, Scientology methods were an essential part of her life. She received assists (a Scientology process to help a person confront and eventually resolve physical difficulties) from her parents when necessary and used L. Ron Hubbard's study technology as part of her learning at home. She argued that this was essential to her performance at school:

Well, I was much more clear in the head than anyone else in the class. And very, very many times the teachers were just confusing to listen to, and in high school I very many times actually took over maths class because I was much more in reality with what the kids thought than the teacher was. So, I mean, a few times I was actually thrown out because I was—they thought I was trying to show off or something, and the kids would actually come with me outside so I could tell: "look——," "this is——," you know, and just help them with their misunderstood words, which is just a basic L Ron Hubbard technology.

I didn't have "misunderstoods,"[18] I didn't have these things I didn't understand, I always clarified everything. Sometimes this got really annoying, teachers [saying]: "why are you asking all these things," you know. But I wouldn't go past these misunderstood words whereas the other kids would. And therefore I was the brightest out of every class.... It's very logical, actually.

As a teenager, Nadine sustained a sports-related injury, and the doctors could not help her. But, she claimed, her mother, through auditing (Scientology counseling methods), found "the command" her coach-teacher had given her and which had somehow been "embedded in her brain," causing her body to respond accordingly at inappropriate moments—allegedly interfering with her own neurological commands. The injury was treated through assists by her mother, and disappeared. When Nadine was fifteen years old her parents went to East Grinstead, the Scientology headquarters in England, for two months of courses. Nadine accompanied them. This trip coincided with her teacher telling her that she was not talented enough to perform her sport at a professional level, and criticizing her body shape and weight. "And that's the moment where I decided: I found here what I really like, I am being granted the beingness of what I am, I am actually granted [as being] important as opposed to being put down all the time," she recalled. "And I called—'I am not coming back.'... I was fed up with being thought of as a piece of meat, you know." Nadine was in her early teens, just as Sally was, when she chose to become more involved in the movement. She had had positive experiences as a child, and preferred the values above those she encountered in the secular world. This perceived discrepancy of values proved a push, and the beckoning possibilities inside a pull.

This process was also reflected in the story of Kevin.[19] Kevin was born and raised within the Unification Church; he is a blessed child. When he was fourteen years old his parents left the movement, but he and his younger sister chose to stay. At the age of seventeen he moved away from home and came to London in order to attend college. He moved into the house of the Collegiate Association for the Research of the Principle (CARP; principle refers to the "Divine Principle"). He chose to live in this house because it was familiar; he knew the people who lived there well, and some of them were his friends. Even though Kevin had gone to mainstream schools, his closest friends had always been church members. This was partly because he had moved to different schools a few times, but also because the workshops for blessed children had managed to create a strong sense of community and fellowship among them, as well as a community of experience and meaning. He noted, "and being together, relating, that just kind of kept, or strengthened, the friendships and all. Because we all had a common base; the same kind of upbringing, same ideas, all this kind of stuff. So, yeah, I do have my closest friends in the church." These friendships among blessed children created during the workshops were also maintained outside them as the young members sought each other out.[20] The shared values, experiences, and ideals made fellow members more familiar and, consequently, more reliable and desirable friends.

> [Being a blessed child] that kind of set up a common base between us. We all thought BCs...create a community, BC community, able to relate to each other, share what's going on in our lives, like, issues to do with school, college, faith, whatever, just that kind of relating, you know, via letters, via e-mails, talking together on the phone, whatever. So that kind of BC setup just, I suppose, helped and created that kind of safe community, that we could support each other, that, you know, if you did feel slightly different to outside people, friends at school, because you felt uncomfortable to share or talk to them about certain aspects of our lives or faith, whatever, that we could be relaxed and be ourselves with each other. And that's how it has been for me, I suppose.

Kevin did feel confused when his parents left the movement, and during his late teens he believed that he had to figure out for himself "where the truth lies." Hence another reason to move into the CARP house was to find out for himself where he stood vis-à-vis the church, the lifestyle, and the leadership (aspects of the movement that had been criticized by his father in the past few years). "So I was just trying to figure stuff out for myself," he said. "But still inclined towards the Church, because that was my only understanding. And my understanding or feeling that it was true, coz that was what I was brought up with." But he moved out a year later. Kevin respected, and valued, many aspects of the Unification Church, but there were also aspects he had problems with. It was as a result of the latter that he moved out of the communal house, and that he openly questioned some aspects of "the way things are done." Kevin was a rebellious blessed child, unlike Nadine, for example, who adapted to "the way things are done" in her community. The extent to which a young member accepts and internalizes the norms and values and conforms to them distinguishes the ones who stay from the ones who leave—and among the ones who stay, it is especially acceptance that distinguishes the goodies from the rebels.[21] All the people I have mentioned in this section referred to the outside as a place they had difficulty adjusting to—be it the values or the people. Both Sally and Nadine referred to people outside in a critical manner, as "weirdos," not as intelligent, certainly preoccupied with different issues (Tom Cruise and makeup rather than making the world a better place). Sam and Kevin both referred to different value systems, and not appreciating the outsiders' ones as much. There was a general inability or unwillingness to relativize the moral and social dimensions between the two spheres—rather a tendency to polarize the two. There were references throughout their accounts of them not feeling adjusted to the outside, but feeling quite adjusted inside—feeling "at home."

How Do They Fit In?
Adapt to Fit: The Goodies and the Activists

Adapting and fitting in require not only successful internalization and externalization of the norms, values, codes, and expectations but also an acceptance of them—an acceptance of the way things are done. Of course this adaptation and acceptance is a complicated (and for a large part unconscious) process of trial and error in exploration around acceptable and unacceptable conduct. Sectarian communities are idealized constructions and through interaction over time this construct is fine-tuned and members united. This process is especially important in groups where tradition has a high priority, such as the Amish. Amish have to adhere relatively strictly to the rules of the community, or they will be shunned. Since this community practices adult baptism, children have more leeway, and receive a substantial amount of freedom during their period of *Rumspringa* (a Pennsylvania-Dutch term that, roughly translated, means "running around").[22] It is a traditional rite of passage in the Amish religion, and signifies a period of months or years, beginning at the age of sixteen, when adolescents are released from the rules of the church. During this period, these young adolescents are allowed to live among "the English" (non-Amish North Americans) and experience the outsiders' way of life, and they are afforded a large measure of flexibility by the Amish. After this period, if they choose to join and be baptized, they have to accept the lifestyle and the rules, and adapt to them.[23]

Although the Bruderhof is also an Anabaptist community (practicing adult baptism), it has a slightly different authority structure, inherited from the Hutterite tradition. In the Bruderhof, only baptized members who are part of the prayer circle may vote and have a voice in community matters—and there are further distinctions for single members (who may not vote on issues that touch on sexual issues) and non-decision-making Brotherhood members (those who are seen as suffering from an emotional disposition or effects of old age).[24] Transgressions are punished by shunning and, in cases of serious transgression, exclusion. Those who are being shunned (small exclusion) are not allowed into the prayer circle, and hence cannot vote. For those who want to be part of the community, this kind of exclusion is a grave punishment. For Anna, the idea of not being in the Bruderhof was frightening, and exclusion was a difficult place to be for her: "And you can't be quite out because you're not feeling 'out' inside. You're still a Bruderhof person. And you dress like a Bruderhof, and you want to go back to the Bruderhof, so you don't do anything to damage that." Hence Anna did everything she could to be accepted as part of the Bruderhof, and tried as best she could to adapt to the lifestyle. She copied the behavior of successful members who were already a part of the novitiate and the prayer circle, and, as a result, accepted as part of the brotherhood. "[I had] actually earlier confessed about masturbating to [the housemother] because... in the Brotherhood, young men would get up and confess about impure thoughts," she said. "So I thought that in order to get into the Brotherhood and the novitiate I had to confess all. So I went to [housemother] and confessed." But for Anna it did not turn out as she had hoped, and according to her she did not receive the same positive attention as the young men in the Brotherhood did: "When you go in and confess you get lots of love and attention. Not at all when you're rebellious. And I was deprived." By trial and error Anna adapted to the behavior she thought would get her ahead in the Bruderhof.[25]

Similarly, Sally capitalized on the talents and attributes that she knew would get her into the jobs and missions she liked in the Family. She had honed the skills she knew were desirable, such as secretarial skills and the outgoing personality useful for leadership and provisioning. Sally adapted to the necessary give and take of communal life and occasionally joined missions she found less interesting but where her skills were needed, as such sacrifices, according to her, were compensated for by the occasions where she could go to her preferred missions. Sally liked being on the front line; not only was she a goodie, she was an "activist" for her movement. This term came up while I was interviewing Kevin, who described the goodies within the Unification Church. He referred to them as the "hard-core BCs"—the ones who do all their public missions and who are on the front line of the movement. They are activists for the UC. Nadine could be described as an activist for her organization as well. A majority of the interview was devoted to her explaining the logic behind Scientology and how it could save the world. She also explained her plans for the future, which involved working her way up to one of the largest Scientology centers.

Change from Within: The Rebels

The rebels are those questioning and challenging the status quo, and they are frequently also the innovators—it is because of their rebellion, depending on the strength of the group's boundaries, that they can make changes and stretch the boundaries of the group. As they gain influence among their generation, they gain a certain kind of power that solidifies their position and influence. In this way the young generation can create its own career opportunities within the movement and gain voting power. Both the Family and the Unification Church over time developed new and exciting missions for the young generations. These young members could now gain access to leadership positions. Also, with these positions came voting power, giving them the power to change ideas or practices with which they disagreed, or at least discuss them with the first-generation members.

Kevin went to live in the CARP house in order to deepen his faith after a time of confusion, a result of his parents leaving the organization when he was a young teenager:

> I suppose, like I said, I just still felt connected because of my upbringing and the friends that I had. And that... is practically all I knew so I just felt—to go with that. It was difficult, because it was

> like: "oh, my faith is being ripped away from me" and I was left on my own and not knowing where to go, so the easiest and safest option was for me to go back into it, to feel safe and secure, have some kind of platform underneath me.

But living in the CARP house, Kevin also came across aspects of membership in which he did not believe, and with which he did not want to continue—he did not discern a personal benefit. He also felt awkward about how much of his life he had to report to the "central figure," a person within the house who was in charge of the household and issues of faith.

> And after a while I felt, you know, why do I need to be telling everything that I am doing, you know, that kind of restriction. So I probably felt a bit of restriction there, living at the CARP house. Twice, during that year, I went through two severe moments of losing my faith, or really going against it and not wanting to do anything with it. And they caught on to that because I was being, for their eyes, negative, because I was questioning a lot of stuff, trying to get answers to certain things that didn't make sense, so I just did my personal research on certain things, talking to my dad, reading different books, and just doing my own kinda thing.

The central figure believed that Kevin had a problem that needed addressing, and Kevin was advised to do a "condition"—which is the process of deepening one's practice in offer to God while helping one's own spirituality in the process. The activities have to follow a certain pattern based on providential numbers, as specified in the Divine Principle. Kevin agreed, even though he was skeptical of this helping him spiritually. "They're offering me to find my faith, but it's kind of hypocritical, because I'm not finding it my way. I'm finding the faith that they want me to find, you know." So Kevin continued to lose his faith in the eyes of those around him (but, interestingly, not according to him). And the demands for conditions and further measures continued. Kevin was told that he had to "sort out his faith," and that if he continued the way he was going, he would end up leaving the church and losing his friends. Kevin was upset over this statement, as he himself had not thought of leaving the church, and the prospect of losing his friends was distressing to him. He has decided with hindsight that the leadership was not prepared for blessed children questioning the church or the faith. "Coz I suppose their idea is that second generation, coz we're born, coz we're there—we go to workshops, we're just being fed, and its easier for us to get trained, I suppose, and take on our parents' mission, what have you. But, they didn't know how to handle me kind of questioning stuff." Hence he left the CARP house, which "kind of created an upset.... It somehow created a negative nametag for me, to be like: 'oh yeah, [Kevin] is on the edge, he's leaving the Church. He's got negative ideas.'" Kevin did not like this label, and as a result he has been out of touch with the other CARP members since he left the house. He does, however, keep in touch with his friends and other members not necessarily associated with the CARP house. He does not attend the activities that he does not believe in, and goes along only to the ones in which he does believe.

> I'm not sure whether I feel inside, outside, or just connected, or associated, or whatever. But what I do feel, I still feel a BC, because that's been [spoon-fed] into me and I have this BC community that I'm really part of, and I have my best friends in this BC community you know, throughout the UK and throughout Europe. Some of my other friends are kind of on the verge, like me, and are leaving or distancing themselves from church activities.

Kevin was always involved in a variety of leadership positions in the youth missions and workshops. But, he said, he was taken out of those roles of responsibility because of what was perceived as his loss of faith, which the leadership feared he could transfer to the other blessed children. Yet, he argued, as a result of his energy and motivation, he always ended up in a leadership position somewhere, despite some people trying to prevent this. And he wanted to continue to be a part of the church, and have a role in leadership positions for his generation.

> I still feel connected, and still feel involved with things, but, like I say, in my choice and what I wanna do, and if I do want to go to a service, or a workshop, I'll go along. But also because I feel I want to help and support the younger BCs, to kind of help to give them a choice or to kind of open their minds up to create their own faith instead of always just taking in and taking in, but to be able to handle stuff, I suppose.

Kevin stressed that he did not want to do this in a "negative way"—he did not aim to undermine the leadership, he wanted to be involved, but on his own terms, not under the control of the central leader or the UK leadership. Senior members had been flexible enough at least to allow him to be on the fringes and still be involved with the movement on some level. Hence he still was an active and prominent figure within the blessed children community when I spoke with him:

> Which I still kind of am, but, like I said, with this kind of nametag on me. Which I don't mind, coz I still enjoy bringing up discussion, or to show them the fact that I still am on the borderline, kind of involved, and showing that I do have a choice, which is what I want to allow other BCs to have. Rather than my feeling of them being controlled or dominated because of this upbringing and being fed this information that they have to do certain things because that is their responsibility as a second generation, you know, to take over the first generation's responsibility of whatever. I just think they're kind of weak people, personally.

Senior members set an ultimatum for Kevin, but he refused to meet it. Yet at the same time, they did not excommunicate Kevin. They have allowed him leeway to rebel.

> But I suppose, if they had been stricter, or really forced me, I would have become more negative. Because I felt as if I was being pushed a bit too much already, and if they had pushed me a little bit more I would have become really angry and gone all out against them. And I probably could have done, but I myself as an individual feel that wouldn't do any good for any of us.
>
> It wouldn't benefit me, or them, or any of my friends. It would just create more problems and difficulties, and break friendships, I suppose. I mean, coz I'm still friends with them. And I myself, as an individual, feel okay and comfortable with people of different faiths.

Nametags and Their Work

Despite Kevin being very active in the BC community and in the church, he still had a "nametag," or a label—he still was considered a problem. He placed this, in his own words, within a larger framework, and distinguished between different types of members. The committed members who want to be on the front line of their missions he referred to as the "hardcore BCs." Then there were those who were "on the edge," who were "really negative." Kevin was one of the latter (both by prescribed label and, eventually, by self-definition). This categorization becomes an important part of sectarian life, as boundaries are drawn between those who fit in, and those who do not, and distinctions made to single them out. Sally, who is in the Family, makes a similar distinction between members, although along different lines. Whereas Kevin explained his problems in terms of the rigidity of the leadership and its lack of understanding of young members and their spirituality, Sally explains the problems of some other members and former members, as she perceives them, in terms of their personalities. Sally explains the difference between "the ones who make it" and "the ones who don't," and in her explanations the "ones who don't" are labeled as lazy or shy, or simply the ones who are not the "go-getters." It is interesting here that Sally, a goodie, places the problem with particular members, while Kevin, a rebel, places the problem with the structure and leadership of the movement.[26]

According to Sally there are different types of personalities; some people may be more interested in reaching out, others may be shy. And in a movement of missionaries who rely on provisioning, being a "go-getter" is an important and desirable quality.[27] The shy ones, upon leaving, would, according to Sally, never suddenly become outgoing go-getters. The go-getters, upon leaving, would be more likely to get a job and be successful outside the Family:

> Okay, we both know that there's the ones who are successful when they leave the Family, and the ones who aren't.... The ones who left the Family and didn't really get anywhere were the ones—they were always like that.
>
> Many times a lot of people, when they leave the Family, they kind of think that maybe it should all be easy for them, like, the work, and—you know, it's not all handed to you on a silver platter. Coz you have to plan on being a go-getter to get yourself going, you know, your parents can only do so much to help you get set up.

The responsibility is placed with the ones who leave; if they fail, that means they were not go-getters. The movement and leadership bear no responsibility in Sally's account; individual (former) members are to blame for their own predicament. "A lot of times, I am sad to say, I know quite a few young people left the Family that wanted to make money quickly—they just didn't want to have the financial stress that many times we have in the Family. So they just wanted to make money quick. But you can't be lazy and make money quick. Everyone wants to make money quick, but you have to work for it."[28] Sally was always a go-getter; her brother was the "bad boy." And although she admits that some people "maybe got frustrated" with the Victor camps, it was never an issue for her. She was occasionally disciplined, but believes it happened in a loving manner. She admits, however, that some had more negative experiences, and that they left the Family as a result of what happened at Victor camps. But these people, as she explains it, were "bad" before they left. That is why they needed disciplining, and that is why they did not fit in the Family. "One girl, a tomboy, she was always being bad," she said, "[and] she left.... She left because she didn't like it. She left before the Charter came out, before her rights came up. She was always the bad girl, and I guess she kind of got tired of getting all the correction, people telling her how to do things, so she just realized maybe this wasn't the life for her." Sally's stories give an impression of the Family as a lifestyle not appropriate for all. Hence second-generation adults (referred to as SGAs within the Family) have to decide whether they are "cut from the right material," hence, a go-getter or of similar persuasion. Although the Family can accommodate different styles and personalities, some literature has made it clear that the young members have to be "revolutionaries" who are ready to "fight" for the mission.[29] Sally's ideas on the role of personality also gives an impression that some former members, who have not made it in the system, are considered to have personality issues that would have impeded them regardless of being in or out—and such personality issues may be why they left. They have been under pressure to "shape up" or leave—the Family leadership has initiated purges to filter out those who were not "pulling their weight" and were accused of "sponging off" the others in the community, allegedly expecting the Family to "carry them."[30]

A Meeting Halfway
Staying by Different Rules

As previously mentioned, when the children of the founding members gain voting power and the ability to negotiate rules, they can become members by different rules. This is by and large the result of adaptation to the demands of the children, or adaptation after a failed process of trial and error. For example, in the Unification Church, the second-generation members were supposed to be blessed at birth, hence there was no need for them to undertake the same missions required of their parents. Furthermore, as the group was still run by the charismatic leader, he could make decisions and make changes on the spur of the moment—particularly when changes or adaptations fit within the framework of the Divine Principle or other Unificationist theology.[31] Doctrines often prove remarkably elastic following new revelations or interpretations.[32]

The first-generation converts were required to have three "spiritual children" (converts to the UC) before they could be blessed by Moon with a spouse of his choosing. Eventually young adults in the Unification Church were allowed to choose their own spouse, although in some cases the parents chose. The blessed children had to fill in lists with specifics such as demographics, educational achievements, spiritual questions, and so forth. Each geographical region (i.e., America, Europe, Korea, Japan) had its own lists. Parents were allowed to match from the lists, and some parents allowed their children a role in the choosing process. With the involvement of the parents, the system had opened up, as many included their children's wishes. The blessed children could be matched for blessing by their parents or their local leader, and they were allowed to be blessed (in marriage) from the age of nineteen. They did not have to accumulate a certain amount of "spiritual children," nor did they have to separate after their blessing (marriage). Because they are blessed children by birth, they owe less indemnity than their parents do. They still were "strongly encouraged" to do certain missions, but theoretically did not receive the same level of pressure their parents had to endure. However, more recently pressure has increased on second-generation members to do their missions. But this time peer group pressure conduced toward urging people to be seen to be a goodie, a "hard-core BC," rather than someone with a "negative" attitude.

From 2000 the blessed children have been advised to complete a public mission, fund-raising, and witnessing for the duration of one or even two years in order to prepare for their blessing (marriage). In Europe the missions for the blessed children were called the European Task Force. In the United States they were referred to as the Special Task Force. As Kevin described this, "It's mainly doing front-line mission for the second generation to experience Rev. Moon's heart, what he went through, and so you can understand what the church is all about." Since these task forces started, there has been "quite a push" for blessed children to take out a year and join the forces. Kevin had this assessment:

I don't know, because it feels like the leaders say that the first generation failed in their responsibility, the second generation now have to do it. I was thinking and understanding that we should have been able to just continue, just be successful in study and do well in that kind of circumstances and not have to go through those difficulties which our parents did, and most of them are now in difficult financial situations.

Now it's like, of course, advising, but it's quite a push to go, because you're thought of as not good or not conforming or not showing that you're really into the church if you don't want to do ETF.

The European Task Force typically lasts a year, which includes four months of fund-raising, for six days a week, and witnessing in east European countries, such as Slovakia and Hungary.[33] Thus, although the blessed children had, theoretically, less indemnity to pay, they were asked to involve themselves in fund-raising and witnessing missions. This has not always been the case, but the UC has, over time, involved the blessed children in the day-to-day life of the church and its activities. Hence, despite the different rules regarding the blessing, the lives of the second-generation members were now coming closer to the lives of their parents in the fields of fund-raising and witnessing. The latter were missions with a dual purpose, as they also functioned to create a sense of community and meaning for the blessed children. The label applied by Kevin to his peers involved in these missions, "activists," summons up an image of dedicated involvement and belief in a cause. The church may have found a way in which to involve the blessed children, by giving them leadership opportunities and career options within their own cohort, and letting them organize their own missions. Otherwise indifferent and disempowered young members are now motivated activists, excited about their lives and their work.

The Family has managed to motivate its young members in similar ways. Certainly, the second-generation adults had a different lifestyle from their parents. The sizes of communities have changed throughout the history of the Family, as have theories over the perfect size of a home. Berg, although deceased, is reportedly still sending messages through prophecy, as are Jesus and other major biblical figures.[34] A further dramatic change in lifestyle came with the Charter. Whereas the early history of the Family was typified by trial and error, the publication of the Charter solidified certain responsibilities. As Sally said, "You might enjoy sexual liberty, but then something else comes with it." After the advent of the Charter, a couple who conceived were strongly encouraged to get married, in accordance with the Law of Love.[35] Sally used the word "suggest" rather than strongly encouraged, and followed this by saying that if they did not want to get married, then at least the father has full responsibility for the next twenty months—throughout the pregnancy and until the child is one year of age he has to look after the mother and child. After this one year, if they still do not want to marry, then their decision will be respected. Although birth control is not endorsed, young members are encouraged to act responsibly and think of the consequences of their actions. Consequently, young members tended to have fewer children than the first generation, and some did use birth control.

Staying on a Different Level

Aside from membership by different standards, different levels of membership are also an important marker of the degree of adaptation of a community to its children. The more sectarian the community, the fewer membership options there are: one is either in or out. But as groups adapt to their children over time, flexibility increases, and the second-generation members can go beyond setting new rules. They can sometimes create their own levels of membership, and set new social boundaries in the process, changing the level of insertion of the group into society. Second-generation adults in the Family, for example, could be fellow members.[36] It enabled members to be a part of the movement, stay in touch, and receive literature, without being a full-time member and living in community. Alternatively, they could be even further on the fringe by becoming "active members" or "general members"; staying in touch or having a general and distant interest. Since the reboot things have changed more drastically, and membership requirements have become minimal and only relevant for core followers.

In the UC, the birth of the blessed children automatically brought with it new hierarchies within the movement, as a distinction was made between them and those not born to blessed couples—the Jacob's children. The former are the second generation, the latter were often referred to as the "1.5 generation." The Jacob's children were born before their parents received the blessing, and as a result they are first-generation members according to lineage (they were not born blessed), while being second-generation members within the community by virtue of their parents being members. This distinction creates a stratified system, as Jacob's children may only be matched to other Jacob's children or converts. (Jacob's children will have to go through the holy wine ceremony in order to purify their bloodline.) Whereas blessed children should only get matched to other blessed children in order to keep their lineage pure. This distinction between different categories of children is considered necessary to keep the "lineages pure." Another level in the hierarchical system is made up of the blessed children who have "fallen"—they have lost their "purity" in similar fashion to how Adam and Eve fell. Through their fall they have created a new lineage; as blessed children they are still in the true parents lineage, but by having had a sexual relationship outside of the blessing, they have lost God's lineage. They cannot receive the marriage blessing like pure blessed children. Fallen blessed children never lose their blessed lineage position, but their course has changed, hence they have a different fate to follow in order to restore their lineage. Fallen blessed children have to marry other fallen blessed children, so that they can work on restoring their lineage together, without defiling another's lineage. Eventually they can be restored by taking a series of workshops in Chongpyong in Korea. These new levels of membership involve members who otherwise would have been excluded by virtue of having transgressed the most important rule in the UC—the maintenance of purity. Now, however, they can remain within the movement (albeit as fallen children), under the understanding that they have to restore their lineage.[37]

Kevin, a blessed child, was trying to create a new niche for himself within the blessed children community. He did not want to be an activist and do the European Task Force, yet he still wanted to be a part of the movement. He wanted to create more connections with the European blessed children community because these members were, according to him, "more relaxed" and "open." He considered the UK community to be very insular, including the blessed children. I asked whether he would have liked there to be more flexibility within the UC. "I am feeling that, yeah," he replied. "Yeah. Everything that I know of my life is [the] UC movement. The teachings and the ideas of the church and the beliefs and faith, a certain percentage I do believe in, and I do go with. I have difficulties with organizational—the structure of the movement and the leaders." And as a result of his difficulties with the existing structure he believed his future in the movement to be uncertain. It depended on the extent to which he could carve out a niche, combining the aspects that he liked with avoiding the aspects he did not like.

> But I still feel that throughout my life I'll be probably on the line, in and out, maybe an associate, I don't know, that's just how I feel.
>
> I don't feel extremely negative, you know, to totally leave or bash, because I feel and know a lot of positives out of what I've learned and the relationships that I have with people. And I'm still good friends with BCs who are on the verge, who are really in, who have left, or—I can handle that, you know, I'm cool with that.

In a sense this is when outside influences affect the sectarian communities, and the children demand to be allowed to pick and choose their allegiances to the community. And some demand to, as it were, sit on the fence and speak to both sides. This would not be acceptable behavior in strict sectarian communities such as the Bruderhof has been at times in its history, but has become acceptable, to degrees, in more adaptable communities.

One example of an adaptable community is ISKCON. This community has had a problematic history with its children, after which it has evolved and somewhat adapted to the changing attitudes of the children.[38] Whereas initially the assumption was that the children would be raised to become monks and work in the temples, the reality proved to be very different. Some children in India and the United States were abused or neglected; consequently, some of them wanted as little as possible to do with the temples. But according to members and teachers I have spoken to in the United Kingdom, the children who have not become devotees are still welcomed at the temples, and some do occasionally visit.[39] This change required a process of adaptation. A major turning point for ISKCON was when married couples were asked to live outside the temples, as "householders." To one member, who had been a devotee since her teens, this felt like she had been "kicked out." Suddenly she had to be self-supporting and ascertain how to run a household, ascertain, in her words, "how the world works." But she, her contentment, and her comfort had had to be sacrificed to other processes—the ashrams needed to change. And as a result, for the children born since then, it meant that the ashram was a place for worship and the place for their education—but not their be all and end all, as it had been for the previous cohorts of gurukulis.

The shift from a movement of monks to one of monks and householders has been significant to ISKCON's social boundaries. As a consequence of the ashrams opening up and the householders spreading the membership to a more widely defined community, the concept of in and out has changed. Consequently, the definition of what it means to be a part of

ISKCON has changed as well. One does not have to be a monk, one does not have to live on the ashram, and now, for the children, the flexibility has continued. According to an ISKCON teacher, "They're still very much part of the community, they're still following—you know, they're vegetarian and they still come in, you know, when there are festivals they will still come in. They're still part of the community. It's only that they're attending outside school, or they're working outside." Hence the concept of the ISKCON community has become much more fluid than it was when the movement had just started. Children can attend outside schools, after which they can take an outside job, marry an outside person, and so forth.

> There's nothing really they could do for us to stop them. We have four principles that we try to adhere by, but *they* do or they don't. It's their choice. At what point do they decide they don't want to be part of the community? As far as we are concerned, they'll always be part of this community, or part of the greater ISKCON community.
>
> They're referred to as gurukul or gurukuli.... Wherever they go in the world, he's a gurukul, or she's a gurukuli, and they're part of the community in that respect. So there's no cutoff point.[40]

Gurukulis can stop practicing, they can stay away from the temple, they can smoke, drink, and live a secular life—but they are still considered part of the larger ISKCON community. The idea is that they may at some point come back. The young members may be going through a rough time, they may have lost the faith, lost the way a bit, but some day they may return. One teacher argued that the gurukulis were not judgmental among themselves, and they forgave each other's trespasses.[41] In general, she found that the older gurukulis in the United Kingdom still had faith in Krishna and Prabhupada. They may not have had faith in certain individuals, and the way they managed things, but these members still had faith in the spiritual side of the movement.[42] Hence, they may go through hard times and not do their practice, but, she predicted, years down the line they suddenly appear at the temple.[43] "It's like a phase.... It's also part of the philosophy—the desires. A person has the freedom to choose. Again, we don't see this as a cutoff point, there is no cut-off point.... A person smoking and drinking may have desires, [it] may be a hard phase. There's nothing stopping that person from moving on.... That's their choice." Hence they don't have to be active devotees, they may break some of the lifestyle and dietary restrictions—but they still are gurukulis. They may consider themselves as having left, but to the first generation they will always be a part of ISKCON. Furthermore, some values and beliefs may be sufficiently ingrained to have become lifestyle choices; for example, very few gurukulis eat meat. Hence, they belong by default. They belong because they have been raised as gurukulis—whether they believe or not.[44] Interestingly, in my interviews with teachers I did not come across special terminology for young members who were considered either good, bad, or rebellious, rather all young members were described as gurukulis, followed by a distinction describing whether they visited the temple, or whether they were "going through a rough time." It appears the one main distinction is between those who may have lost the way temporarily and are perhaps having a hard time: troubled. This points to a significant change in attitude between ISKCON now and at the time of the first gurukulas in the United States and India.

Relativism versus Absolutism

Sects construct communities of meaning that are special and opposed to outside. Hence the group, to its second-generation members, can be seen as a safe haven compared to the world outside. Yet sometimes staying is an effort as the young members grapple with institutional or organizational issues. Then, the discontent with the sect has to be weighed out against the undesirability of outside. It is at this point that the relative flexibility or rigidity of the groups' boundaries becomes important to the second generation. In some communities the beliefs and values are more important than membership and, in some cases, practice. It is more important that the children have been socialized into the beliefs, norms, and values than for them to stay with the group. One is more likely to find this, for example, in groups with a New Age orientation, where teachings emphasize the importance of finding one's own spiritual path.[45] Such religious groups put more emphasis on norms and values, as opposed to "truths." Charlotte Hardman (1999), in a study comparing the moral rules and sense of self of children in the Family, Transcendental Meditation, and Findhorn (a New Age community in Scotland), found that relativism and absolutism were very important and deeply ingrained underlying values that distinguished these children from each other.[46] The Family children were more likely to be absolutist in their outlooks, whereas the other children in Hardman's study were more likely to be relativistic. Children in TM and Findhorn had learned the concept of "inner knowledge," whereas the children in the Family had learned to rely on the teachings of Berg and Jesus. Hence, the children in the Family knew they should abide by moral rules, laid out by God, Jesus, Berg, or leaders within the movement, and they believed these to be objective rules. The children from TM and Findhorn believed that there were no objective moral rules, that all rules were subjective, and a few argued there should not be any rules—that nothing should be imposed. People's inherent goodness, they argued, would ensure harmony. Hence for the TM and Findhorn children, moral discourse came from within, whereas the Family children looked toward an external authority for guidance. Consequently, Family children interpreted right and wrong in light of the Bible, whereas the TM and Findhorn children had more relativistic concepts (right and wrong were seen as subjective concepts) and had an empowered sense of self as opposed to an empowered external authority. Hardman concluded that the Family children were successfully socialized into their parents' worldview, and those who deviated had either to conform or to leave, as there were absolutist moral views. On the other hand, the TM and Findhorn children had been empowered to trust their inner selves, hence they had created their own moral views and may well find their own paths and reject those taken by their parents (240). Despite not following the parents on their path, however, the children had internalized the parents' general worldviews and beliefs of self-realization. This adds an interesting angle, as it underlines how the "absolutist" groups are also more likely to have less negotiable norms and rules, and more regulatory and disciplining methods and agencies. The presence of an external agency (be it God or Berg or Moon) who provides guidance, as opposed to the potential for an "inner monitor" or "inner knowledge," does tend to make rules more nonnegotiable, and consequently infraction of such rules comes at a higher cost. Following this logic, the more absolutist the groups, the more intense the control of infractions and deviancy. Hence it makes sense that baddies come from groups where breaking rules amounts to impurity and danger, where those who leave are considered backsliders or "in disgrace"—their action frequently seen as a betrayal. Whereas groups who have the flexibility of a more relativistic worldview have room for rebels who are considered "groundbreakers," "light workers," and so on. There are no such hard and fast rules to break, and consequently no such deviants. In the case of the UC, however, there was clearly still a significant amount of resistance to Kevin's rebellion; he reported himself that he felt as though he walked around with a label tagged on him announcing his "negativity."[47]

But by and large it seems that the more flexible the group, the more opportunity the young members have to negotiate their own roles within the movement. In this case the labeling is more likely to use the language of rebels, be they somewhat contrary or innovators. The young members can explore and carve out their own niches and expand the territory of the movement without being banished from the tribe. Young members in groups with rigid boundaries do not have this opportunity; they will have to adapt or be cast out. In this case, one is more likely to see polarized labeling; children are either goodies or baddies (and potentially also troubled). Of course these distinctions are ideal-typical—but there is a boundary dynamic that is interesting and that taints the picture of what happens after the young members leave. The rebels and troubled can be redeemed, for example by doing conditions (UC); by undergoing clearances and going through exclusion, which gives them time to redeem (Bruderhof); by word time, writing open heart reports, and going through the Victor Program (the Family); and by undergoing auditing, an ethics program, or other appropriate courses (Scientology). But if they don't redeem themselves and are excommunicated or leave, then they become baddies, which frequently requires physical and emotional distance; disconnection, exclusion, shunning, or other way of not being in contact. The terms of course are generalized stereotypes I created to represent a number of labels, used differently, by each organization. For example, within the Family there are rebels who can still be redeemed, but once they have left they may become baddies if they have become apostates (this was especially the case with the first cohort; some former members of later cohorts remained on friendly terms with the organization). But in conversation they may be labeled as troubled instead as an explanation for their "bad attitude." Stephen, for example, is reportedly a "backslider" and a baddie—but this is explained by his "troubled nature." Boundary maintenance is negotiated through language as well. In a different example, ISKCON teachers argued that "once a gurukuli always a gurukuli"—they may not follow the principles but can always return. But when I asked a former gurukuli whether she and other former gurukuls she knows still consider themselves devotees, she wrote: "Heck no." Of course being a devotee is different from being a gurukuli by birth, but it gives one an impression of where these former gurukuls stand vis-à-vis ISKCON. The maintenance of boundaries is what defines a sect, and what maintains the sectarian stance with society—opposition and isolation. Hence, if the young members leave, they join the opposition, as it were.

PART THREE

On the Outside

There are different scenarios for leaving the group of one's childhood, and a range of experiences among young members who find themselves outside the familiarity of this community. Interconnected with the way young members leave is the type of support they are likely to encounter, and how this support affects them. It has a role in shaping their future attitude to the group and to their parents, as well as their sense of identity. However, not all former members who leave seek or receive support, either from the group they came from or from outside agencies. There are many who have left sectarian religious groups who have found and made their own ways. There is no systematic research or literature on this group of people, or statistics, hence it is very difficult to ascertain what the numbers may be (especially since it also depends on which religious groups we use in the analysis).[1] In short, more systematic research needs to be done on this topic, but for the moment this book maps out a number of trends, relying mainly on interview material. Although I use the labels introduced in the previous chapters, much of the following material is presented in the words of the individuals I interviewed, and focuses on their stories.

6

The Young Members Who Leave

RICKY, PREVIOUSLY KNOWN as Davidito, could not seem to adjust to the outside world. He had difficulty finding employment and settling down, and consequently moved frequently, working low-wage menial jobs. He also became very angry. In what appeared to be a bid to find his mother (who has lived in hiding for several decades) and kill her, he arranged to meet with a close friend of hers, Angela Smith, to find out where Maria was living at the time.

In a video Ricky recorded himself a day before meeting with Angela, sitting at a table surrounded by an array of weapons, he says that he has thought about committing suicide since he was small, and that now he will do this, but not without taking some key people with him:[2]

> But anyway, my main incentive in this is knowing that not only will it make me feel a whole fuck of a lot better but that maybe it'll bring, well if I'm successful, which is startin' to look kind of slim, slim chance right now. But it's worth a shot, because if I am successful. I mean I can just see all those fuckin' thousands of Family kids, you know, who have been abused.... Because what about all of the thousands of us who have been fucked over, literally. What about us? Where's our apologies? They're not even fuckin' sorry! They're not even fuckin' sorry.
>
> I feel like we're in a war here. It's not necessarily a literal war, like *I'm* making it, but it's a war nonetheless. I feel like every one of us who has left and in some way speaks out, in some way tries to help somebody, in some way tries to help ourselves, um, is a soldier in this war.

The following day he killed Angela Smith. Soon after he killed himself.

Some of the people I have spoken to have literally run away—and never returned. They have sacrificed their relationship with family and friends in order to break free from the community in which they were unhappy. (Often they were unhappy with their family and some friends by association.) They left following abuse, neglect, disagreements, or dissatisfaction, and often look back in anger. But of course this is not always the case. Some had mixed experiences, and after leaving frequently doubted their decision. Others move away with a feeling of "this is fine for some, but not for me" or "I want more" and move on. In some cases young members could sit on the margins and float in and out, although they could only do this if the community allowed them to do so. For others membership was part of their ascribed identity, whether they practiced or associated with the community or not. For example, gurukulis in the United Kingdom are generally still regarded as part of the community by their parents and other members of ISKCON, no matter the lifestyle and beliefs of the young adults. Some people moved away only to later move back. The Family had, since 2002, "rejoinees"—second-generation members who had returned to the movement after having left.

Why Do They Leave?
Look Back in Anger

Those who look back in anger are generally those who have experienced their childhood as unhappy, or even abusive. They tend to be the ones who were previously labeled the baddies within the group, although others were quiet and "biding their time" while planning to leave. These are the young members who were generally labeled deviants, who were frequently disciplined for transgressions, or who were scolded for not "being in the right spirit" or "lazy." Frequently they were disillusioned—feeling that the parents and the group as a whole did not live as they preached. This was frequently coupled with doubts about religious doctrines. Upon leaving they often had no or very few connections with the group and their family and friends; they made a choice and there was no middle way. Their difficulties adjusting to the outside world often left them frustrated, and angry with the community from which they came.[3]

Nora was raised in the Unification Church, but she was not born into the movement; she was born to an unwed mother before the mother joined the church.[4] She was known as an unblessed child, and as such she was excluded in a variety of ways. During the Sunday morning prayers, she was not allowed to partake in the pledge of the families, not belonging to a blessed family herself. During big celebrations (such as God's Day) seats were reserved for blessed children, and Nora mentions that she was allowed to sit there, but not without being told that this was an exception, as these seats were really only for blessed children.[5] Although blessed children would often go to Korea (this was considered an honor and akin to a rite of passage) she was never asked to go. And blessed children were, at first, exempt from fund-raising and witnessing, but she was not. Nora had to pay indemnity; she was not a blessed child. For blessed children, according to Nora, jobs and higher education were often mediated and sponsored by the church, whereas she had to depend on student loans and welfare. This discrepancy left her feeling inferior and inadequate, but rather than focusing on her own perceived inadequacy, she projected an image on those around her as being "gibbering morons." She returned the "otherness" imposed on her onto "them," and, over time, somewhat emotionally removed herself from the community as she learned to shut out the group's discourse. Hence, for Nora, leaving was not as great a jump as it was for others who had felt more integrated into their communities.

Marianne was born and raised in the Family, but left with her mother and several of her siblings at the age of twelve.[6] As a child she and her family had spent a lot of time in "the mission field," which is, in her words: "any third world country...who were ripe and ready for the message." In Marianne's case it was India, where she lived with her mother and stepfather. When Marianne was seven, her mother, pregnant with her seventh child and, according to Marianne, still suffering from postpartum depression from her previous child, returned to her native country and moved in with her parents. Marianne remained in India.

While back home, Marianne's mother began to doubt her membership in the movement, and when the family was reunited for a holiday, she took the children and left for a women's refuge. Following this, Marianne's maternal grandparents bought a house for them, and, away from the Family, the children went to school for the first time. This is how at the age of twelve, Marianne found herself out in the world. "I was suddenly thrown into this different world, you know. Not just culturally, because obviously I was thrown from India to [a Western country]. Not just that. But, you know, I was suddenly out of everything I knew, community-wise, and suddenly I was the dad in the house, looking after all my brothers and sisters, you know, my mum fell to pieces. We didn't have any help." As a result of her family responsibilities, Marianne had little time for homework, and did not perform well at school. She reported having been bullied, because she did not fit in. And although she had been reading from a very early age, she found that the Family's education had not prepared her adequately for school.

> I never got education. I learned to read and write but by the time I was six I was looking after children. When I was nine I had, after my chores in the kitchen, to cook breakfast for like forty people, and then clean up afterwards. And then make the bread for dinner, for forty people. I mean, we're talking flour here, and water, we're not talking about going out and buying bread. You know, after all my chores in the morning I had to take school, when I was nine I had ten toddlers to look after.... I was a teacher at nine years old. I wasn't taught, you know, my education stopped when I was—as soon as I could read, you know, that was my education stopped.

Marianne's teachers were not aware that she had never been to a conventional school, and she received no special support. At the age of sixteen she was pregnant, and moved out of her mother's house into her own accommodation. In her own words: "It was a lot easier to move out and look after one child than stay at home and look after five." This was also prompted by what Marianne considers to be a lack of respect for her mother—a lack of respect developed within the Family. She believes she was never taught to respect her mother. "I am talking about unconscious respect, I'm talking about: here's this woman who has totally fallen apart, she's basically my mother, you know, she should be cooking and cleaning and stuff, not me. Is that a mother? That sort of lack of respect." Marianne argues that her mother, who joined as a young teenager, must have "stopped developing" when she joined, after which her communal tasks were mostly to do with looking after her children and those of others. In contrast, Marianne argues that children who were raised in the Family are very mature, because they take on responsibility for tasks from a young age. Consequently, she found it difficult to relate to other teenagers, and she did not manage to make friends easily.

> I can't think of myself as twenty-one. I'm not twenty-one. I don't feel like twenty-one. There's no way. Mentally, I mean, there's something wrong with me where I don't feel my age—I feel a lot older. When I was nine, I felt twenty-one. See, I'm comparing myself to people outside, you see, it's natural. I'm looking at normal, average twenty-year-olds, and I think: bloody hell, I was like that when I was four.

Marianne also firmly believed that the sexualized environment in the Family added to what she terms her "accelerated life"—children grew up very fast. Having witnessed sexual relations from a young age, Marianne feels, in hindsight, that she knew too much prematurely. Marianne herself was involved in sexual relationships as a child, both with other minors and with older men.

> It's affected me in every single way you can think of—especially sex. And especially devaluating yourself. You know, not allowed to say "no." I used to get punished, locked away and made to read mountains of Mo letters on not being selfish and giving sex for love and, you know, if I said "no" to somebody or squirmed away from someone: heaven forbid, because I wasn't in the "right spirit," I wasn't sharing and caring, and I didn't have the love of Jesus.

As a teenager outside the group, she had a difficult time adjusting to a different value system. Behavior that seemed normal to Marianne stigmatized her among her peers. "Sex to me wasn't a big deal; I used to have sex with the boys, just like having a cup of tea. So I was labeled a slag. Just everything was too weird." Another former Family member I interviewed, Stephen, spoke of similar experiences.[7] Stephen, like Marianne, also asserted that during his childhood the Family was a highly sexualized environment. He spent most of his life in large communes (called combos and jumbos at the time) in India and the Philippines, where sharing was a normal part of the routine.

> I remember, in India, walking into a room, and seeing some people doing [a sexual act], and they didn't even notice I was in the room. And it was, like, totally common. Just walk right in. And I remember people having sex all over the place when I was growing up. And also having sexual contact with grown-ups as well...a twenty-five-year-old beautiful woman comes up and wants to give you a kiss, and she's got no clothes on—you're not gonna say "no" when you're twelve years old, you know. And those kind of situations happened a lot in the Philippines. And I know of people who were on sharing schedules in the Philippines as well, and India. A schedule on the wall says who you're gonna share with that day.

As a child Stephen thought this was the norm, and when he later left he, like Marianne, had difficulty adjusting his behavior. His ideas of normative behavior were significantly different from those around him, and this caused a few broken relationships when he was a young adult.

> But being in, you know, a normal Christian society, or I should say secular society, where those kinds of practices are taboo, it was actually quite hard...in relationships. And it took me about four or five years to realize that that portion of my socialization wasn't gonna work in the future. And it wasn't gonna work in any sort of relationship—long-term relationship anyway. So over the last three years I have changed my mind and attitude towards sexual practices, I guess.

Throughout Stephen's childhood there was a need for constant adaptation: he regularly moved between his parents and foster parents, and he regularly moved between countries, as well as homes. Stephen's parents separated when he was seven years old, after which he alternately lived with either his mother or father. By the time Stephen was ten, he was given the option to go to a teen training camp in the Philippines, which was an honor to him. But the camp turned out to be different from what he had imagined, as the Family had started introducing new ways of disciplining their "wayward teens," and experimented with these new practices in the training camps. At the age of fourteen Stephen began planning to leave the Family, and he left at the age of sixteen.

> I promised myself when I was fourteen that I would leave when I turned sixteen. And the reason why I set sixteen as the date was I knew that if I'd leave before I turned sixteen that I—and I didn't get away with it, or if I got away with it for a few months and they'd catch me, then I'd probably get sent to a Victor training camp. And I knew that if I got sent there, I'd just become a vegetable. For one, I'd become a vegetable, and for two, I really didn't like the idea of going there.

Hence Stephen behaved very well by the standards of the Family and tried to not put a foot wrong, out of fear of the Victor camps. He applied for missions that would take him abroad as part of a small group, rather than living in a combo, jumbo, or other large communal structure. But all the change and fluctuation never quite offered the option of a fresh beginning—something he was craving.

> [They] always used to tell us that, you know, when you move to a new home your records are destroyed and you've got a clean slate.

> But they'd also send a little manila envelope with you wherever you went that you were supposed to give to your shepherds. So—and it was quite obvious from the way you were treated in your new situation...that, basically, you were put in a category and you pretty much were kept there, unless you made some extreme amounts of progress, in some, you know, unbelievable way.

Despite this, Stephen learned how to stay out of the Victor camps. But not all his friends managed to do this, and Stephen felt that the camp changed some people dramatically.

> And it seemed most of them had just completely adopted whatever they had been taught at those training programs, and were the most likely to rat on us. It's funny, when I left I read 1984 and there were so many parallels, specifically between the ones, you know, the ones that you can trust and the ones you can't trust. There was a whole setup of people like that in the group...our age—there was maybe about 10 percent of the kids you can trust, with your actual feelings and your actual attitudes on things. Then there was the mass that you really didn't know, and you weren't going to take a chance, and then there was about 30 percent you wouldn't say anything bad to, or anything questionable to. And those were mostly the ones who came out of the training programs.

According to Stephen, "getting the Victory" was akin to losing one's personality—those who "got the Victory" were the ones who, later, were "toeing the Family line." In Stephen's words, "Getting the Victory is when the rat is eating your face—[when you finally submit] and then they can use you for whatever they want to use you for." Hence, he chose his friends wisely, trusted only a select few, and left at the age of sixteen.

Stephen argues that those who were treated badly in the Victor camps had a more difficult time letting go of their beliefs. Whereas Stephen, and some of his other friends who managed to avoid some of the more severe disciplining, had over the years developed a form of disillusionment.[8] He became disillusioned with what he began to see as hypocritical individuals (mostly leaders) as well as questionable teachings. Stephen says that there was a difference between what they believed and what they were taught to believe in. He asserts that he and his peers had doubts about many of the teachings.

You know, we were taught to believe that it was all one wife and one family, although we saw that it wasn't in many ways. We saw how families that had higher status, as in leadership families, were treated differently than families that had a lower status. So that sort of was, you know, it didn't really fit with that whole philosophy.

But basically what I'm saying is that there's a difference between what I professed to believe and what I actually believed wholeheartedly. And there was a period of time when I did believe that I was going to heaven and that—and I was really looking forward to that. But by the age of thirteen or fourteen I had sort of major doubts about that as well.[9]

According to Stephen, some pretended to get "the Victory"; they figured out what to say and how to act. "You learned how to write the right reports... because you knew it was all a matter of coolness, and if you were cool you were a revolutionary."[10] He pretended, until he left. There were others who remained rebellious and left because they never "got the Victory."

This Is Not for Me

In the cases mentioned so far the former members were unenthusiastic about their childhoods and left disillusioned with the group in which they were raised.[11] This was not always the scenario—in some cases former members had no particular grievances with their childhood communities, but nonetheless wanted to move on. They have "been there, done that," and now want to experience new things—things the group did not offer, such as higher education, a different lifestyle, or a certain vocation or employment. Of course this was more likely to be possible in groups that were flexible enough to allow the young adults to leave the fold without their jeopardizing relations with their parents and friends. As I described in the last chapter, these young adults may have still been on the margins of the community, or members by different rules or on a different level than their parents once were.

Sam, whom I mentioned in the previous chapter, did not, at the time of the interview, foresee himself leaving the movement.[12] He believed the morals and values of members to be superior to those of nonmembers, and thought he had benefited from the movement throughout his life so far. Yet he did not plan to have the same level of involvement as his parents, who were missionaries. As a consequence of their involvement in the Unification Church, they had not had enough money for Sam's schooling.

> I had to go out and make my own money to go to school.... All my other friends have gotten help and in our society most parents help their children through school a bit.... I've just gone out and done it myself, which has made me that much stronger, but I don't want my kids to go through that. So I wanna make sure I'm really successful at what I do, so they don't have to go through some of the hardship that I went through.

Sam stressed that he would not work for the UC full-time. Instead, he plans to tithe or support a particular project. This is a significantly different level of involvement from that of his parents. Although he still believes in the movement and what it stands for, it does not quite offer him the future he wants—the group will be relegated to a marginal position vis-à-vis his professional life as something he donates or tithes to. When asked whether, in the future, he plans to be an active member of the church, he answered, "No, I'll be working full-time." And when asked whether he still planned to be involved in any way, he answered, "Yeah, I'd like my kids to get some of the values I've learned. I think it's really important they grow up with some moral standards." In response to questions about future family life, Sam said: "I want my wife to do whatever she wants to do, as long as we get along.... If she wants to be involved with [the Unification Church], she can. She can do whatever she wants. I know what I wanna do. I'm not gonna do what my parents did, which is full-time—their work, their life, everything is for [the Unification Church]. But if she wants to do that, she can do that." Sam envisaged a membership at a significantly different level from that of most of the first-generation members. This is only possible because the movement has adapted to the second generation to some extent and has stretched the rules for its members.

Is This the Right Decision?

The previously described experiences are almost stereotypical opposites—to "look back in anger" or realize that, although fine for some, "this is not for me." It is not always such a clear-cut experience. For some members their experiences are a mixture of positive and negative memories, and clear-cut decisions are difficult to make. Hence, some stick with the community, and leave later in life. Some are never certain whether leaving was the right thing to do. The latter was a position that came up repeatedly with former members of the Bruderhof. Anna, whom I have mentioned in previous chapters, left the Bruderhof. Despite loving the community as a child, and believing it was the place for her as an adolescent and young adult, later in life she left the community and its people behind. Over time she had come to realize that the ideal community of her childhood had some institutionalized problems. This realization was a source of disillusionment, she said in her 2001 interview.

> You had these teachings about faith, honor, and honesty. At the same time you have this unspoken increasing power thing, where if you questioned power within the Bruderhof, you were actually questioning—they put it that you were actually going against God—because they were the representatives of God, and Christ. So it was extremely serious, anytime you were angry with them. But they could get as angry as they wanted to. Then it was justified; it was like Jesus in the Temple when the servants did it. But if you did it to them—and I was one of those people, I could take it so long, and then I'd scream... it was too much. Of course it's not that they can't handle a person who's angry, it's that the person has evil spirits. So suddenly you had this immature person being blamed for her immaturity and insecurity—totally blamed for her emotional sickness, as it were by a doctor.

Anna came to realize that the blame always fell onto the individual, never on the Brotherhood: "So, if you believe in a system where you can have people who've got more power than God, more power than the pope over individual lives, and if [individuals] question that, then they're evil. And you've got children absorbing all that."

The issue of power and abuse of power in the Bruderhof has arisen repeatedly in this research. Janet, also a former member of the Bruderhof, spent most of her childhood in Paraguay, and she was also caught up in the Great Crisis as a young adult.[13] For her, the crises revolved around power relations within the leadership:

> And always these big clearings, as they called them, these spiritual clearings [were] always based on the fact that the Arnolds were trying to get power and then there was another clique trying to get power.

And it all started back with the founder Eberhart, as he had three sons and two sons-in-law, and when he was dying he said—his sons basically he hadn't elected to be the bosses, he had elected his two sons-in-law. After his death there was fighting about that, endless, but it was never out in the open.... And that's what undermined the whole community.

When Janet was a young adult, her parents were sent back to England. She was asked to stay in Paraguay, which she did. Despite the invitation to remain, she spent most of the time in exclusion for reasons unknown to her. At the time of the Great Crisis, the leadership decided to close the Paraguayan community, and Janet was caught in the subsequent mayhem as Ibatea, the community where she lived, was due to be closed. Many people were excluded, and sent away to their home countries, while a small inner circle was allowed to stay. The latter were sent to another community, and would eventually be moved to America.

And then all the people around me began to shift, move, and I was left there. And my roommate came home one day.... She was packing her things without saying a word to me. She just completely closed me off. She would come home and say nothing to me, wouldn't talk to me. They were treating me like a leper. She said: "Oh, we are all going to Isla." I said, "Oh, am I going?" "I don't know," she said, "you will be told." And then marched out. Well, then along came one of those American blokes, and he told me that I had to stay there. And that's all; I had to stay there. And I actually watched the exodus. I was the only single girl, the only unmarried person left in the village.

And then, as time went on, and I couldn't tell you how long it was—one week, a few weeks. I would just wander about in the day, not knowing what to do, where to get food from—they just deserted us. And I found out that these people that were here and there, couples and a few families, were going to leave and were going back to Germany, or England, or France, or wherever they had come from; were being kicked out. And I thought: where does that leave me? And I was so sick with horror over what my supposed brothers and sisters were doing to me, I actually packed a case, and I was going to walk away from the community to a Paraguayan family and, I thought, even if I can't understand them or talk with them, I'll be happier with them than in this. I was going to walk away.

Eventually a young couple was sent to pick up Janet and take her to the new community, where she stayed with a family, doing menial work. She was still in exclusion, not allowed to speak with anyone. Then one day a minister wanted to see her.

> [The] minister asked, "What's the matter with you [Janet], what's the matter with you?" And I didn't know. I thought, well, you ought to know, but I didn't know what to say to him. And it was so frightening, so fearsome, that he was being all sweet this time instead of shouting and screaming, I couldn't figure it out.
>
> Eventually he said, "Would you like to leave here?" And I thought, "yeah, I want to go to my family in England." And before I could say that he said, "Would you like to go to the States?" And I was so frightened to say, "no, I want to go to England," because I thought that's how I'd gotten trapped in this mess, alone in Paraguay. So I said, "Yes, ok." And three weeks later they sent me to the States, still in exclusion.

Janet still did not know why she was in exclusion. Eventually, in the community in the United States, a minister asked her why she was not coming to meetings. Janet told him she was in exclusion, but that she did not know the reason why. He told her to "forget about it" and join in the meetings. But eventually she left. Under the guise of looking after a relative she left the community (and lived with this relative), which enabled her to eventually make the decision to not return.

Support

Passing from one status to another is both psychologically and socially a significant event. Historically rites have been markers of status passage to underline its real and symbolic importance. But the process of the passage can be varied, and "agents" who help the "passagee" through their process of change (and who may define and control the passage) may be more or less beneficial (Glazer and Strauss 1971). In the following section I discuss the roles of the sects, secular organizations, and former members as agents in this status passage, and the ways in which they may affect the passage.

Support from the Groups

Sectarian religious groups generally do not offer extended structural support to first-generation members (converts) who leave. After all, they are defectors, and these members are going back to something they know. Furthermore, why should they support those who negate what they stand for? Although some groups have agreements regarding those who leave after they have made significant contributions to the community, other groups, somewhat controversially, do not. Although most groups mentioned in-depth in this book eventually offered some form of support to second- or subsequent-generation members who left, this has generally been a rocky road.

In some cases the members who leave are considered to be undesirable—because they are spiritually "lost" and need to find their way before they can return, or because they are thought to be, or have proven to be, a bad influence within the community. These former members may be barred from contacting members, and vice versa. Of the twenty former members raised in religious communities who contacted Inform, and whose stories I analyzed to add to this research, seven were former Jehovah's Witnesses who had been disfellowshipped and consequently had very limited contact with former friends and relatives (except for one who still had contact with his mother). Such shunning practices (employed by the Bruderhof, the Jehovah's Witnesses, and some Hutterite groups) have parallels to the attitude of Scientologists toward those they term "suppressive persons"—those who speak critically of Scientology. Meredith, for example, who left the movement, could not raise criticism about or speak badly of Scientology to her relatives who were still members, and had to promise she would not criticize the organization or else they would have to disengage from her.[14]

Those movements that aim to isolate themselves from their surrounding community tend to have teachings and rules regarding what they consider negative influences—these can include critics of the movement as well as relatives of members (for competing allegiances) and former members. Publications in the Family, for example, have described former members as backsliders and as "Vandaris," a form of demon who uses former members as vessels to destroy "the pure" (Maria and Amsterdam 2002, pars. 135–163). In a Family children's publication that summarizes information from Family publications in cartoon format, the term has been defined as:

> Van-dar-i [vən da´ar e´e] noun: SPIRIT WORLD: Agents of the netherworld; evil demons; hitchhikers; evil lords of the netherworld; set on preparing the ignorant to worship the son of perdition; bent on destroying what is pure; they seek to mar the truth; dark ones; work through vessels who yield to darkness; vandals of the spirit world. [The "van" is derived from the word "vandals," the "dar" from the word "dark," the "i" spelling of the last syllable signifies "I," denoting self or selfishness.] (*Vandari Repellent* 2003: 24–26)[15]

The existence of Vandaris had apparently been revealed in a vision and communication from the Lord, in response to Peter and Maria's questions about what to do about those who are out "to destroy The Family" (Maria and Amsterdam 2002, par. 39). They explain this is an especially difficult question, as these are friends, children, and sometimes parents of Family members, and, consequently, there may be competing emotions at play. But the revelation, entitled *Pray, Obey and Prepare!*, clarified that there was "increased enemy activity," and the "emissaries of Satan" can take many forms (Maria and Amsterdam 2002, par. 141). This labeling is significant in light of the discussion in chapter 4—young Family members were told about and read comic-book-type publications where they were warned about the powers and dangers of these "polluting" and "evil" people who were categorized as "enemies." Sources of criticism and opposition are reified and anthropomorphized, validating the group's ideology while suppressing debate. I quote at length from *Pray, Obey and Prepare!*:

> I saw a clean-cut, handsome-looking man, around his early 30s. He looked like a nice guy, well-groomed, together, confident and on top of things. Then all of a sudden he morphed right in front of me into the most grotesque creature! He turned blood red from head to toe, starting from his head down. His clothes were no longer defined once he morphed, but rather it looked like he was covered in some type of blood-red cloak that was clinging to his body—it was like a hood over his head, and it covered him like a long cape all the way down to his feet.
>
> His eyes look very bloodshot. His red cloak looks somewhat like the traditional cartoon picture you see of a ghost—the typical ghost covered in a sheet—only this covering is clinging to him and it's blood red. The horrible thing about it is that he seems to be dripping all over with blood. It looks like he's just come up out of a

swimming pool or some body of water, like the ocean, and he's dripping wet. Only the outstanding and yucky thing about this is he seems to be dripping not water, but blood—from his eyes, his nose, his lips, his arms, his hands.

It's totally grotesque, and if I didn't know the Lord is protecting me, it would be downright frightening. It's horrible, disgusting! One minute he's this handsome-looking fellow, then he's this horrible, red, dripping creature. Then there were rats, of all things—horrible, big, filthy rats running all around! (pars. 135–137)

There are antidotes, as Maria adds later in the same publication:

The Lord knows we need this information to combat our enemies' attempts to destroy the Family. We need to pray both against the Enemy using our detractors and apostates, as well as misguided officials, sensationalistic reporters, deluded lawyers or publishers, and against the specific evil spirits, the Vandari, that inspire these people's ungodly actions and stories. Use the keys and the key promises to pray against our enemies, and against these vile, disgusting vandals that live in the filthy, putrid sewers of the depths of the netherworld! (par. 163)

The comic books for children and teenagers assert that prayer and the word of Jesus is the "key" that can protect them from the Vandaris (*Vandari Repellent* 2003: 27). It is significant that this information and advice was published in reading material geared toward the children and teenagers within the Family, as they were likely to have older friends and siblings who had left with whom they might otherwise want to remain in contact.

This belief that former members are polluting influences, both to current members inside and to officials outside, is an obstacle to leavers receiving the necessary support from the religious groups from which they came. With the more socially isolated groups, the first cohort of members leaving their communities generally had the most difficult time—the groups were not accustomed to dealing with this issue, and in general offered no support. Also, there was little motivation to support those considered to be "backsliders," "traitors" or "renegades," or "polluters." Either the young members ran away, or they were cast out like bad fruit. Over time the groups, having learned through trial and error from the first cohort of their children leaving the fold, generally adapted to incorporate some form of support—be it structural, spiritual, or emotional. But there is a large variation in the support given, some minimal and inadequate, and some substantial. Some young former members have received a certain amount of cash to help them find their way, others were introduced to a friend or relative on the outside they could stay with for a while—or even work for. In some cases parents chose to change their level of membership (i.e., from missionary to fellow member in the Family) to enable their children to go to mainstream schools or adjust to nuclear households. But efforts on the part of the group to help its young members can be counterproductive. Parents feeling under pressure to change their level of membership to accommodate their wavering child may put significant pressure on this young member, who may feel guilty about uprooting the family. On a different level, meetings with elders or other religious leaders to help children who may be "spiritually confused" can leave these children very confused indeed. After all, they may not necessarily know what they want (beyond a general feeling that "this is not it"), and more theological arguments may not help them understand (if they already think that they "don't get it"). Also, young members may not want spiritual or emotional support from a source they do not trust anymore, a source they may accuse of hypocrisy.

Spiritual and Emotional Support

Several of the people interviewed for this research spoke of having long talks with senior members and elders about their doubts and reservations, and almost every one thought that this had been fruitless, and in many cases frustrating—it seemed that senior members always had an answer ready with doctrinal justifications. Although this may have been helpful for some, for others this was not always a beneficial form of support. In some cases, such conversations may lead to problems, as senior members may report those who question teachings. Andrew Holden (2002) has written about such cases within the Jehovah's Witnesses, where questioning doctrine may be seen as apostasy, an offense that can result in disfellowship—and, consequently, shunning. But in most cases there will be room for continuing discussion so that the "confused member" may "understand." This may take the form of Bible study, courses or other programs, or in-depth discussions with an elder or another in a leadership position. Members of the Family may be asked to spend more time reading Mo letters and writing open heart reports so that they may find a parallel to their questions in doctrine, and realize what they are struggling with. Similarly, teachers and senior members in Scientology may employ special procedures to "help" children who are disruptive, questioning, and voicing uncertainties about their situation. At Scientology's Walsh Manor School for Cadets a senior member said that if a child wants to leave or is having a hard time, "they will go in and have a look."[16]

> Not because we're trying to keep them here, but just from the point of view of "well, hang on a minute, that doesn't make any sense." Then we'll come in and try and see if there is any problem that's being encountered here. Normally we get them through a complete word-clearing action first, and see how they're doing. And if they're doing better but still maintain a wish to go or whatever then the parents get consulted or they go and stay with the other parent or with family members or whatever.[17]

If the child does not want to be in the little cadet school, or even in Scientology, the parent becomes "unqualified" to be a Sea Org member. The senior member interviewed said there are strict rules regarding Sea Org members and their children:

> If a child doesn't want to be here then a parent is called before a board and looked at. And obviously there's things done internally to try, like word clearing and applying ethics technology and so on to the child in the hope that he may want to stay here. But if he's really adamant that he doesn't want to be here then the parents would be asked to go as well. Because a family is a very important thing.[18]

In theory this appears to be fair, although in practice this could put significant pressure on young members who may not know exactly what they want aside from feeling that the current situation makes them unhappy. But the knowledge that their decision may uproot the parents, or even the whole family, could be a significant burden to carry. Furthermore, the meetings, courses, and auditing sessions involved in "checking" whether the uncertainty or desire to leave is not about a "misunderstood" or "ethics" issue can be taxing on a young member. One young former member of the Church of Scientology, Meredith, told me that, although "ethics" is said not to be punishment, it did feel like that sometimes to her.[19] She took longer than others to accomplish her courses and goals, and had started to feel like she was known as a problem student. Meredith said that she was afraid to go past any unidentified word as she had been taught they may cause problems in understanding and progressing in life. She was therefore scared of "misunderstoods," and very diligent about avoiding them. So much so that she frequently did not read past a word or section she was not entirely certain she understood. Once she entered the Sea Org this became a problem, as supervisors occasionally interpreted her diligence and repeatedly asking for explanations (after being told to "look it up") as a behavioral problem. For Meredith, some concepts did not make sense. Consequently, Meredith was sent to "ethics." There she also had problems with tasks, such as the overt withhold, which means that the member is believed to be covering up for an "overt," a harmful act toward Scientology, and is asked to write up her or his behavior and subsequent "denial." The problem was, however, that she did not know what was causing her to not understand her study materials, not "get it." In hindsight, after having been away from the organization for a while, she told me it may have been that she did not agree with what she was learning—even when she looked up every single word, she still "did not get it." But at the time, she spent weeks writing overt whithhold letters, trying to "get her ethics in."

> I was a good person, I didn't have anything to write up.... I wrote down things like "I looked at a guy." Is that an overt? No. But me, being so conscientious, I was trying to—thinking that I had done something wrong, thinking I had to write something down. And then checking every time with the e-meter—and it wasn't it. Then I was thinking it had to be something really big, that I wasn't even thinking of. But it wasn't. I got really annoyed by that.[20]

Meredith was "down stat" (which means that her productivity statistics were not up to par) and was not allowed to go into town for personal errands. She had left school prematurely so that she could take more courses at the Scientology headquarters. Soon after, however, she regretted this, and went back into education to get her qualifications. This gave her an excuse not to be "on staff," and to distance herself from Scientology, and a few years later she took the decision to "become disaffected." Despite the best intentions, such spiritual or "career" support, whether to help the young members make up their minds to find out what they really want, or what is bothering them, can sometimes be counterproductive. Those in leadership positions may have the intention of helping a "lost young members," yet they impose the group's views, norms, and standards while those young members may be trying to define these for themselves. The pressure to "get it" and to conform does not always result in assimilation and integration—and when not successful can have the opposite effect and lead to alienation and estrangement instead.

Material Support

Material support could be more useful, and more needs oriented, for the young member who wants to leave. But such support is not always readily available, as some religious movements may not have the necessary means, nor do they always prioritize leaving members as deserving beneficiaries. The Bruderhof, after the Great Crisis, was struggling financially, which, allegedly, was part of the reason for shutting down the Paraguayan communities (Oved 1996). Frank had been born and raised in the Bruderhof, and had spent most of his childhood in Paraguay, and despite some emotional and physical hardships, he had loved the country. In his own words: "There was something really, really wonderful about my childhood. Also some terrible things, but the fact is: there were some good things." As an adult in an American community he was not so fortunate.

> I had been falsely accused by a man in '62, and what he wanted I can't tell you now. He was a minister. He wanted to know, and I don't know what he wanted to this day. Anyway, I was out of the Brotherhood, and I was out sixteen years....
>
> I wasn't allowed to come to religious meetings, I wasn't allowed to break bread in the Lord's Supper; I was shunned. I was told I was not allowed to marry, I had to give that up. And they would carry me, in other words: fellowship. You can stay here but that's it.[21]

In his sixteenth year of exclusion Frank decided to write down the things that were bothering him, but most drafts ended up in the wastepaper basket. Some of these notes, however, also ended up on an elder's desk. Frank was excommunicated that same night.

> They gave me an old Beetle, which couldn't get through Pennsylvania State testing, because Pennsylvania is far stricter than New York.... They gave me $150 for insurance, and they gave me three nights' lodging in a hotel. And a box with Heinz beans.... But I had no spoon, I had no tin

opener, I had no scissors. I was allowed to drive so long on New York plates, then, I had to send the plates back because they belonged to the community.

When I left I didn't have any clothes to bring but I did bring [homemade] wine, three boxes.... That kept me warm, because I had no blankets.

Although Frank had trained as a mechanic, he did not have a diploma. He had taken the theoretical examinations, but not the practical segment necessary to receive a diploma—the leaders at the time had said he did not need the diploma, and he had had enough practical experience working in the community. Hence, after leaving the community, Frank had no papers, curriculum vitae, or references, and had to settle for low-end jobs with minimal wage.

Janet had been sent away for a period of time before she eventually left the Bruderhof herself. At that time she had with her a few items of clothing. She was sent to work for a doctor's family where she could work in exchange for her lodging. Similarly, Anna had been sent to care for an elderly couple. She, too, received free lodging in exchange for her work. They both received a small wage typical of those lacking certificates or other necessary papers. More recently, in the new millennium, a young woman left under similar circumstances; she was given £200 and housed outside the community with a friend of the community.[22] Her parents, not keen for her to communicate with outsiders, refused to give the contact details of two elder siblings who had previously left the community. In this case, however, the young woman had the necessary qualifications to be able to choose whether she wanted to further her education or rejoin the community.

A lack of formal qualifications was a theme that came up repeatedly in interviews with former Bruderhof members, and it has also been a topic of discussion in *Keep in Touch* newsletters distributed among former members. It has also arisen as an issue for some former members of the Family and Scientology. In the case of the former, some young members had been raised in the mission field or inadequately homeschooled. In the case of the latter, training within Scientology had, for some, been a priority over more mainstream educational qualifications. All the former members whom I interviewed knew of others who had also struggled without formal credentials. One of the former Bruderhof interviewees told me of her brother, who had trained as an architect in the community. He received enough training to be able to work as an architect within the community, but not quite enough to receive the credentials. Anna told me in her 2001 interview that this was normal practice, and that members may be able to get the necessary qualifications if they get a job and finance it themselves: "They'll fund you for two years and then you have to make a decision as to whether you join the Bruderhof—otherwise you're on your own." Anna herself was not given permission to study what she wanted to study, but instead was asked to concentrate on something that would be more useful to the community.

For these former members, leaving the Bruderhof was challenging materially and emotionally. They left with a sense of inadequacy and low self-esteem, which was aggravated by the fact that they owned nothing, including material evidence of their training in the form of certificates or references. As Janet pointed out in her 2001 interview:

> You'll find that most of us are saying that we were kicked out, sent out. I think what happens is, psychologically—remember that we have nothing. When you're there you have no money, no bank account. In fact, nothing that you own is your own, you see. So that brings a much bigger fear about upping and going, because you have nothing! To get up and walk out is next to impossible. You have to first line up a job, which you can't do if you're still in the community. It's a very difficult thing.

The former Bruderhof members I have spoken to felt alone and deserted when leaving the community—there was no significant or helpful support from the movement.[23] Rather, many believed their childhood in the movement had set them back. Some had relatives they could go to who helped them adjust to the different surroundings, but this was not always the case—and those who did not have relatives outside were, they believed, out on their own.

The first wave of young members who left the Family, during the 1980s and early 1990s, generally received little support. They also tended to be very critical of the organization, and several of these former members have been accused of being Vandaris. Such deviant typifications can be a point-by-point antithesis of core features of the group that fashions it—Vandaris being accused of being filled with evil and polluting the faithful. But the Family adapted over time to the reality that their children were leaving (during the 1990s between half and two-thirds of their children were leaving).[24] The movement eventually established ways to support young members who did not want to join in the missionary lifestyle. In some cases parents left the mission field and became fellow members so that their children could go to mainstream schools. In other cases the young members moved to another community or stayed in another home. Eventually the Family set up a special education pack for young members who were leaving, which had information on the everyday aspects of life from which they had been largely shielded. The booklet contained information on how to open a bank account, rent a flat, buy a car (and what to look for in a secondhand car), and write a CV and offered suggestions regarding job interviews, as well as information about diet (alcohol in moderation) sexually transmitted diseases, and how to practice safe sex.[25]

The Unification Church has also changed in this respect, and its structure became more conducive to supporting its young members. The leaders, movement, and parents by and large have become more flexible and the children and teenagers generally have more room for negotiation.[26] ISKCON has undergone a similar structural change in which the group switched from a communal lifestyle to a more nuclear one. This has made a significant difference for the children, who then moved from ashram schools to "outside" schools. Furthermore, this shift empowered the parents, who, as a result of moving from the ashram to their own households, suddenly had more say over the way they raised their children. This empowerment of the parents appears to be a significant factor, as the role of the parents, or lack thereof, was an issue that came up repeatedly in this research.

Parents as "Middle Management"

Susan Landa introduced the idea (and terminology) of parents in cults serving as middle management in an article published in 1991, and this approach has since then been referenced by others.[27] Landa's article was geared toward helping those in the legal profession dealing with "cult" cases, especially child-custody cases. Landa (9) argued that parents, as a result of mind control, are unable to protect their children from the cult's child-abuse practices.[28] She asserted (9) that the parents suffer from "learned helplessness response," which is emotional numbing and maladaptive passivity of the cult member, who has realized that surrounding events cannot be controlled except by the leader's command. Landa argued, "To the outsider the cult member, like the battered woman, does not appear as helpless as he or she perceives. However, due to this perception of helplessness, the member no longer has the knowledge or ability to prevent the abuses from happening to him or herself, let alone to someone else" (9).

This is a simplistic generalization—and one that I do not find useful or representative.[29] But the general idea of parents as "middle management" is perhaps evocative, and does parallel some of the comments made by members as well as former members during interviews, which hinted at competing loyalties or even priorities. In the Bruderhof, for example, the structure is authoritarian, and several former members have commented that the parents did not have as much say as the leaders did in child care and child-raising issues. According to Anna her parents were good parents, but their loyalties lay with the movement rather than with their children—there was a hierarchy of priorities:

> I think most of what my parents were sent away for is that they were not good enough parents. Well, we were never abused, we were never treated badly, they just weren't strict enough with us perhaps. Appalling. They were good parents. They were totally married to the cause and they weren't there for us. And the Bruderhof, as soon as something goes wrong with the children, they blame it on the parents. My parents never questioned any criticism of us, any punishment, nothing. What the Brotherhood said, went.

Janet has a similar opinion: "When times were hard and going all wrong because of their ideals, our parents would not come to our aid. They wouldn't defend us, ever." Anna has never been able to respect her father because she blames him for the fact that her family spent significant amounts of time in exclusion. (Hence the Bruderhof has, according to her, managed to drive a large wedge between her and her parents.)

Frank remembers that his family was accused of having "emotional ties" within the family when he was a child, and that consequently he was away from his parents from the age of sixteen.

> I had the impression we were kept deliberately away from our parents. They accused [my family] of having emotional ties in the family. And with me it was that way, but I was a lot by myself and did my own thing—I couldn't care who my parents were.
>
> I was away from my parents from the age of sixteen. I worked away from the hof and then came home weekends, then I had to stop that, then I was sent to Woodcrest; they were sent to Evergreen.

> Then my father was sent away, my mother followed him. They were away eight years, outside. And I didn't dare to side with my parents because I knew I would be kicked out.

Janet puts these sentiments in context: "The communal life was such an ideal in our parents' minds that individual attention and love and kindness, in their minds, was so unimportant compared to this communal 'we all belonged to the community' sort of thing, you know." Janet's brother spent a significant amount of time in exclusion as a young teenager; moreover he was physically sent to the margins of the community, not to be contacted by anyone.

> My parents let it happen, they didn't defend him. If somebody did that to my children, I would slaughter them. Out of the window would go all ideals of Christian nonviolence.
>
> And I'd like to say, all these ex-Bruderhof people my age and younger and older, they all like to defend their parents and what's happened, but the truth is, I say, unless you can be angry at your parents and then still love them, you've lost it, because you're covering up the truth of the place. And the truth is that each parent is actually responsible for their offspring.... And the thing is, our parents didn't defend us.
>
> And my parents didn't just up and leave these two farms that were only a stone's throw away—but I didn't know they were there. They didn't just get up and say "we're not having this." They waited until they could see it through with the Brotherhood. There were so many times in my life that this kind of thing happened.... The parents never ever went to defend you.

Similarly, Sam spent a significant amount of time away from his parents, who were missionaries for the Unification Church. As a teenager he lived in a house with school and church friends and their elder sister—she was in charge of the household. This is a similar scenario to Family homes that teenagers can move to while their parents are in the mission field. Young members who have grievances with the religious movements (or beliefs) frequently have grievances with their parents as well—simply because "they weren't there," did not "defend them," or had other priorities. This reduces the young members' avenues for support should they want to leave.

The Cult Scene

If the young former members cannot always completely rely on their religious community or their parents for support, whether that is because they do not want contact or because the group or parents have limited means or inclination (that is, the "rogue" member is shunned), then whom can they rely on? The religious diversity that has grown exponentially since the 1900s (especially after World War II), and organized reactions to it, often referred to as the "cult scene" (Barker 2004), is an ideologically fraught scene where the different strands often argue they have "Truth" on their side and hence are not willing to accommodate and meet halfway on moral and spiritual issues. Since the 1960s, as the spiritual diversity in the West has grown, accusations of moral depravity and spiritual danger have been abundant within this cult scene. This scene became polarized as seekers looked beyond the traditional spiritual options, and critics of the new religious developments organized into groups and communities, criticizing the "cults" and extremists and warning of their alleged powers of mental manipulation (Beckford 1995; Melton 1995; Barker 2004). This collection of groups and communities of critics is often referred to as the anticult movement (Barker 1986; Shupe and Bromley 1994; Melton 1999; Shupe et al. [2002] 2003). This movement's approach, generally, is one of attack rather than accommodation—one of accusation rather than communication. Often this approach comes from an emotive (the personal experiences of parents of members or former members) or doctrinal (apologetics) standpoint focusing on differences and incompatibilities, rather than from a value-free approach seeking explanation or interfaith-type communication (Barker 2002).[30] Depending on their standpoint, critics will tend to rely on different types of information and have different aims and methodologies (Barker 1995b; 2002; Cowan 2003). Consequently, there are different types of support available for those who leave religious movements, each with its own biases. For example, support from other religious organizations (such as churches) may involve theological criticism as well as spiritual support. Psychological support is likely to focus on the former member's well-being, although some counseling may still involve a particular religious or spiritual bias. However, counselors may not be knowledgeable about religious minorities and associated issues or about the particular issues and problems young former members may have. Secular support is more likely to be needs oriented and less likely to concentrate on issues of religious doctrine and practice (unless this practice is illegal or harmful), hence less likely to be able to offer spiritual support (which some people might seek).[31] Again, depending on the type of aid, secular organizations may not be familiar with the unusual issues sometimes associated with new religions. Lack of religious bias is not always considered the most desirable factor in support for former members—the latter often prefer to speak with people who have had similar experiences.[32]

Religious partiality, however, can come with its own difficulties. Arguments that the beliefs, or the interpretation of doctrine and practices, are the reason for the abuse can cover for other (often institutionalized) problems. The leader(s) and the parents are frequently blamed as those who have "misinterpreted" doctrine or "misused" religion to justify abuse. They may have, and I do not intend to downplay either the leader(s)' responsibility regarding doctrinal interpretations and religious teachings or the parents' responsibility regarding the way they choose to raise their children. However, doctrinal content (the content of a group's doctrine frequently is blamed as the direct source and reason for the practices) and practice are not always perfectly causally related. Religious texts do get interpreted and reinterpreted constantly, and certain sections are highlighted while others are downplayed, depending on how liberal or literalist the movement. And interpretations and emphases are strongly linked to culture and structure. Hence the usual legal practice in Western countries to judge according to behavior rather than beliefs, and the insistence of research-oriented bodies on criticizing problematic practices when present while steering clear of criticizing potentially problematic religious beliefs when there is no evidence of these directly or even necessarily influencing behavior. Such a distinction, however, is generally not granted by anticult and countercult groups, who tend to assume that problematic doctrine (which can be very subjective) translates into problematic behavior, and who frequently assume that past behavior predicts future behavior without recognizing and accounting for changes within the groups. Those coming from an anticult or countercult position frequently argue that distinguishing between beliefs and practices, and not passing judgment on the religious beliefs and doctrine, amounts to "cult apologetics."[33] Hence there is a polarization between different positions in what is often termed the cult scene (and in most cases it is a position rather than a movement or group).

The cult scene has changed with the maturation of the second generation of the most infamous NRMs.[34] Most of the institutions and organizations that are critical of cults have had conferences and meetings or have written reports on the topic of those born in NRMs.[35] The argument, in general, is that whereas their parents were, to some extent, consenting adults, these young members were not. (Although the degree to which the converts consented has been debated by many anticult organizations and authors, who have claimed that converts were deceived into joining without knowing the full extent of the cult's beliefs and practices, frequently with the use of "mind control" methods or other forms of manipulation. See, for example, Conway and Siegelman [1978]; Hassan [1988].) Many of these organizations offer much-needed support for "born-into" members who have left; they offer themselves up as agents to the status "passagees." As the second- and third-generation (or, in the case of nineteenth-century sects, the third- or fourth-generation) members have come of age, many of them have left their communities (although of course the numbers differ per community). Of these, many have inadvertently remained within the cult scene by either joining anticult organizations or creating their own self-help organizations to help their peers. The latter have chartered their own passage and are offering themselves as agents for the next cohort of passagees. This has been an important development, as these former members can offer the knowledge and specific support that young former members need. These are a type of self-help and campaigning groups that have emerged as institutional expressions of anger and grief, in a sense not dissimilar to those described by Paul Rock (1998) in his research on self-help groups, in which he describes them as victims' organizations striving to reassert meaning and control in a world that has been turned upside down.[36]

Teenagers and young adults leaving sects have often not lived outside their communities before, and finding other former members offers a sense of comfort as they speak the same language (in the sense of word choice and matters of speech) and have an idea of what the former members have gone through and where they are coming from. Those who leave tend to prefer the familiarity of other former members to whom they do not have to explain their past and their problems, and to whom they do not have to explain their worries and fears. They frequently fear the "outside"—a society with which they are not familiar and of which they have often been told disparaging and frequently fearsome stories. Hence this type of support can be exactly what they are looking for. As Rock argues (1998: xxiii), the survivors claim an existential understanding that is different in kind from other forms of knowledge. Such self-help organizations claim that they are the only people who can understand, and that by their experience they are qualified to help others in similar circumstances. In some cases, however, such support comes with a bias, as those providing the support often have had a problematic involvement themselves—these people have had their own reasons for leaving the group. Although this gives them an expertise on the one hand, it can also provide an emotional motive for wanting to discredit the religious community. According to Rock this dynamic is not unusual among self-help groups. He describes the self-help movement of the 1960s: "Individuals who had hitherto been separated by grief, confusion, fear, and rage came together and they experienced in that encounter a shaping, affirmation, and collectivisation of a powerful passion that created an emotional field, identities and identifications, sensibilities and motives, and boundaries between the 'us' of the survivors and the 'them' of the world outside" (324).

Such binary opposition is reflected, too, in the self-help groups for former sect members. It creates a sense of community to those who belong, but is alienating to others, especially where support frequently emphasizes "wrong doctrine," and doctrine is conflated with practice. This puts the focus as much if not more on text rather than individuals and the structure that has been created that has allowed abuse to occur. Such an emphasis on content is more likely to alienate the former members from their parents and the religious community as a whole rather than to move them toward identifying the "bad" and being open to dialogue or accommodation with persons and aspects that were perhaps not so bad.[37] Of course this binary position is a generalization, and not all former member self-help groups can be easily classified like this. Below I describe in more detail the two main former member support groups I have come across in my research that are mostly geared toward those born into the religious movements the founders originated from.

Support from Former Members
KIT

One former member of the Bruderhof, Ramon Sender, started a round-robin newsletter initially meant to bring former members together in order to keep in touch with one another; hence the name, *KIT*, which stands for "Keep in Touch." He had been motivated to do this after finding out that his adult daughter, who had remained a member, had died; he had not been notified at the time. He wanted to research her life, as he had not been told of her marriage, children, illness, and other major life events either, and attempted to do this by contacting other former members who may have known her while in the group. The communication via *KIT* increased, and soon the initiative developed into the Peregrine Foundation (a nonprofit organization that aimed to illuminate the nature of experimental social groups and assist those who want to leave them) and within it the Carrier Pigeon Press (a publishing house that has published and distributed the memoirs of former members of the Bruderhof). Over time the network expanded and in 1995 individuals associated with the Peregrine Foundation founded Children of the Bruderhof International and initiated a toll-free number for people inside and outside the Bruderhof who wanted information or assistance.

Within two years of the foundation of *KIT*, the resulting network's members started meeting at conferences. One of these first meetings, in 1990, led to an open letter from approximately fifty former members (many of them second-generation members) addressed to the Bruderhof communities. The open letter pointed to the frightening prospect of expulsion. It requested guaranteed financial support and the right to contact relatives in the community for those who wish to leave, and that children be educated, "acculturated," and given meaningful choices, including the choice to leave without fear of being cut off. The open letter asked the Bruderhof to address physical and psychological abuse, and offered to help the organization address these issues.[38] The contents of the open letter were largely rejected by the Bruderhof, who were of the opinion that the requests were unreasonable and out of line with their religious tradition (Oved 1996). This marked the beginning of a period of antagonism, an antagonism that increased dramatically with the founding of Children of the Bruderhof. The Bruderhof filed a civil lawsuit against the organization the year it was founded, and reached an out-of-court settlement a year later that ended its work.[39] The antagonism continued and culminated in another legal case in 1997, a defamation lawsuit initiated by the Bruderhof against the founder of *KIT*, the Peregrine Foundation, the main initiator of Children of the Bruderhof and a leading academic who had been commenting publicly on the Bruderhof and *KIT*.[40] In this suit, the Peregrine Foundation was described by the Bruderhof's legal representation as being established "for the sole purpose of undermining the goals and membership of the Bruderhof," with the aim being the dissolution of the Bruderhof communities.[41] Sender was described as the chief proponent of the dissolution of the Bruderhof, along with others.[42] The case revolved mainly around the information disseminated by the Peregrine Foundation, considered defamatory and libelous by the Bruderhof. The suit was dismissed that same year, and the Bruderhof dropped its appeal and withdrew the lawsuit against Sender.[43]

Moving On

The website movingon.org was specifically created for the second-generation members who had left the Family International—it was created by second-generation members for second-generation members. Not an organization as such, the website revolved around supporting former second-generation members by providing information and offering a discussion forum.[44] Like *KIT*, movingon.org would post critical comments about its relevant group, the Family (including open letters to the organization and the leader). Movingon.org developed over time and the founder established the Safe Passage Foundation, a nonreligious and not-for-profit organization. Like *KIT*, the foundation aims to use its network of former members and friends to offer material as well as emotional support to those who have left their religious community. It also offered information and advocacy. The Safe Passage Foundation offered to help people who have left what it terms "high demand organizations"—it extended its support to those who have left organizations other than the Family.[45] Having adopted the United Nations' Convention on the Rights of the Child as the statement of its guiding philosophy, it was geared toward helping those who, as children, have had these rights denied and who, as adults, need help in adjusting to "the system."[46] The foundation and movingon.org certainly have disagreements with the Family, although none has gone as far as the courts.[47] But there are competing websites from young members within the Family contesting the information provided on movingon.org, and open letters from former members to current leaders, and vice versa, point to the ongoing differences of opinion and point of view.[48]

There are many other, similar organizations—it appears that each minority or marginal religious community eventually creates its own "anti"-community. The Watchtower Society has its renegades who have created the silentlambs.org website, which discusses child abuse and sexual abuse (as well as child sexual abuse) among Jehovah's Witnesses. Former members of the Exclusive Brethren created peebs.net, which had a large list of "helper locations" across the world where there are Exclusive Brethren communities, to help those who wished to leave (it has since had to shut down). Ex-Scientologists can choose from many online discussion forums they can join, anonymously, to discuss and criticize the teachings and practices, something they cannot do overtly with their relatives and friends within the organization without being penalized.[49] In 2008, a few young women who had been born and raised in Scientology left and created a website, exscientologykids.com, by and for second-generation Scientologists who had left or were thinking of leaving.[50]

Interestingly, this is not a trend specifically linked to cults or new religious movements; older and more established religious minorities can elicit similar responses. The communities of the Fundamentalist Church of Jesus Christ of Latter Day Saints who practice polygyny have their communities of critics in the form of antipolygamy activists such as Tapestry against Polygamy.[51] In Israel and the United States there are organizations whose aim is to help those who have been born and raised in Orthodox Jewish communities and want to leave, such as Footprints in New York and Hillel in Jerusalem. Similarly to *KIT* and the Peregrine Foundation, Hillel is an organization that aims to help young members who leave a particular religious community to adjust to life outside. In Israel there are young Haredis who are disillusioned with the scholastic path they are expected to follow. Despite being enrolled in their yeshivahs they wander the streets and explore the secular world. They are referred to as *shababnikim* (Haredis who have secular thoughts and attitudes). Leaving, for them, involves many problems also experienced by those who have left the Bruderhof. Adjustment to the outside world is complicated following an "inappropriate" education and socialization (the educators had a different end goal in mind), and consequently former members struggle to find employment. Once their "rebellion" is known, they are often not welcome in their communities, as they have ventured into a world forbidden to them. They are, then, not only school dropouts but also exiles from their community.[52] Hillel was created to help such young Haredis in Israel who have left Orthodox Judaism. Hillel helps by offering host families (when possible) and assisting in other immediate needs including education, professional training, preparing for military service, and so forth. As with *KIT*, Hillel is also made up mainly of former members, Haredim in this case, who frequently work on a volunteer basis. The main difference between Hillel and *KIT* is that Hillel does not seek to criticize Orthodoxy, nor does it want to change people's minds. Although Hillel does not criticize the Orthodox, it does get attacked by them.[53] And in many ways its presence exaggerates any rift between the Haredi and those who have left. In this way the dynamic is very similar to that between *KIT* and the Bruderhof.

There are a variety of approaches and consequently a range of levels of antagonism between the religious groups and their former members. But despite the differences, there is almost inevitably antagonism, because both the religious communities and the former members have different requirements and different priorities.[54] The former members are frequently drawn together into new communities.[55] In this case, the young former members have frequently had hurtful personal experiences, and they do tend to seek one another out and create a community of "renegades" who have something in common. They are critical of the religious community they came from, which instantly puts them in a position of antagonism with these very communities who try to protect their members from outside "pollution." In what is generally an antagonistic relationship, the former members frequently expect to initiate the changes they want within the religious groups from outside or even from the margins. Over time, they can expect change. The outside presence of young former members can initiate changes within groups over time, as the parents and the group realize that some of their children are unhappy and aim to accommodate them more and minimize criticism. But with rigidly sectarian groups this is not always possible. The presence of *KIT* did change dynamics within the Bruderhof but these were not the changes *KIT* requested—the group intensified its rigidity and became litigious toward former members and critics. However, it did eventually develop more flexibility toward younger cohorts of former members.

Cohorts of Leavers

Over time both the Family and the Unification Church changed levels of membership to accommodate those who wanted more options and flexibility. The Family produced stricter rules to regulate sharing and the disciplining of children after complaints from young members (and the rules were further tightened after outside intervention, as mentioned in chapter 3). ISKCON also developed internal controls and structures to safeguard the children within the organization. These were constructive developments, and they did have consequences. As a result of these changes there are cohorts of young (former) members who have had significantly different experiences. As the religious group moves toward a position of more responsibility toward its youngest members, akin to H. Richard Niebuhr's ([1929] 1957) theory of denominationalism, this results in a stratified second generation, as the first cohort of children has had significantly different experiences from the second cohort.[56] In a sense, the older cohort of children has paved the way for the younger "community siblings," who now frequently have more options, and who have benefited from the introduction of new rules and measures to safeguard them.[57] Consequently, the younger cohorts of children tend to have better relations with their parents and with the religious community than their elder community siblings who have left. Having had different experiences, they lack a shared understanding of the community. In some cases, and often in line with teachings and stories they have heard from parents and other older members, the younger cohort have blamed their elder siblings for causing problems for the movement.

For example, a discussion among devotees and former devotees in ISKCON centered on the argument whether one should be allowed to blame Prabhupada for the abuses.[58] In this case, several cohorts suffered abuse, but only the older cohorts had memories of Prabhupada. First-cohort gurukulis felt that many of the younger gurukulis were blaming Prabhupada, and rejecting his teachings along with the practices of which they were critical. Young gurukulis were accused of hating ISKCON, Prabhupada, and anything Indian—this being the result of being "too young to know," and hence not understanding. Raghunatha in particular argued that the young gurukulis were too young to have known Prabhupada, hence could not distinguish the organization from the guru (Anudasa 2000). This discussion pointed to a significant difference between cohorts of the second generation. Similarly, within the Family there was significant criticism from young members toward another second-generation member whose round-robin letter had been published in a Family distribution entitled *The Professionals* (Amsterdam 2002), as described in chapter 3. The responses illustrated a difference between cohorts of members, as well as between goodies and rebels—or, in this case, the one who overcomes obstacles and the "loser." One respondent to the initial letter, Steve (aged twenty), in a reply titled "You've Got to Have a Real Gut Hatred for the System!," wrote:

> I can't help but grow a bit weary of all this whining that keeps going around amongst our spoiled second generation. (I take liberty to say this as I myself am of the second born.) I wonder, when are these certain people going to realize that we've grown tired of hearing about these insignificant complaints and all this nauseating "poor me"?
>
> I mean, really brother, who wants to hear about how you've had such a drrrreadful past, and how you're destined to such a drrrreadful future, and every single one of your actions will be conditioned

> negatively, because of "this horrrrrible way in which you were raised?" I don't know about everyone else, but I've heard about as much complaining as I can possibly take.
>
> In this world and throughout life anywhere you are going to encounter a great many obstacles; those who use these obstacles as a justification for not doing anything with their life and who choose to live in the past are commonly known to most as LOSERS. Yet those who choose to use even those same supposed obstacles in their favor and who are determined to make use of what God gave them are sooner or later bound to succeed in some aspect or other of their life. And furthermore, no one out there is going to stop and feel sorry for you (don't be fooled), so quit taking advantage of the fact that people in the Family are so loving and concerned about your needs and are willing to hear you out. (*Speak for Yourself!* 2002)

Of course the elder cohort has criticisms of the younger siblings as well; the young members are considered innocents who do not understand. As one former member put it, "Do you really expect us (your much older brothers and sisters who grew up in your same group and who are now living very different lives) to believe you know what you are talking about?"⁵⁹

The *KIT* network is mainly made up of a very specific cohort of former members—those who experienced the Great Crisis. Many of the *KIT* members were either excluded during this crisis or left after the upheaval that followed. But over time some fault lines appeared within the Peregrine Foundation, and another similar discussion group began appearing, Bruder Christo, which was for the former members who still considered themselves Christians. This new group, according to Justin, one of the former members associated with *KIT*, became more popular among the later cohorts of former members of the Bruderhof: "I think the young people that leave now take away with them the idea that people outside that are against the community, such as *KIT*, are very, very evil."⁶⁰ Justin argued that young people who were leaving the Bruderhof at that time tended to keep a low profile and stay away from *KIT* so that they could occasionally come back to the community and visit their parents. They were likely only to contact people whom they knew, and who they knew were Christian. As for support outside, Justin argued that the communal lifestyle has engendered a closeness that remains, and outside they were likely to seek support with others of their generation, rather than someone from the older generation who has been vilified within the Bruderhof.[61] But Justin did not seem to think this is a problem: "If they have no contact with *KIT* they'll probably be able to visit back and they'll have at least emotional support from their parents."[62]

My research suggests there may be other cases where members of the younger cohort ignore their elder siblings who have left, either because they believe these former members have lost their way (the elder members of their generation have often been labeled and demonized, as I have discussed in chapter 4) or because they know that when contacting someone from this elder cohort they may jeopardize their own position with current members. Consequently, members from a younger cohort who want to leave often choose to stay away from their elder siblings. This is problematic when the only support available for them is organized and run by members of this elder cohort who have left. This type of support, as useful as it may have been for many former members, may also alienate those members who did not have the same experiences as their elder siblings. Seeking this support could have a high cost, and they could find themselves in a position where they have to choose to either lose contact with their parents and community or ignore the only other community of people out in the wider society who have a somewhat similar background. In ignoring the elder cohort the younger cohort may be able to keep some form of contact with their parents and community, a situation that offers more continuity with their past.

Stephen has argued that the better you "land" when you leave the cult (for instance a family takes you in), the more likely you are to hold on to some of your old beliefs and integrate new ones. Whereas the worse the transition is (having no support, being on one's own) the more likely the former member is to reject everything, and become "an atheist." Stephen equated this with the level of trauma associated with being "out there on your own" and the resulting anger. This sentiment was also reflected in the Inform cases, where most of those who called were looking for some form of help in adjusting to the outside, either in the form of a support group or counseling. One former Jehovah's Witness reported having entered an abusive relationship the moment she left, because, she said, she had immersed herself into a world she did not understand. Another former Jehovah's Witness was looking for someone to talk to because she could not stop worrying over whether she had made the wrong decision in taking her young children with her, and possibly condemning them to an awful fate—to be alive in the end times yet not as Jehovah's Witnesses. Yet another former Jehovah's Witness was seeking help because he could not relate to the people outside. Stephen suggested that young members who leave should be taken in by another family outside the movement, so that at least they may find themselves in a stable environment. This sentiment was shared by a foster carer, Joyce.[63] She argued that the young former members need to be fostered—they need to enter a family environment they can rely on in the long term.

> They need to be fostered and it has to be a long-term commitment. It can't be we're taking care of you for a couple of years, it's got to be someone they can trust to be there for them, to stick up for them, to be in their corner for them, you know, so if things go wrong and they lose their job, with pressures that come later on in life and they find all this bubbling up again, it's got to be someone that they can go back to.... So you do need a commitment from somebody who's going to love them and make a lifetime commitment, because I cannot get across to anybody how very very disturbed these youngsters are. They are so shattered and so wounded in every way.

Joyce's comment here is interesting in its emphasis on the commitment and the extent of the support necessary. One can understand why young former members are likely to seek each other out and form a community of support. And many of them do; the Safe Passage Foundation, as *KIT* did, aims to create a network of people who are willing to take a former member in. But it appears to be locked into a position of antagonism with its "parent community," which, in turn, appears to have an effect on the relations between the cohorts as well as on the desirability of this support for the later cohorts.

Other Support

Support other than self-help support is hard to find. Young former members further complicate this matter, as they often have an unusual combination of ordinary and specialized needs—on the one hand they may need very straightforward directions (such as how to apply for a loan and how to enter the education system) while also requesting very specific spiritual and emotional support (such as discussions about religious doctrines that are often obscure and strange to the nonbeliever and pressing questions about the truth or falsity of these doctrines). Consequently they are challenging clients to any support organization—certainly secular ones. As Joyce has argued, when talking about the kind of support young former members need: "They need grounding, you've got to really ground them, you know, but it is hard. And of course they have so much fear. They're frightened of the devil and they're frightened of God, you see, they haven't got a leg to stand on, have they?... Frightened of the world, frightened of themselves, it's a life of fear and of course, fear does awful things to people." Joyce herself tries as much as possible to steer clear from religion and religious teachings when she is fostering a former member, as these have often been connected to abuse as well as to the people from the former members' past.

> Although I am a Christian and can articulate a good theological argument against many of the teachings of [this particular group], I know, from my own experience and from the experience of helping others, that this does not work. With spiritually abused people I always work from the premise that it does not matter what others say about God or religion, it is what best integrates wholeness within an individual which will work for them. It is difficult not to get entangled with fierce condemnations of doctrines and philosophies which have resulted in the abuse I am trying to heal. On the other hand, it does no good to simply condemn people who may be very dear to my client; on the other hand, it would be dangerous for me [to] allow certain ideas to go unquestioned and unchecked when they have clearly resulted in such personal devastation. I tend to try and focus on the character of God himself, rather than what "God people" of any sort say about him. This is by far the safest route and helps the person to make a genuine faith link for themselves which ultimately strengthens them.

Support for young people who have left sectarian religious movements is a complex issue, and one on which opinion is divided. One of the first organizations in Europe specifically geared toward helping children born in isolated religious communities that incorporated personal experience and knowledge as well as a legal and human rights approach was the Norwegian Go On, funded by Save the Children Norway.[64] The idea for Go On was born when a few teenage former members of the Family and one of their outside relatives contacted the Norwegian authorities, lobbying for more research on the subject of children growing up in isolated religious movements. The project leader, Turid Berger, a lawyer, contacted Save the Children for funding to look further into possible infringements of children's rights. Save the Children offered start-up funding for three years for the establishment of Go On, a small charity aiming to help children reintegrate back into Norwegian society. A representative from Save the Children agreed that some of these children were losing their rights in a difficult and complicated landscape where children's rights are balanced against their parents' rights.[65] Hence Go On was established to safeguard children's rights, and ensure that children who had been socially isolated would receive help in integrating into Norway's complicated welfare system. According to Berger, Norwegian law and the children's rights were the starting point for the project.[66] Berger argued that, in the stories of the former members, she had heard a variety of infringements of their rights; from restricted access to information, curtailed freedom of expression, lack of privacy, censorship, and lack of education to physical and emotional harm and unsatisfactory health care.[67] In the end, Berger concluded, the rights of parents are pitted against the rights of children, and one is left to wonder, which convention is definitive—the European Human Rights Convention or the Children's Convention?[68]

Go On had a carefully chosen perspective; its members did not aim to be therapists or counselors. Instead, the objective for Go On was to be a center that would help young former members to solicit help from other offices in Norway's welfare system, and to provide society with more information on this topic.[69] The main focus was to "create a new future for young former members," but the project failed to find more funding and ended after the three-year start-up funding ran out. Go On was frequently criticized for its position—trying to be nonsectarian and human-rights-oriented in an area where this is considered, by many, to be impossible and undesirable. A Go On conference summarizing the evolution of the project and its conclusions provided several perspectives: whereas some involved with the project remained within the framework of children's rights, other speakers ventured toward criticism of religious beliefs and practices—many of which supposedly fall within parental rights. Hence representatives from certain religious communities who were present argued that they felt discriminated against and that there was a focus on "negative issues"—arguing that they have been practicing within their rights according to freedom of religion clauses. But stigmatizing the movements was not necessarily the aim of the former members who initiated the project: "This is an important point, that we're not interested in attacking religious groups or making it difficult for small religious schools or something. We just want to say that children also have rights, and those need to be acknowledged and recognized. And that also goes when it comes to religious groups."[70]

But in such a sensitive arena this is a very difficult balance to negotiate for support organizations and charities. Even academics researching NRMs, who frequently opt to adhere to a value-free methodology, are likely to be accused of being either anticult or cult apologists at some point in their career. One particular publication that highlights this divide sees academics accusing one another not only of questionable research and methodology but also of accepting money from NRMs—all this being linked to ongoing discussions about theory and definition, especially around the idea of human susceptibility to "mind control," this itself being a hotly debated concept (Zablocki and Robbins 2002). Such disagreements, combined with the view that a value-free approach is nothing but an unwillingness to take a position on issues of morality, of "right and wrong," frequently make the research-oriented approach unpopular among some. Paul Rock found a similar distaste for the academic approach in his research on self-help organizations, in which he observed the discrepancy between the anger-fueled passion of the self-help groups versus the more "rational," or removed, approach of outside researchers: "I suppose I should never have imagined it could be otherwise but, to those who want passion and advocacy, sociology can appear to be a distancing discipline, the sociologist a stranger, and print a cool medium" (1998: xxiii). As Stephen said, "It is discouraging for second generation [e]x-members when they read statements put forth by the Family's leadership trying to portray the [movement] as an innocent Christian missionary organization, and when we see that the 'experts' [academics] are so easily fooled by the façade that is [hereby] portrayed."[71]

The Inevitable Conflict

Religious diversity can create conflict; and this conflict becomes especially challenging when the rights of parents and those of children clash. Religious freedom is fairly ambiguous in the best of circumstances, but in this case, one hears arguments for "freedom to" as well as for "freedom from"—freedom to, for example, act on such beliefs as "spare the rod, spoil the child," rather than freedom for the child to grow up without (supposedly) biblically prescribed corporal punishment. Of course some countries have developed rigid laws surrounding child disciplining, but there is always a minority of parents who argue they should be allowed to raise their children according to their religious beliefs. And in general, they do have the right to take their children along on their spiritual journey and, in some cases, reinvent "conventional childhood"—but occasionally this right clashes with the children's rights. Thus members of religious groups and their children may simultaneously believe their rights have been trampled on. This rift continues as the children leave, and deepens as factions of society take a side in what is then presented as a moral debate. Many of the former-member support groups and those set up to help the young members who have left argue that the religious community should apologize, make amends, rectify wrongdoings, or repent in some way. In some cases the religious groups have not made significant changes; for example, the Bruderhof have not significantly adapted their rules to unify first-cohort former members with their relatives in the communities. This would be in contravention with their beliefs, and the leadership has decided against this. Similarly, the Exclusive Brethren in Australia have requested amendments in the Family Law Act to "ensure that a child is not subject to a radical lifestyle change without compelling reason."[72] They requested special treatment in family courts to avoid the "outside" parent receiving visitation rights, as the parent who was no longer a member of the community could subject the children to different views in contravention to those of the Exclusive Brethren. More recently a mother has ignored a judge's orders on visiting rights for the father of the children, and denied the father access.[73] In many cases, however, the religious groups in question have made changes; ISKCON has set up the Child Protection Agency and the Family has created the Charter.[74]

Yet despite the changes in some groups, accommodation between the group (and the parents) and the children still appears to be a complicated issue. The Internet is a cornucopia of websites, discussion groups, blogs, and more, giving voice to a large spectrum of views and opinions about religious groups, many of them the views of members or former members. Viewing the websites created by former members alongside the sites run by the religious communities—the parents—can be disconcerting. Usually the stories do not add up—they portray widely varying realities. Furthermore, there are many accusations, from both sides, that the other is lying or, at best, being economical with the truth.[75] Both sides offer their own monologues—but they rarely meet to form dialogue or communication. The religious groups and the parents tend to separate any act of violence or neglect from doctrine and tradition (the child "was a bad apple," there was a "misinterpretation," and so on). The former members, especially those who have been the subject of abuse or neglect, tend to not make this distinction (especially if they have been in touch with other former members or organizations critical of the beliefs and doctrine, and have had their beliefs and feelings validated, as I mentioned in the previous section). Hence they may now generalize and consider the group as a whole a "destructive cult" or blame a "perverted cult leader" of disseminating "false teachings."[76] This is understandable, as in some cases the young members' experiences were traumatic life and identity-defining events. They do not want to move on without there being some sense that the group and the parents repent, apologize, or are doing something to prevent this from happening again. On the other hand, the religious groups tend to look ahead, protect their members, and chart their course of future action. While history is written by those who were victorious, in this case there are two histories, written by both sides of the conflict. Mismatched stories and accusations of lies and apologetics are typical of this discrepancy. In a larger, sociological context, they make sense—they are human and institutional responses to the problematic histories these people and organizations have shared, which I have discussed in the conclusion to chapter 3 in light of Stanley Cohen's research on denial. The Family, as an organization, is in interpretive denial, while former members argue there is implicatory denial—the extent of the abuse having been largely denied while the "bad apples" were blamed. The situation is exacerbated when labeling is used to discount the other's story (as mentioned in chapter 4). Frequently critical former members are devalued (as, for example, having adaptive problems, spiritual problems, anger issues, being troubled, and so forth) or accused of making money from selling their story.[77] Similarly, members are labeled in such a way that their beliefs, opinions, and priorities are devalued in the eyes of nonmembers. They are described as brainwashed, indoctrinated, ignorant of "what is really going on," and so forth. In this way both sides are undermining the other—and increasingly so as the discussion intensifies.

Both the Family and ISKCON have not addressed the issues to the satisfaction of many of their former members. A "generally agreed upon" knowledge of what happened (that is, despite what the group maintains, "everybody knows") is never going to satisfy the young former members who have been harmed or neglected. As Cohen writes (2001: 225), "There is a distinction between knowledge and acknowledgement." The young former members want acknowledgment, an official admission that something went wrong. "Acknowledgement is what happens to knowledge when it becomes officially sanctioned and enters the public discourse," Cohen asserts (225). This is significantly different from "everybody knows"—a knowledge that comes from the grass roots (usually the Internet, where many different claims to "the Truth" compete) and which has not been acknowledged and sanctioned. As Cohen (226) notes, a final justification for truth telling lies in the sentiment "never again": the eternal hope that exposure of the past will be enough to prevent its repetition in the future.

Solidifying the Gap Rather than Building Bridges

These various forms of denial, comprehensible as they are, jeopardize the building of bridges. The main complaint from former members is that the religious communities "cover up" their problems, or offer justifications or excuses—that they either deny the seriousness of the issue or deny full responsibility. In the case of the Family, a long and drawn-out court case was necessary to generate a public admission that abuse occurred and that some of Berg's teachings were not appropriate. Yet this was not a public apology specifically intended for the victims, and in the internal literature a different tone was taken. There had been a prophecy from Berg, who by that time had passed away, that it was acceptable to "bend" but they should not "break"—they could blame Berg here and there as long as they did not deny him or the Law of Love—that would be considered "breaking" (Maria 1995). The Ward case was followed by a new revolution and missionary zeal, and the movement focused on the essence of its tradition and teachings, the Law of Love, by instituting the *Loving Jesus Revelation*.[78]

In the case of ISKCON, special organizations were instituted to provide support and compensation for the children who had been abused. ISKCON leaders argued that they were dealing with the problem and making amends. Internally, there was much "soul-searching" and discourse regarding the writings of Prabhupada and the extent to which these may have created a context. The conclusion generally agreed on was that some "bad apples" do not necessarily spoil the bushel, or in this case the larger message and the aims of Prabhupada and ISKCON. The perspective of some of the young former members was generally, to paraphrase, "*plus ça change....*" Two former gurukulis and victims of abuse I have communicated with have never received support or financial compensation from the agencies set up by ISKCON. They argue that the money goes into salaries for devotees, and that some of the perpetrators are still at the temples as highly respected devotees. Their view is shared by other former members communicating on the Internet.

Similarly, former members of the Family argue that several of the main perpetrators are still in the leadership—and that in reality "nothing has changed."

This course of events and their interpretations work to solidify two camps with two different perceptions of their history, and one is left to wonder if ever the twain shall meet. The young former members are accused of only focusing on the negative experiences (and of embellishing them), while the groups argue that such experiences do not reflect the essence of their beliefs, and in some cases they may argue that they have changed their behavior. On the other hand, one has to respect that these problematic experiences have had a profound influence on the young former members' childhood and on their formation. This miscommunication and misunderstanding is perhaps most profoundly illustrated by the horrific event that took place in 2005 when Ricky Rodriguez, previously known as Davidito, killed Angela Smith, after which he killed himself. In a telephone call to his wife after having shot Angela, he voiced his frustration that, as Angela lay dying, she still did not understand what she had done wrong (Goodstein 2005). This gap in understanding widened after the horrible event when other former members, commenting on forums, communicated understanding for his act of anger and revenge, while Family members denounced the act and equally denounced and blamed "vindictive apostates" for influencing Ricky after he left (Goodstein 2005).

Reconciliation of different realities is a delicate matter, but when religion is involved it often seems near to impossible. By its very nature, religion is not a topic that devout followers can easily discuss objectively and dispassionately, and it frequently is interpreted as speaking of absolutes. In a scenario where there has been abuse or neglect and families are divided, the issues become touchier and fraught with emotion, and the proverbial bridges fewer and far between. A member of the Family interviewed for this research said about the Go On project:

> It is a good thing. People do need help.... You get a young person who has grown up differently than the majority of the people, and they're gonna have an adjustment.... Maybe their parents lived in the embassy, they lived abroad. Maybe they worked for a multinational company and they lived abroad. Or maybe they're part of one of the less popular religions; they're Orthodox Jews or they're Muslims or whatever, and they come to a Western country, and there's gonna be an adjustment. And it's not the fact of their upbringing, it's just that they're moving to a different way of life.... So giving them practical

help to make the adjustment, yes.... But if, in the midst of that, you then sit down and knock their upbringing, and even put them in a position that they feel that in order to get this very practical help they have to criticize their parents, their families, their former life—I personally think it really hurts their self-esteem. And then they can't go on with their life. Because if you're ashamed of where you come from, how can you be a happy, well-adjusted adult?[79]

The miscommunication intensifies when one side is concerned with a group or community, while the other side presents a personal perspective. In the words of Stephen:

The problem for second generation [e]x-members when trying to deal with their past and find some way to either correct the mistakes or gain recognition that abuse took place, is that the Family has been working for ten years or more on its public image. The Family has had teams of experts working with their own teams on [court cases] in a number of countries. They have restructured the laws of The Family (hence the Charter) and written statements that are well developed and pre-planned to debunk any form of complaint or accusation. The abused party in this situation, the second generation [e]x-member, stands more or less alone. If she is lucky she has a loosely connected network of other second generation [e]x-members who have experienced similar abuse. However, that is hardly what is needed to combat a well organised organisation.[80]

Stephen points out some of the "tactics" he has identified, used by the Family, to neutralize negative media portrayals and diminish the appearance of wrongdoing.

The primary tactic is to blame whatever wrongdoing has occurred on individuals and say that such action[s] are against the laws of the Charter. This is fine when dealing with wrongdoings that have occurred after 1995 when the Charter was established, but it in no way counts for The Family's actions before that time. It does not nullify the actions that were done by individuals who were acting in accordance with David Berg's "Revolutionary Laws" which is when, and by whom, most of the abuses occurred. To say that these were just isolated incidents is absurd and blatantly false.[81]

Blaming the individual often involves blaming the parents, and Stephen objects to this, arguing that:

> In most cases, however, it is not the parents that we have had our main griev[ances] with, but rather The Family and The Family's leadership. It was when we were away from our parents and under the supervision of The Family and treated by Her 'One Wife' principles that things started to go wrong. To put the blame on the parents is irresponsibility on the part of The Family's leadership and points to their cowardly behaviour in their relation to second generation [e]x-members.[82]

In contrast, parents whom I have spoken to in the Family have either stressed the personal problems of young former members (i.e., mental or spiritual instability) or argued that a particular case of abuse was an isolated incident. One parent argued that young former members had personal issues against the parents and she compared this to mainstream children having grievances with their parents, either as the result of divorce, an overbearing parent, a working parent, and so on.[83] It appears that one side refuses to put the religious group into the picture, while the other refuses to leave it out.

Continued Sectarianism

The cult scene consists of a large variety of groups, organizations, and communities, many with strong ideological or social boundaries—and, in the case of cult-watching groups, a variety of methodological approaches. In the case of the latter, the majority of instances of external support increase the polarization between the parents and the religious groups on one hand and the young former members on the other. There is a reason new religious groups are stigmatized—there have been horrific cases of abuse. The perpetrator groups are a small minority within the diversity of religions, but these are real cases nonetheless. The external support at the moment is, in general, still heavily influenced by this generalized stigmatizing stereotype. The attitude of the sectarian groups is that the outside is polluting, and too much contact with it will affect the purity of the group. Hence, the Family wards off Vandaris, and Scientology aims to keep away from suppressives. As a result of these two different perspectives, young members who leave such stigmatized groups find themselves in a difficult limbo. They have to, in general, choose what side they want to be on, and sacrifice the other side in the process.

In many cases the support that second-generation former members received when leaving their religious communities, helpful as it may have been, also removed them further from the relatives and friends with whom they may otherwise have remained in contact in some way. In using the self-help approach for former members, the groups offering external support apparently with relative ease viewed matters from the dualist perspective endemic within the cult scene, and demonized the "other" side. As for the young former members, their immediate needs may be met on one level, but on another they are also alienated from their childhood environment, primarily because they were unhappy there and now, in a different social environment, they realize that their childhoods were not quite "the norm." In some cases they may turn against their childhood as part of a process to "better integrate" into what they perceive as the norm and values of the outside society. In this different social environment, the religious groups from which they came are usually stigmatized, and the former members, eager to move away from their past and adapt to their new surroundings, tend to "join" the other side's worldview and begin to view their past as "freakish" and deviant. The more socially isolated and doctrinally rigid the group, the more likely the former members feel they have to make such either/or decisions. Consequently, the sectarian divisions intensify. The groups who have adapted have, over time, managed to create foundations for some sort of bridge.

Later cohorts of children have often managed to negotiate different levels and terms of membership—they have generally been able to do so without as much sacrifice of old relations as earlier cohorts made.[84] In some cases they have received support from the religious community to enable them to more easily make the transition from the group to the outside. This is a constructive development, although it does not always work out as intended. Material support is essential, although in many cases it is not sufficient. The Family's information packages were useful, and a transition via marginal membership into "the system" provided young members with adjustment time. Spiritual or emotional support was not always well received by the former members interviewed for this research. As I have mentioned before in this chapter, such support, or measures to help the young members realize what they want out of life, can often be counterproductive and become another reason to leave. Stephen asserts:

> I think in a practical sense, it's good that a child who is leaving doesn't have to worry too much about [his or her] economical situation... and can learn all the practical things. But that doesn't necessarily mean

that that is gonna be the most important thing for the child at the time. And often, I think, if the kid decides to leave, he'd almost want to make a break with the entire organization. And that's why I feel its important to have some sort of setup where they can get all the aid from something that's detached from the group. And I would say that it doesn't necessarily help their...mental or their psychological or their philosophical problems at all, that sort of situation.[85]

Aside from the psychological and emotional problems that may be associated with the group, the world the young adult plans to enter is the world the parents and the sectarian religious groups have consciously rejected— usually because they believed it to be problematic in some way. Are they, then, the best ones to be preparing their children to enter it? The agent accompanying the passagee from one status to another can control the process and affect the shape and quality of the passage.[86] As Stephen argues: "In the liminal stage the important thing for them to be, I think, is under the guidance of the society that they will be entering. Not the society that they will be exiting. Because the whole idea in the liminal stage is that you have, at least from historical perspective,...some kind of mentor [who] will guide you into your new status."[87] Generally the groups that have adapted and made changes to accommodate their children, either for them to stay by different rules or to provide them with some support when they leave, have developed a better relationship with their young generation over time. But in some cases this has led to a schism between the cohorts of second-generation members, who often believe they do not share the same experiences, and disagree with each other's view of the religious group and their past.

There are other variables that make the limbo of second-generation former members difficult: the link that has been established between religion and abuse or neglect, and the stigmatizing labels that have been applied to them by the group leaders, their parents, and their peers. For many of the former members the abuse they suffered has been connected to God—God has been a powerful part of the equation. In power relations when God is perceived to be on someone's side, that then becomes the more powerful side. And it is difficult to go against God if you believe in this God. Hence the former members frequently believe that they have to leave their God behind as well—or redefine God according to their own ideas. This cuts into their very sense of who they are—their identity. Furthermore, they have been identified as being "bad," being "rebellious," not being "in the right spirit," or having the wrong attitude. This affects them as they leave their communities, and after.

7
In the Wilderness

ONE OF THE biggest issues for the young adults who leave sectarian religious movements is finding themselves alone and in an unfamiliar place. Terms that have arisen in interviews and communication with second-generation former members about the outside were all indicative of a strange and foreign place: "out in space," "a jungle," "out there," "in limbo," and so forth. These descriptions have in common that the outside world was perceived as an alien place in which the former members felt like exiles, akin to the Israelites "in the wilderness."[1] This chapter describes aspects of this journey from the old to the new, some of the different forms this journey can take, and possible consequences for the young people undertaking this journey.

The idea of being in the wilderness came up in a variety of ways throughout the research and interviews with those who had left or been cast out of their movements. Themes that arose repeatedly were of former members feeling they were in exile, abandoned by their family and their God. And many did describe the feeling of wandering in exodus, a space they did not know, in which they felt "fragmented," lonely, and unable to blend in. This symbolic comparison to being in the wilderness also ties in to their sense of identity, as these young former members have been frequently labeled as rebels, bad apples, or "bad" in the sense that they were "in the wrong spirit" or a "bad influence" on others. In many cases they have been accused of "murmuring," and often they no longer completely and wholeheartedly believe in the God of their childhood—like those in the wilderness (Heb. 3:19).[2] As a result the exiles often no longer knew what or whom to believe and trust. Nora wrote:

> The best illustration I can think of to illustrate this dilemma is that of a small animal, locked up in a cage most of [its] life, and then suddenly set free to manage as best as it can in the jungle. Or, as another cult kid I read about in a Norwegian newspaper described it[,] being raised in a sect is like growing up in a spacecraft, protected

and confined, and then one day leaping out into space. Compared to the chaos, the overwhelming freedom and incredible loneliness I encountered out in the big cruel world, being an Unblessed Child in the Moonies seemed like peanuts. After all, at least I was part of something, even if it was the lesser part of an otherwise perfect family. Orbiting the Outside World, having cut all ties linking me to the Mother Moonie Spaceship, I felt utterly and completely alone.[3]

Some of the people interviewed described a feeling of being in limbo, not sure who they were and where they belonged. They described what sociologists may refer to as anomie, a state of being where an individual may experience deep and profound dread, a feeling of being out of control (normlessness), that he or she cannot trust anyone, has had his or her emotional insulation removed, and perceives the world as being in disarray.[4] The changes experienced when moving from their childhood communities, and the discrepancies in structure, organization, standards, and meaning, have often left them feeling confused in regard to "how things should be." Stephen, in the last chapter, spoke of the liminal stage he felt he was going through when he left. Others interviewed for this research have spoken about the urge to find a new community, new labels, concepts, rules, and most importantly, a new identity. This involved leaving the past behind—a challenging endeavor. And it describes a desire to leave behind what is essentially an anomic state and find a structure where "things," and "they," make sense.

Branded by the Past

Joyce, being a foster carer, has met several young adults who suffer from what she refers to as "personality fragmentation"—they feel as if they do not fit in.[5] This feeling is deep-seated and, according to Joyce, affects them at the core—they feel "branded" by the group and their past. Her term is comparable to other descriptions of identity crisis and "fragmented identity" that point to a sense of discontinuity and disconnection in the storied selves that make up a narrative identity.[6] Joyce illustrated her concept with an anecdote about one of the young women she fostered, Isabel: "She said on many occasions that she felt different from anyone else; she felt as if she had been tattooed or permanently marked in some way and that because of this tattoo she would never be normal. I asked her what the tattoo was and she said, [the name of the group]." This is reminiscent of Erving

Goffman's *Stigma* (1963), where he described the Greeks' practice of tattooing "stigmas" onto the bodies of those who they believed should be identified as outcasts, that is, slaves, criminals, and traitors, and drew a parallel between this and processes of devaluing people. A young man in Joyce's care, Allan, also felt that he had been "branded" by the community, and that, as a result, everybody could see where he was from. This was tied in with feelings of inferiority and of "not fitting in." Joyce said:

> For a long time it was difficult to get him to go out, but eventually I hit on the idea of him walking a dog and we borrowed one daily for this purpose. He said he felt more normal walking a dog. When I asked him to expand on this, he said, "I feel I've got no right to be walking down the street, as if I'm doing something wrong and I keep expecting someone to pounce on me and collar me and drag me off." Allan told me that he had never been allowed to go out in public without an escort lest he should become tempted by the world.

Allan, reportedly, had no concepts of rights, opinions, or choices—notions that were not valued in his particular religious community as much as they are in society as a whole. Furthermore, having been raised communally he had different concepts of agency and ownership from those he encountered outside the community of his childhood. Joyce explained the difference:

> He found the experience of having an opinion/choice both fascinating and frightening. Allan did not seem to understand boundaries and frequently allowed people to step way over his boundaries without stopping them. He did not consider that he should own anything and was always giving possessions away.
>
> On coming out of community I noticed that, for Allan, everything was a big thing. The smallest things we take for granted like being able to go for a walk, decide what we will wear, what we will eat etc. were mountains he had to climb.... For many months Allan could not decide what biscuit to have from a plate because he was afraid that too luxurious a choice may have been indulging in the sin of gluttony or vanity. Allan lived as if his salvation depended upon every move he made.... Even when he was recovering a little and was behaving normally, inside he confessed that he felt he was "only pretending to be normal" and that he felt like a "reject" and a "freak."

Others described similar experiences and feelings, especially those who had joined their parents in a missionary lifestyle. For example, Nora recounted:

> Nevertheless, for me, the most enduring and overwhelming side effect of growing up as a cult kid is the relentless, almost haunting yet mostly exasperating feeling of never quite fitting in, *anywhere* (having been set apart from society at large and carefully protected in a dogmatic cocoon for the most part of my formative years). I have yet to discover whether this is a blessing or a curse, probably a little of both.
>
> Still, it is as if all this moving about[,] learning new languages, making new friends, adapting to different environments only to be torn away from it all and repeat the process all over again... somehow turned me into a weird little muddled misfit. I was doomed to feel like a perpetual stranger, forever the foreigner, like some bizarre product of shoddy enculturation, sloppy socialisation or whatever one wishes to call that process through which young children experience a sense of belonging and identify with their nearest and dearest.[7]

As I have explained in the previous chapter, Nora struggled with feelings of inferiority at two levels. She believed she had taken a secondary position within the Unification Church as an unblessed child and a secondary position in the outside society as one who does not fit in. She was, in both cases, marginal. "Understandably," she wrote, "after many years of this kind of treatment, there is always the danger of feeling vaguely inadequate and prone to a slight sense of inferiority with respect to those Holier Than Thou."[8]

From One Culture to Another

The feeling of being in the wilderness is also tied in with a necessary shift from primary to secondary socialization as the young adults move from one culture to another.[9] As mentioned previously, the community of their childhood has had a significant influence on them. Many have either escaped in some form, or feel they have been rejected by their communities. This has an impact on the way they perceive themselves—they did not "fit in." Furthermore, they often did not easily assimilate into the wider culture, hence they did not fit in there, either. The feeling of not fitting in anywhere often makes them question their identity. Some former members have referred to feeling brainwashed, not necessarily in the sense of their previous knowledge having been "washed clean," rather they believed, in hindsight, that what they perceived or assumed to be their intrinsic individual will and identity had been "whitewashed" and subverted while the group's doctrine and culture had been imposed.[10]

Is this a conscious decision on the part of the cult to impose "mind control" (to use the language frequently used)? In some way it is, of course, as the groups wanted to socialize the children within the culture and norms and values of the community, while keeping their children distant from the supposedly contaminating impact of the larger society. The parents wanted to raise their children within their (chosen, in the case of converts) worldview, as is their right. This is a process of which we are all "victims"; each social community has its own socialization, which has its effects and consequences—we are all shaped by the environment in which we are raised. In contemporary society the diversity ensures that there is a large variety of modes of socialization—all with common grounds, but many also with their own distinct aspects. Muslim children in Western countries, for example, might attend madrassas after school and on weekends, in order to receive supplementary education that is not provided in the majority of mainstream schools. The same is true for many other children, whose parents believe that the existing socializing forces are not providing sufficient education. Hence children may attend a Sunday school in church, or classes at a temple or mandir, or, indeed, courses at the Scientology center, camps run by the Unification Church, and so forth.

Yet some forms of socialization are deemed more acceptable than others. There are cases where international human rights organizations unanimously condemn infringements of rights over and beyond cultural values and differences. Generally, it is agreed (by, for example, the European Convention of Human Rights and the Convention on the Rights of the Child, among others) that there should be no child soldiers, children should not live in poverty, and children should not be trafficked or sold as child prostitutes. But there are gray areas where public opinion is divided. For example, although corporal punishment is banned in many countries, some parents still believe that if they "spare the rod" they "spoil the child." The tradition of arranged marriages is found throughout the world, but in some instances, when one of the spouses is considered to be under undue pressure to comply, it becomes "forced marriage." In June 2014 it was made a criminal offense in the United Kingdom, punishable by up to seven years in prison. Polygyny is the norm in many countries, but illegal in most

Western countries (where it is considered a form of bigamy), yet different countries enforce these laws in different ways. The question of what is legal is contingent; it varies according to geopolitics and is often parochial. There are significant variations, not only globally, but also within Western countries.

Diversity relies on accepting the cultural relativity of values and the rights of parents to pass their own values on. But at the same time a state has the responsibility to ensure that the rights of children are not being overlooked. This, of course, is another gray area, and there are many debates surrounding what exactly counts as an infringement of children's rights when minority religions (or so-called cults) are concerned. This debate aside, there is one aspect where those born in isolated religious groups can be at a disadvantage. Those who have been raised in sectarian religious movements have had a significant portion of their primary socialization within the religious movement. This is a different experience from adults who have converted to a religious movement, but who still have their primary socialization to fall back on should they leave. The former can be left, as mentioned before, in the wilderness—shaped by a socialization not designed for the place in which they ended up, and feeling like strangers in a place that is often, on paper, their "home."[11]

Shaping the Field of the Possible

Stephen Lukes (2005), when describing what he termed the first dimension of power (as the premise to a more nuanced discussion of power), defined power as A exercising power over B when A affects B in a manner contrary to B's interests. The premise is similar to Weber's definition, which forms the basis of many other discussions centering on unequal interaction. The concept of unequal interaction forms the basic theme of many of the arguments that are critical of the so-called cults. The leitmotif in these works is that cults (and their leaders) exert power over their recruits, and as a result these recruits, against their better judgment, do things that are contrary to their interests. In some literature the word "power" is used alongside terms such as "brainwashing," "mind control," and other terminology that brings to mind a victim whose morals, ideals, and dispositions have been overruled by those in power. In some of the older writings the process is described as a sudden, irresistible, and irreversible change of personality as someone succumbs to the power of a stronger (or even sinister) person in power.[12] Academics have questioned, and occasionally even disputed, such theories, and over time the tone and language has developed a less dystopian tone (Wright 2007). The term "brainwashing" was largely replaced by more moderate terms such as "mental manipulation," which pointed more toward a process rather than an instant "snapping" from one mental state to another.[13] Notwithstanding the terminology, the discussion of "unequal interactions" does beg the question: to what extent can different structures influence the minds, identities, and thoughts of those growing up in them? When looking at social structures, one is inevitably looking at ways in which individuals can be enabled or limited depending on the social arrangements around them (Foucault 1980). There is always an interplay between agents and structures; agents can choose to comply or dissent, but choices can be restricted in several ways, by other agents as well as structures. Hence one may speak of active and passive power (Lukes 2005).[14] According to Lukes, power is not necessarily a direct influence from someone in a superior position (active power); it can operate impersonally by "shaping the field of the possible" in which actors are more likely to make certain choices (passive power).[15] But how can the researcher study such subtle "influencing," this "shaping the field of the possible"? How can a researcher conceptualize such power in a meaningful way distinct from the concept of socialization, and how does it provide a context to this particular research?

Just as brainwashing theories from the 1970s and 1980s are, in hindsight, too simplistic for the complicated process of conversion, Lukes, upon reviewing the criticism of his first edition, considered that his first definition of power was too simple and binary. Hence he developed the concept of the third dimension of power, which includes the possibility of power mechanisms working against people's interests by "misleading them, thereby distorting their judgement" (2005: 13). This is not necessarily an intentional process "done unto" them by those in power—it is a byproduct of the social structure that has developed historically.[16] Hence the third dimension of power becomes a structural theory of socialization.

Although such a structural approach can be useful, it is important to remember that individuals are more knowing, reflective, and critical than such theoretical approaches often leave room for. There are, after all, baddies and rebels. Young members can go along with the status quo, they can rebel, they can leave, they have the option of a variety of actions and choose those within a context of imagined consequences—both this-worldly and otherworldly (from "my community will shun me" to "I'll go to hell"). However, the imagined consequences, options, and interests will have been shaped by the surrounding (power) structure. Hence, power becomes a complicated entity enmeshed with the social structures and an integral part of socialization. Its definition then becomes subjectively tied to the process of influence—if we like the content it is labeled education, if we loathe the content it is labeled brainwashing, mind control, and other terms that suggest a negative action "done unto" the "victim." As Eileen Barker (2007) has argued, allegations of brainwashing are often more about content than they are about process. Parents have by default a position of authority, a responsibility for their children. And, crucially, in a signatory country to the United Nations Convention on Human Rights, they have the right to raise their children within their religion. But the way parents choose to raise their children has consequences—they are, in a sense, partly shaping the field of the possible for their children. I say partly, because they do so in conjunction with other socializing influences, such as teachers, peers, and others (although in some cases the majority of these other forces may be part of the same religious community). Some fields have been shaped differently than others; this is part of the diversity of contemporary society. Furthermore, individuals have historically consistently transgressed their imagined "field of the possible."

Much of the research on which this book is based has explored the extent to which the social structure and culture of a religious group may have affected the (perceived or imagined) field of possibilities for the subsequent generation. Rigid sectarian groups tend to have strong ideological as well as social boundaries that are conducive to an "absolutist knowledge-base," meaning that the young members are likely to have been socialized within a specific worldview presented as "Truth," often without a significant comparative context. They tend to have a dualistic attitude, interpreting information in a "true/false" or "black/white" way. Nonsectarian groups have more flexible social and often conceptual boundaries and as a result the members of the subsequent generation have a more "relativistic knowledge base," which includes a larger variety of information from a variety of sources. Consequently these members are more likely to be open to alternative ideas and shades of gray (although of course they may choose absolutist views on some topics). The concepts of formation of "absolutist" and "relativistic" knowledge bases are similar to the "formation of character" resulting from internalized constraints as described by C. Wright Mills (1959), and the "adaptive preference formation" of Jon Elster (1983).[17]

The concluding part of my research was concerned with the ease or difficulty with which young members who leave integrate into the surrounding society. Here certain questions arise: How "rigid" is their knowledge base, and how does new information fit into their preexisting worldview? How deeply entrenched is their primary socialization? Does new information easily integrate and help develop a more relativistic worldview? Or does new information have to replace previous discourses because it is incompatible with the old absolutist principles? These questions parallel those of Charlotte Hardman in her essay examining the ethics and moral rules expressed by children in three new religious groups (the Family, Transcendental Meditation, and the Findhorn New Age community).[18] Hardman (1999) studied the relationship between the kinds of moral rules the children expressed and their sense of self and authority—whether their sense of self was constructed within a framework of belief in one absolute Truth or whether there was a sense of relativity. She found that whereas children in the Family learned to "surrender their egos to God and community," those in TM and Findhorn were more individualistic—the emphasis being on self-realization rather than submission (233–234). Furthermore, the children from TM and Findhorn had a relativistic attitude toward moral and conventional rules that was unthinkable to those in the Family (235). As Hardman writes:

> The implication of these findings is that Family children have a hard time conceiving of someone being a "really good person" without being a member of The Family, having "been saved," and adhering to Family rules. Yet, for children in TM or Findhorn, moral discourse comes from within, and they wholeheartedly accept the notion that someone can be a "good" person *without* being a member of their respective communities. (240)

For those who come from a background with a necessarily exclusivist religious worldview where there are absolute truths and falsities, there is a distinct difficulty in integrating competing information. The latter requires, to some degree, a "change of mindset"—an adjustment of one's cognitive framework. It requires a shift in meaning system, as well as an adjustment of norms and values. For example, a young person from a traditional and sexually conservative upbringing may have to adjust his or her behavior toward the opposite sex when leaving an environment of matchmakers and arranged marriages. Conversely, those from a "free love" background will have to adjust their expectations when dating in a more conventional environment, as reported by Marianne and Stephen and discussed in chapter 6.

Having to "switch," as it were, between two worlds frequently comes with questions of allegiance, of where one belongs.[19] The old culture, knowledge, and norms and values are often a far from perfect match with the new environment. This experience may lead to what is often termed an "identity crisis" or what Joyce referred to as "personality fragmentation."[20] Those who had run away or been exiled from their sectarian communities aimed to discount and suppress the past and sought to blend into the outside by forging a new identity adapted to that of outsiders. The result was often a self-described fragmented identity consisting of noncompatible segments. This frequently involved a process Goffman (1963) has termed "passing," the management of undisclosed discrediting information about oneself. Passing entails concealing information about one's real social identity while receiving and accepting treatment based on false suppositions concerning oneself. Burke Rochford (1999) has described "passing" of young ISKCON members who removed stigma symbols that associated them with the organization—trying to pass as "regular" pupils at school and blend in.[21] There was a feeling that the past identity was not compatible with the new identity needed to integrate into the outside world. Of course "whitewashing" one's past identity is hardly entirely possible, but my discussion here is about the desire and aim conceptualized and voiced by young former members who sought a method to adjust to their new surroundings. In some cases former members had great difficulty in conceptualizing and voicing their feelings. For example, one former member who contacted Inform put his partner on the telephone (whom he had met since leaving the Jehovah's Witnesses) to speak on his behalf and tell me what she thought the issues were, because he could not articulate what was bothering him beyond the general statement that he felt that, since leaving, everybody was against him.[22] This process of switching from the "old" to the "new" was often a complicated adjustment, and required an understanding of the "new" world. Ironically, this process of "unmaking" and "making" identities is not unlike the process of conversion.

Between Two Worlds

The young woman I call Isabel whom Joyce fostered was born and raised in a communal evangelical Christian group and came to Joyce at the age of seventeen. Isabel, according to Joyce, felt confused, alone, helpless, and afraid. She felt tremendous guilt about her "sins of the flesh" and felt she was innately evil, which had been underlined, reportedly, by the treatment she received from her father. But according to Joyce, there was also a part of her that "knew" her father was wrong, although this was difficult for her to admit and accept. "She did not know who were the 'goodies' and who were the 'baddies' in her life and she did not know which category she fitted into either," Joyce said. "She was beginning to suspect that there was something deeply wrong with the way in which she was brought up and with the philosophy of her family and those around her yet she felt that without them, life would be unbearable." A doctor diagnosed Isabel with depression and anorexia and advised that she should separate herself from her parents and the community. Isabel's mother argued that she was demon possessed and needed to repent and undergo deliverance at church to deliver her from these demons. According to Joyce, Isabel was caught between the two worldviews, and consequently was never confident she was doing "the right thing." She could not easily integrate the two worldviews and believed she had to reject one or the other, which led to confusion and anxiety. This sentiment was also reported by a former Jehovah's Witness who contacted Inform, and said she did not believe in those teachings anymore—except when watching the news, after which she always assumed the world would soon end—and agonized over having made the wrong decision in leaving.[23]

This theme of being caught between two worlds has arisen repeatedly. For example, teachers and parents in ISKCON have told me about children having had a difficult time adjusting to outside school or outside friends when changes within the organization demanded ordinary activities of daily life for "householders" be moved from the ashram.[24] One teacher relayed an anecdote from what she termed the early days, when everyday life was within the ashram where members lived and where children went to school. She spoke of a young member in her early teens whose plans for the future were either to sing in the ashram or take care of the cows. These were the only two options she conceived of and considered at the time (alternatives, in a sense, to other young teenagers who may want to become a pop star or a veterinarian).[25] As mentioned previously, life in ISKCON has changed, and, since the 90s, most members have lived in their own accommodation rather than the ashram, and most children have gone to local schools rather than gurukulas. For those children who started their education on the ashram and then had to change and attend outside school, this was a significant and often stressful shift. It was a shift in which, according to Rochford (1999), former gurukulis often sought to adapt and fit in with their new surrounding culture.

This was frequently at the expense of ISKCON traditions they had been expected to conform to in the past, such as particular clothing, comportment, and diet. This was a challenging adjustment and not all previous values and traditions were replaced by all former gurukulis. One of the teachers spoke of her son who went from the ashram school to an outside school, and she described the difficulties he had and his feelings of not fitting in. It took him a long time to adjust to the uniform, and the concept of keeping his shoes on all day while indoors. He did not know how to present himself, and the unfamiliar dress was not helpful. Other teachers repeated similar stories, and they raised other issues as well. The main issue for many of the pupils was lunch: the children could not bring themselves to eat meat, and many did not join their outside friends at the lunch table because they could not be near these friends while they ate meat.[26]

One former ISKCON member from the United States said:

Some (like me) decided to simply conform to society as quickly as possible, become somewhat of a wallflower in society, blending right in so no one knows of my past. For some, blending in meant befriending whoever they were able to associate with first who would accept them.

We had no training. I told my teacher she was going to [hell] for eating a hamburger. I was sent to the principal in tears, I never understood ANYTHING about the outside. It was so scary. I could recite the entire Bhagavad-Gita in Sanskrit, but couldn't tell you how many states were in the US, or who was the president of the United States.[27]

Nora, the former member of the Unification Church, said that she has never overcome the feeling of being a "misfit": "Children, as a rule, don't like to stand out, and Lord knows I did my best to fit in. I made friends easily, was unusually outgoing, learned languages and dialects in record time, joined the girl scouts, the swim club, the ski club and even a [chorus], I wore the right clothes and probably liked the right things, but to no avail, that feeling just never left me."[28] Anna asserts that young people in the Bruderhof are not enabled to leave—let alone create a life for themselves and earn a living. Consequently, she argues, it is frightening to leave. She also assigns difficulties she encountered to the different value system in which she was raised. In the Bruderhof, humility is a great virtue, and a brother or sister would not dwell on his or her talents and skills. This is significantly different from the values of contemporary middle-class English society, and, for Anna, this difference particularly causes difficulty when looking for work or when faced with competition at work.

> I think about every time I go for an interview. I use a lot of the "being confident about myself" and "believing [in] myself," and all this stuff—and every time I write for an interview I am wincing. This is wrong with my upbringing, saying: "I'm good at this." Still now, having some of these thought patterns that are sabotaging my going out fully to do what I really want to do most.
>
> In the community you just don't choose to have power or to acquire a job with more power. It's about humility and modesty and all that kind of stuff, and others make those kinds of decisions for you—if you've got what it takes. If you desire it, it's a selfish ego-trip. And ambition is wrong—whereas in our society, ambition is right and encouraged.[29]

Anna still struggles with the values she was raised to believe are the most important, but that are not helpful to her in her current life. For example, she has a difficult time standing up for herself, something she considers a necessary skill in her career, but that was frowned on within the Bruderhof. Janet has had similar problems that she attributes to her Bruderhof upbringing. In one case her boss wanted her to apply for a certain promotion, but she told him she could not possibly do that. Janet blames this on the Bruderhof mentality. Also, she notes, interview settings make her very nervous: "I've never known a bunch of people assembled unless it was to tell me off and to shout at me."[30]

The discrepancy between what the young former members are used to and what they actually encounter when leaving can be problematic. They may have a hard time understanding meanings—cultural contexts may be lost to them. Their different sets of norms and values are likely to put them at odds with the perceived mainstream in a variety of ways. Anna, after having been in exclusion for a few years, away from the community, noticed that she had been having difficulty making decisions (which is hardly surprising for one emanating from a hierarchically authoritarian organization where individuals' lives are micromanaged). She never was quite sure whether she was doing the right thing, and had recurrent doubts about her decision to leave. But over time this slowly changed:

And I was starting to listen to my inner monitor. We don't have an inner monitor. Children in the Bruderhof have no idea that they—well, I mustn't generalize, but that was my experience. You don't know that you have your own inner monitor. That you don't have to run to an authority figure every time—every time that some small decision needs to be made.

I think my biggest fear [in] leaving the Bruderhof was "getting it wrong," totally not realizing that I had my own inner monitor—to get comfortable with it and operate from it.

For some, adult issues and responsibilities were topics they never prepared themselves for; they did not imagine themselves as "grown-ups." In the Family, during the 70s and 80s, teachings centered on the belief that the world as they knew it would soon end. Stephen recalled this era:

I was taught that the world was gonna end. I mean, when I was a kid I never thought I'd live to be sixteen. And when I was sixteen I never thought I'd live to be twenty. And when I was twenty I never really thought I was ever [sings] "what are you gonna do when you get to be twenty-five"—I never thought about that.... That's an impossible situation for me to be in....[31]

I was expecting the world to change fundamentally, and I mean to a point where the person I am today is not really the same person. It's a person that has powers that are completely different than the kind of powers he has today.[32]

Shaping Identities

The sense of a "self" and of one's identity is tied to a frame of reference in which people locate themselves by reference to actions or performances and expectations, both about themselves and others, in particular social settings. Individuals tend to position themselves by reference to a previous pattern of behavior recognized by significant others. In this they rely on constructed stereotypes of generalized others. Hence identity formation is also a process of construction of meaning. Identification is a process of naming, of placing ourselves in socially constructed categories (Mead 1967). Psychological and sociological views of identity place different foci on the idea of an internal identity—an inner self—or an external identity forged through the internalization of social roles. The latter can change and mutate as people's sense of self changes as a result of different social experiences. Hence identity can be fragmented (different identities, according to gender, ethnicity, class, etc., as well as roles), and undergo alterations as social reality changes. By and large, identity is socially bestowed, socially sustained, and socially transformed (Berger 1963). The socially dominant group projects its own experience and culture as the norm, rendering invisible the perspective of those it dominates, while simultaneously stereotyping them and marking them out as "other."[33] In chapter 5 I discussed this in reference to the young members born in religious groups who were labeled according to their behavior and the extent to which they rebel or conform. The idea of defilement that Mary Douglas (1970) links to the enclave culture of the tribes in the wilderness (in the book of Numbers) is in a way an appropriate metaphorical parallel to these individuals. Upon leaving they have often been labeled as problematic influences on the community to which they initially belonged—defiling to the community of believers. Their identity has been dominated; they have been identified (as, for example, rebels) by the majority of their community, or at least the leadership.

There is no single interpretation of domination, however. Domination is more than just subjecting populations or minorities or individuals to external coercion and constraints that restrict their options to live as they choose. There are also internal constraints that complicate the picture—the formation of preferences, internalizations, and hegemony. These formations are also influenced by external pressures, but they interact differently with each individual's personal characteristics, hence the variety of choices made by members as they grow up, and the variety of ways in which the members negotiate their roles within the communities. There are ways to subvert the dominant paradigm—covert subcultures of dissent as well as more open, but disguised, transcripts of dissent, such as gossip, satirical jokes, folk tales or urban myths, and so forth—actions that Lukes (2005: 125) refers to as the "theatre of the powerless." These are the everyday actions of those who resist the group identity. There are many forms of dissent to be found within culture, in literature, art, media, and so on.

Within sects one can see parallels with the forms of dissent initiated by the young members expressed in online discussion groups, in gossip and interactions at camps and other events for young people—some seeking to stretch the boundaries of the status quo and change things from within, and some dissenting so much they opt to leave altogether.[34] Such dissent notwithstanding, there is no doubt that these young members will have been significantly shaped by the dominant influences in their environment, especially through their primary socialization. As Lukes (2005: 134) puts it, this process involves the shaping of agents' desires and beliefs by factors external to those agents, the shaping of their preferences by a lack of alternatives, and the resulting adaptation of desires adjusted to the limits of what is seen to be feasible. States of mind, therefore, can be byproducts of "domination by default" (the social structure that exists), as well as domination of a more purposeful kind—manipulation from one social group over another (136). There are countless examples of such domination, often unquestioned for a long time as a result of lifelong socialization and absence of information. Religion can have a significant impact as well by taking the level of this shaping to another level—by suggesting that certain choices may be detrimental to one's spiritual career and salvation. For believers, this adds a risk factor to one's choices.

Other persuasive examples of such molding and manipulation, partly but convincingly religiously induced, are constructs (and internalized concepts) of gender and the almost global and historical dominance of men over women.[35] Martha C. Nussbaum (2000) argues that Indian women have accepted what she considers their unequal fate as normal; the outcome of lifelong socialization and absence of information. John Stuart Mill ([1869] 1989) argued that, at the time he wrote, the subjection of women consisted of a combination of external and internal—and internalized—constraints. Pierre Bourdieu (2001) regards masculine domination as "symbolic violence"—a gentle violence, imperceptible and invisible even to its victims. It shapes the *habitus* (internalized and embodied dispositions that become an unconscious part of the worldview and are considered natural) and as a result is deeply embedded. Other examples of dominance, or symbolic violence, are, for example, ethnic dominance (i.e., in the United States before, as well as after—in different ways—the civil rights movement) and religious dominance (i.e., laws and norms against conversion in India and many Muslim countries, regulations against minority religions, and so forth).[36] It is important to note that the processes discussed here, whether they are referred to as mental manipulation, indoctrination, or shaping the field of the possible, are neither new nor unique to religions, let alone sects—they permeate society. The issue here is whether and to what extent such processes may be more powerful in some isolated communities, and the difficulties this raises for those who move away from their communities. The process of adaptation to a new environment involves a number of shifts, including an almost inevitable shift or adaptation in identity.

From the Old to a New Identity

As Nora says, "I was never really on the inside, just like I'll never really be on the outside, you'll find me floating in those fuzzy grey zones, in between."[37] In some cases, the shift from the identity the young former members had within the group to the one they had to establish outside the group has to be considerable. The meanings, interactions, and expectations outside are significantly different and the previous roles that partly made up a young member's identity may not exist outside. The young members may, when leaving the sect, not be able to continue their "roles" as missionaries, end-time teens, or blessed children. They have to address many questions. Can they just drop some of their old roles and beliefs and add some new ones, in a "pick and mix" fashion? Can they build onto their old identity and knowledge base? Children in mainstream society generally are subjected to a variety of socializing influences. These children encounter different nuances, whereas children in socially isolated communities may have been raised with restricted and censored socializing influences. This affects their "knowledge base"—their conceptual and imagined field of the possible. At the Go On conference a child psychiatrist argued that the word "isolated" was the most crucial word, as the children develop and construct their reality without having been offered alternative views—hence they come out with an incomplete picture of the reality accepted by the mainstream.[38] In some cases the young former members believe they have been lied to, and that everything they know must be wrong. In many cases religion is seen as part of the problem, and in the case of absolutist belief systems, new ideas and beliefs may not be compatible with the old ones—hence the young former members may feel that rejecting the old is an easier solution than attempting to blend seemingly incompatible concepts. Also, as I mentioned in chapter 6, the previous religious teachings may have vilified the culture in which these young former members now live and have to operate. Hence some opt for a radical rebirth—they attempt to replace all their old beliefs, norms, and values with new ones. This, of course, is radical indeed, and is very demanding both emotionally and intellectually. What does one do with the beliefs, norms, values, and roles that have been the context of one's life so far? The approach appears to depend partly on the emotional and spiritual connection, or lack thereof, the former members kept with their childhood beliefs and community. Some who had made a clean break, such as the baddies and some rebels, had later become atheist or agnostic. Some others had a religious experience outside and joined a new, but loosely structured, religious community.

Stephen has, as he puts it, shifted from one paradigm to the other. He has become an agnostic—rejected all the old and accepted a new paradigm according to what he learned in university.[39] Hence he is now critical of the Family's teachings about the end times.

> First it went from being three years to being five years, then it went from being five years to being ten years. And then it went from ten years to being about forty years. And now I'm thinking, my grandfather tells me he wants to be a hundred, and he's eighty, and I'm twenty-five. Sounds good. But I don't think about it like that anymore. I mean, of course I know the different paradigms, and I know how different they are. I only believe one of them. I don't really believe the other one, although I've been taught to believe the other one.[40]

But the process of "changing his mind" has been challenging:

> I describe it initially as total chaos and really not knowing what to do for about the first year and then I sort of just put it out of my mind for a while. But when I started dealing with it again at the age of nineteen, it took a lot of work and a lot of actual research and reading all kinds of humanistic literature and philosophical literature to sort of figure out what parts I was gonna keep and what parts I was gonna throw away.
>
> But I realized later on that a lot of my notions were still determined by that socialization, specifically the idea that there is a right and a wrong. That was something that took a long time, for me to discard that. That it's not just a matter of finding the truth, but it's a matter of finding a perspective. That was something that took a long time to understand.[41]

Hence, in Stephen's words, "I didn't really stop believing it, I just sort of changed my belief about it."

Marianne still considers herself a Christian: "Because I'm too afraid not to be.... It was drummed into me in the group all my life, that Jesus was gonna come back in '93. That was it. He was coming back in '93. The world is gonna be destroyed in '93. All my life that's what I thought. '93 comes, you know, and it goes." By 1993 Marianne had left the Family, but part of her still believed Jesus would return: "Yes. Deep in the subconscious, yes. On the outside, I was like 'crap, I couldn't give a shit, all the lies—bollocks.' But subconsciously, it's there, because you were told it's important. It's your whole make-up for the rest of your life."[42] But she has adapted her beliefs after years of living away from the Family. She argues that according to her old beliefs she, as a backslider, would go to hell. But she does not believe in that anymore. She has adapted her beliefs to something more conducive to her current lifestyle:

> Whatever happens, happens. I mean, I'm a good person.... And if there is a God, then God will know my heart. And he'll know that I can't do better because of the group.... I'm confused, I'm hurt, and I'm suffering. And he'll know that I've had no help, and he'll know—he'll just know. Because God is God, in the end.... So if that is the case, and there is a heaven and a hell, and there is a God, then he'll know me. And he'll make sure I'll go to heaven. He won't want me to go to hell. He won't want me to suffer, you know. He won't make me suffer. He knows I've suffered enough. And that's how I feel, you know, I'm quite content with that.

The changing or significant adapting of the religious beliefs is for some unavoidable, because their past is so closely intertwined with religion, any criticism of their upbringing involves criticism of the religious beliefs, practices, or at least interpretations of these beliefs. Hence young former members occasionally believe they have to "drop all the old." Of course this depends on a number of variables, and it is best to avoid generalizing. Having said this, there are a number of themes and clusters of shared experiences that have come up over the course of this research.

Those who were baddies within the group were more likely to, when out of the group, have a black/white approach to their past as well as their religion (i.e., "it's all rubbish"). They are more likely to have been raised in an absolutist and dualistic environment, where the "true" path is singled out and all other paths are rejected as "false"—not leading to the "Truth" (be it heaven or a similar concept). As a result of such doctrinal (and often resulting behavioral) rigidity, nonconforming children were labeled as baddies (and probably as rebels on the way to becoming baddies). These baddies were likely to have left on bad terms, frequently they either escaped or were cast out. If they found and received support, this support would have been likely to be critical of their upbringing as well as the teachings of the community (often for good reasons). Hence, baddies are more likely to drop the vast majority of their old norms, values, and beliefs, and look for new ones. This may leave them, in a sense, temporarily "normless," without familiar roles and a sense of what is "good" or "bad." To quote one former member who described the kind of switch she had to make: "It was a matter of becoming somewhat of a chameleon in many ways. If you fit in, you were accepted. If you were funny, did drugs, had sex, all of the above, you were sure to be accepted somewhere. All we knew was that EVERYTHING we had been taught about the real world being so evil was now our only choice to survive[,] so yes, most of us have conformed."[43] Both drugs and sex (not for the purpose of procreation) were supposed to be taboo in ISKCON, the group in which she was raised.[44] The former Jehovah's Witness who had left and instantly entered an abusive relationship asserted, in hindsight, that this was not the result of a lack of beliefs—rather the result of not knowing who she was. She asked me upon what people based who they are, and whom she could trust.[45]

Joyce has encountered what she termed a sense of normlessness and lack of roles on several occasions with young former members she fostered who came from a very strict communal group. She attributes this to what she calls the lack of freedom they had when growing up.

> And the freedom that they've missed is awful. And giving them permission to have that freedom again is very very hard to do, because to them it's like stepping out on their own, it's the great unknown. And the freedom to make their own choices. They've had all their choices made for them, they've never chosen their own clothes. It's like if you don't do something, you don't have the ability to do it; if nobody teaches you to write, you can't write, can you? Well if nobody teaches you to make decisions, you can't make them, so you grow up incapable of making decisions, you know, and that's a terrible thing, cos that makes you so vulnerable you're just constantly at the mercy of other people, who can make the decisions for you. So even if you get out of the [group], you're still looking for somebody who can make the decisions for you....
>
> They wouldn't know what to do, they really wouldn't. This is a hard thing for them, and as I said, they'll come in and say things like, "shall I put the lid on the toothpaste?" "Which colander shall I use, shall I use the plastic one or the metal one?" "Well it doesn't matter." "Yeah but which one?" "Well it doesn't matter which one

you use, darling, use which one you want." "Yeah but which one do you want me to use?" "Well I don't mind, you use which one you want." By this time the potatoes are getting cold, the peas are getting cold, you know, but I will never give in, I will not make a decision for them that they can make for themselves, so we go on like this for half an hour. I say, "which one do you want to use?" And they say, "well I don't mind, I'll use whichever one you want me to use," and it goes on and on... but you can't give in. You have to say, "look it's getting cold now and I'm not going to make a decision, so if you're not, we're not going to eat, so it's up to you." And then after we've ate, they'll say, "do you think I should have used the plastic one?"

In some cases the young former members she fostered had no sense of ownership because they had been raised in a community where all things were either shared or allocated. As Joyce put it:

So there's never that sense of anything belonging to them and this, it has an impact, and when you try and get them out of this you realize that they think they don't deserve anything of their own. And so when you buy them their first lot of clothes and possessions, you've got to be very careful cos they give them away, and you say, "what happened to that sweatshirt?" "Oh I gave it to Adam." What did you swap it for? "Oh I didn't swap it I gave it to him." And in the end I had to go and rescue everything and explain to people this is all he's got. But they feel reluctant to own anything and it's a sense of unworthiness, "I'm not the sort of person who can own things, that's too much for a person like me cos I'm not worthy of that." And it's the same when they've earned their first pay packet, they'll give it all away. And you have to monitor their friends a bit because if you're not careful, the friends will catch onto this, you see, and they start taking them for a ride. And they'll buy a packet of cigarettes and smoke one and then give the rest to their friends. They're easily taken advantage of so you have got to watch out a bit. And I knew what was going on and I would say to his friends, "look, you can stop taking all his money off him and you can stop taking his cigarettes off him and you know you can take advantage of him but I'm watching you."

And this affects their sense of self and related concepts of self-worth, and what Anna referred to as her "inner monitor." Joyce said:

It's that thing that somebody else always knows best and it makes them doubt themselves terribly, and that's why they're so full of self-doubt, full of self-doubt.... They will bow to another opinion of themselves very easily, especially if that person's opinion is negative of them, but they find it very hard when you praise them and to teach them to stick up for themselves is murder.

On the other hand, those who have left more relativistic groups, including the rebels, tend to have had a less extreme experience in the sense that there was more negotiability in some way or other (if not in belief, then possibly in practices or level of social isolation). In such groups there tends to be more than one way to reach the "Truth," or there may even be a number of truths. As a result there is less rigidity, and, often, more space for children to experiment and find their own ways. Hence, they are not necessarily nonconforming children or baddies, they are more likely to be seen as rebels (as discussed in chapter 5). This relative flexibility means that they are more likely to have left on a better note than their baddie contemporaries (or those of the previous cohort), with possibly a few bridges (in the form of personal contacts) intact. Such bridges make the need for outside support less urgent, especially if there is some form of support coming from the home community (be it emotional, spiritual, or financial) that is helpful to them (which is not always the case, as discussed in chapter 6). Such bridges also make it less likely that the young former members believe that the primary socialization has been "useless" and that they have to drop all the old beliefs, norms, and values. The rebels and those who have left more yielding groups tend to have an understanding of shades of gray. As a result they feel able to and tend to "pick and mix" new ideas and practices into their existing worldview. Where they feel able to embrace aspects of their childhood there may be some hybridization of their identities blending old and new roles, concepts, and beliefs.

New Identities

The young former members who find themselves in the wilderness undergo a process of enculturation into new surroundings that demand levels of adaptation of their attitudes, roles, selves—their identities. One significant aspect of this is overcoming or coming to terms with their stigmas—their "tattoos," the way they had perceived they were branded and labeled in the past. This is a significant part of what has shaped them, and forms part of the baggage they take with them into the wilderness. Although most reported this enculturation process to be challenging, many did find empowering ways of managing it. The young members often embraced their labels and in this sense developed a resistance identity where they defined themselves on the basis of principles different from, and often opposed to, those permeating the sects from which they came. Those who had been devalued and stigmatized created a subculture of baddies and rebels in resistance, and frequently celebrated their supposed "spiritual troubles." Outside they frequently embraced these previously stigmatizing identities and used them as a cohesive force to bind themselves to a community of other outsiders with frequently shared pasts and experiences. They embraced and reclaimed their labels as rebels and baddies—be it as backsliders, Vandaris, demon possessed, and so forth. Hence they may have rejected the old beliefs and practices and other aspects of their old identity, but they embraced the aspects that put them in a position of resistance to the community of their childhood.

The young former members came from one religion and then joined and sought to adapt to another hegemonic religious culture (where religion may be covert or overt). I have found that, rather than picking and choosing useful beliefs and ideas from both, in contrast, those who left sectarian groups had no desire for such blending. They sought to replace the old with the new—convert instead of hybridize—convert to the culture, the norms, the roles, and in some cases the accepted religion, spirituality, or lack of religion within contemporary society. Inevitably, however, there is a level of hybridization in that not all history can be easily erased, and some has become the foundation to the new roles and identity. One example of this is the way in which the young former members often embrace their old labels and turn them into an aspect of the new identity that they appreciate and are proud of—such as the subversive and rebellious aspects. There is a transposition of negative meanings. Hence there are those who, in hindsight, feel blessed that they were not blessed children, and embrace their unblessed nature. And there are those who are proud to be Vandaris, or fulfilled over their sense of ambition and pride, pleased at their worldliness, and satisfied about drinking, smoking, and promiscuity.

I will conclude this chapter with an excerpt of a poem written by a former member of the Family and posted on the website www.movingon.com:[46]

> We are the Vandari,
> We are red and drool...
> On Zerby we will chew.

Conclusion

THIS EXPLORATORY RESEARCH has brought some issues to light that would benefit from further, more systematic scrutiny. I have argued that sectarian socialization has its consequences—one may speak of a segregated socialization. For those who leave, this segregated socialization may become a stumbling block to (perceived) integration into the wider society. They feel they fit neither here nor there. In a world that is increasingly diverse, it is significant that the sectarian attitude is still attractive to some, and that this attitude engenders another form of sectarianism as well, where a community organizes itself in opposition to another community, or even a people.

A point that needs reiterating is that nothing stays the same, especially new religious movements. As noted in the introduction, the groups in the research that this book is based on have changed significantly, and have continued to change as I wrote this book. This does not, however, change the essence of my argument, which is about processes, group dynamics in light of separatist teachings and leadership, reactions to tensions with society, ways in which young members can be affected, ways in which they may react in turn, and so on. Changes and the attitude to change are strongly influenced by the style and structure of leadership. The Unification Church and the Family, both initially charismatic groups, managed to initiate changes relatively quickly over time, and eventually adjusted to the demands of their children—the Family by establishing different levels of membership, and the Unification Church by allowing membership according to different rules. The Bruderhof and ISKCON were both more resistant to change in an effort to maintain ties to certain traditional ways. ISKCON's gurus who were deemed problematic were not easily deposed, and the Bruderhof refused to allow critical exiles to break the Ausschluss rules. Scientology's charismatic leader installed a bureaucratic system that is very resistant to change—neither former members nor second-generation members have managed to institute significant changes. These efforts of boundary maintenance have been reflected in the types of labeling applied to those challenging the status quo. The groups focused on in this research made for strong examples to highlight these processes, but they can be found in other groups, in other parts of society, and at other times.

Similarly, the experiences of the individuals described in this book are specific to them, but, again, some of the trends and processes indicate patterns. The passage from one such subculture to another culture can be a significant challenge. I use the term "passage" here purposefully and mindfully; the young former members go from one place to another—they are, in a sense, passing through a liminal stage. It is a journey—metaphorically, spiritually, and conceptually not unlike a spiritual diaspora, where the individuals have to travel through different cognitive and spiritual frameworks. Also, it is a passage in the sense that they often feel their journey is an isolated one that they travel on their own, or at least in very small numbers, enclosed from other people's experiences. A passage after which they hope they will be free from normlessness, able to assign meaning and find a structure in a strange world. Finally, it is a passage where the passagee is often seeking an agent who will help, and for some, define and control aspects of the passage.

I have used the term "segregated socialization," because from all the second-generation former members I have interviewed and spoken with, as well as from literature I have read and from discussions I have followed in online discussion groups, it has become clear that the young former members feel like strangers within the society they have entered upon leaving the sects. This sense of being "in the wilderness" was experienced on several levels. Former members have reported feeling a discrepancy in knowledge and skills, ranging from the material lack of qualifications to a lack of information, knowledge, and understanding. They have also reported discrepancies in norms and values, not knowing what is considered normal or deviant, and not knowing how to act in familiar and unfamiliar situations. These feelings combine in a general sense of not fitting in, having been "branded," and fears that people will find out that they are "faking it." Former members reported that they lacked the necessary or appropriate "mindsets," the necessary cognitive framework to understand the world they were now living in. They considered their mental framework "useless" for understanding and operating in the world in which they want to live, hence their sense of anomie, of disjunction. Many former members described a fear of "outside," which seemed evil, "dark," or "black."

This is a significant contrast to those who chose to remain within the groups, who "understood" the difference between inside and outside, embellished it, and used it as an example of why their way andr values were superior. Again there was a distinction between good and bad. The ones who left often came to the opposite conclusion, pointing to the differences, occasionally embellishing them, and using them as an example of why the sect is inferior. In some cases it is possible that feelings of disillusion and dissatisfaction with one's past have intensified as a result of the type of support young former members have received upon leaving—where the sect and their childhood is likely to have been criticized and labeled as immoral and possibly heretical (Shupe and Bromley 1981; Wright 1998). In other cases such criticism follows a childhood where abuse has occurred. It is certainly not my intention to downplay this; on the contrary, these real cases often get lost in the generally overblown cult discourse, where they become part of an overly generalized and frequently theological or moral agenda. In such an atmosphere, different sides are demonized and accusations run high. These discourses are interesting sociologically both for who makes such charges and how they may affect the subjects. For example, some parents in NRMs have argued that the young members who leave "have to" make a switch and denounce or even accuse their parents or the group in order to gain acceptance outside, or to "get ahead"—by selling their story to the news, and so forth. One Family regional leader and parent described some young former members as "pawns" in a political and ideological battle waged between the Family and a particular support organization that criticizes the movement. In this battle, he argued, the young former members are not thinking for themselves.[1] These parents argue that, consequently, the personal issues between them and their children become politicized and the group as a whole is blamed. Meanwhile, the former members complain that the leadership always blame individuals, "bad apples," for institutionalized problems. Sally explained this dynamic in light of sexual transgressions within the Family, and begrudged those who, while having a problem with another individual while in the group, shifted their vendetta toward the groups as a whole after leaving. Sally argued that this happens because "there is something in it for them—they can sell their story." And the feelings intensify—in a statement where protection of her loved ones trumped empathy toward those previously abused, Sally said, "If I could, I would have a list of all the people that had any of that type of abuse and I would make sure that none of them ever came near any of my loved ones in the Family." Young former members are "pawns" on a variety of levels, often labeled one way within the religious community (baddies, rebels), and labeled another way outside the religious community ("victims," "brainwashed"—"they are not thinking for themselves"). This makes it very difficult for the former members to journey between the old and the new community, or to connect the two together in some conceptual and meaningful way. The past and present are frequently like disconnected islands. These young former members have found themselves in an arena where opinions are strongly divided and where disputes are emotionally loaded. Furthermore, their passages have often been colored by agents who have affiliated themselves with one particular side of this polarized debate.

Mixing and matching new information within their existing cognitive framework often does not work for the young former members; they frequently prefer to denounce and reject significant aspects of their old beliefs and habits in favor of new paradigms that facilitate "passing for normal." These former members have not overwhelmingly chosen the pick and mix religiosity of the spiritual supermarket. Many of them end up in virtual communities or networks where they are ideologically and emotionally opposed to the communities from which they came. Hence they have chosen a side of a spiritual or moral argument rather than hybridized the different discourses. Consequently, they become an integral part of the alienating and separatist discourse of the cult scene, a significant kink in the social reality of religious diversity. Akin to what Barney Glaser and Anselm Strauss (1971: 93) have termed a "socially alienating passage" that has only apparent mutual desirability for both agent and passagee alike, it provides meaning only to those involved. As Rock wrote about self-help groups in his research, their work "attacks alienation by giving that inner turmoil an outer cladding of structure, stability, communality and direction" (1998: 325). The way in which those who left put themselves in opposition to the communities they came from shows they have not quite rejected all the norms and values of their childhood. They may have joined the wider society, yet they still put themselves in sectarian opposition to the communities of their past. In keeping with the dualistic and absolutist frameworks of their childhoods, they join the opposition, as it were, and manage to hybridize the framework of sectarianism with a new antisect discourse.

It would be interesting to compare some of the findings from this research with the beliefs and attitudes of those who have left less sectarian religious communities, as well as those who have been raised in established religions but lost their faith. Do young Mormons feel this sense of being in the wilderness when they leave; do lapsed Catholics or Muslims struggle with a sense of normlessness? Do they struggle from what some may consider a "mismatched socialization"? It would also be interesting to compare this research with that on other groups and institutional responses to controversies; are there similar reactions—such as blaming bad apples and labeling victims? There could be a larger conversation about communal and institutional forms of denial and its social consequences.

This discussion may become increasingly interesting when also compared to other subcultures and minority communities. For example, the second generation within immigrant communities (first to be born in the new country) may grapple with some similar issues, such as feeling they are between two cultures, two influences, and that one aspect of their diaspora identity is always devalued by the other side. There is research on this topic; for example, Werner Schiffauer (1999) illustrated the struggles of the children of migrants with the example of a young Turk in Germany, who described a sort of "crisis"— he felt he belonged neither in the culture of his parents nor in the one of his German peers. His world, so far, had been conceptually segregated into Turkish and German, and he carried a stigma from both, hence could not easily integrate into either. Eventually he joined a community of radical young men who combined a political view with new interpretations of Islam. The worldview and conceptual framework explained his diaspora identity and his surroundings in a way satisfactory to him, and this helped him develop strategies for dealing with his crisis.

Similarly, the young former members in my research have been raised in a subculture different from the rest of the surrounding society. There were those who stayed within it, considering it better than what was on offer outside. There were others who left and suffered some sort of crisis as a result of their mixed identity, occasionally geographically diasporic following the missionary work of their parents, usually cognitively different following a sectarian upbringing and education. A further similarity is the stigmatization suffered by those who left who were negatively labeled by their parents and community (for not "fitting in"), and who feel stigmatized by others around them (again, for not "fitting in"). Having left, they were straddling both worlds, much of their identity based in one while attempting to fit in the other, which often left them feeling like "misfits." In a society as diverse as ours, it will continue to be important to be mindful of different childhoods, and socializations, and the ways in which these may have shaped those around us.

Appendix

Amish

The Amish are an Anabaptist Christian denomination known for their plain dress and limited use of what they consider to be modern conveniences such as cars and electricity. The Amish, who have communities in the United States and Canada, separate themselves from mainstream society; they do not join the military, they draw no Social Security and do not accept any form of financial assistance from the government, and many avoid insurance. Members speak a German dialect, although they also learn English in school. There are over two hundred thousand Amish (including unbaptized children).

Ananda Marga

Ananda Marga (which means "path of bliss") was founded in India in 1955 by Shrii Shrii Anandamurti (1921–1990). The movement spread to the West in the 1970s. Through a system of meditation techniques, yoga postures (asanas), spiritual gatherings, and social service the Ananda Margis (followers of Ananda Marga) strive to develop themselves, while also working toward the betterment of others. The movement defines itself primarily as a philosophical or political organization that engages in social welfare and education rather than as a religious movement. Members are expected to follow certain ascetic spiritual practices, practice yoga, and chant to focus the mind on the supreme consciousness. The movement claims to have between two and three thousand nuns and monks. It has drawn controversy when the leader was jailed in a political dispute, and followers set fire to themselves in protest.

Christian Science (The Church of Christ Scientist)

Founded in 1879 by Mary Baker Eddy (1821–1910) in the United States and based on her book *Science and Health with a Key to the Scriptures* (1875). Special emphasis is placed on the eradication of sin and illness through prayer; physical suffering is seen as an illusion that can be conquered by the spirit-filled mind. At times the group has taught a "radical reliance" on spiritual healing, as spiritual healing and allopathic medicine were seen to be incompatible, and could counteract one another. Over time this has changed as the message became more moderate. The church estimates (2006) that there are four hundred thousand or more students of Christian Science in over sixty countries worldwide. There are anywhere between 1,850 to 2,000 branch congregations in the Christian Science church.

Exclusive Brethren

The Exclusive Brethren are a nineteenth-century Christian sect originating from the British Isles and generally described as the Plymouth Brethren (where, historically, their largest congregation was located), and more recently as the Plymouth Brethren Christian Church. They are distinguished from the Open Brethren, from whom they separated in 1848 after one of the leaders, John Nelson Darby, initiated a rift. The distinction between the Open and Exclusive Brethren is that the latter do not share communion with those who do not agree with their principles. They remove themselves from aspects of the world that they consider "evil," including aspects of modern technology. The Exclusive Brethren, currently under the leadership of Bruce Hales, are found throughout Europe and the English-speaking world. According to their own figures, forty thousand Exclusive Brethren meet in three hundred assemblies throughout nineteen countries.

The Watchtower Society (Jehovah's Witnesses)

A Christian millenarian movement founded by Charles Taze Russell (1852–1916) in 1884. Witnesses tend to interpret the Bible literally, and reject much of mainstream Christianity in favor of what they consider to be a restored form of Christianity. They reject the Trinity, and believe that only they will rule with Christ in the millennium. They obey "divine law," which has led to clashes with some governments. For example, they refuse military service, do not vote, and do not salute the flag. They do, however, pay taxes and are told to obey civil law. Yet they refuse blood transfusions, which has also led to further clashes with authorities (although they do accept modified transfusions). Jehovah's Witnesses are represented worldwide, and they claim 6 million members.

New Age

An umbrella term applied to a vast network of individuals and groups with a wide range of beliefs and orientations who share a family resemblance. The range of New Age beliefs and practices is historical and global, stretching to reinterpretations of teachings from pre-Christian times to contemporary teachings, and across the cultures and religions of the globe. There is a generalized focus on the coming of a new age (including beliefs in the Age of Aquarius). New Age beliefs may include concepts associated with holism, alternative and complementary medicine, the Human Potential Movement, paganism, occultism, astrology, and more. Groups tend to be amorphous and syncretistic.

Oneida Perfectionists

The Oneida Perfectionist Community was founded in 1848 by John Humphrey Noyes (1811–1886) in New York State. Noyes advanced his social theory and philosophy, which he termed "Perfectionism." The Perfectionist Community was a Christian Utopian commune with socialist overtones. Noyes challenged accepted notions of a family structure, and implemented a variety of different structures throughout the history of the group. Housing, work, and finances were communally operated and shared. The Oneida Community dissolved in 1881, having only ever had, at its peak, just over three hundred members.

Osho (Bhagwan Shree Rajneesh)

Rajneesh (1931–1990), an Indian who claimed to have been self-realized at the age of twenty-one, founded an ashram in Puna, India, in 1974, where he taught new and radical teachings that mixed Eastern and Western influences. He rejected the ascetic tradition of the East in favor of more chaotic and dynamic practices, one of which was the practice of dynamic meditation. In the early 1980s Osho and some of his followers moved to the United States, where he founded Rajneeshpuram in Oregon. The ashram in Oregon was controversial, and after the movement in the United States spiraled out of control, Bhagwan moved back to India, where he changed his name to Osho. After his death in 1990 the movement divided into several strands, each following different pupils of Osho.

Sahaja Yoga

A movement based on the teachings of her holiness Mataji Nirmala Devi (1923–2011), referred to as Mother within the movement, who claimed to have been born self-realized. She began teaching her techniques to reach self-realization in India in 1970. Self-realization is seen by Sahaja Yogis as both a physiological process and a spiritual transformation in which the Kundalini is awakened within and passes along the spinal cord through six chakras. Emphasis is on meditation. The movement has become syncretistic, as Sri Mataji included New Age teachings and influences in her teachings. According to the movement, in 2001, there were twenty thousand members in India and a further ten thousand members outside India, half of whom were full-time followers. This may have changed after her death, although there are no other estimates.

Sullivan Institute (Fourth Wall Community)

The Sullivan Institute was a self-improvement group within the Human Potential Movement founded by psychoanalysts Saul Newton (1906–1991) and his then wife Jane Pearce in 1957 in the United States. The Institute developed into a commune designed to nurture the personal growth of its members by removing them from conventional structures regarded as oppressive, such as marriage and the nuclear family. During the 1970s the commune began reaching out in an effort to initiate social change; in the following decade it collapsed following internal conflicts.

Notes

INTRODUCTION

1. Throughout the book I have changed their names to respect their anonymity. In the case of Joyce, a (foster) carer, I have not mentioned the name of the group she and some of those in her care came from, at her request. Of course much has happened since I conducted these interviews and the bulk of my research, and as much as possible I have updated the information. But clearly my focus is often on particular eras, and hence the accounts will not necessarily always be the most up-to-date information on particular religious groups. This will be clear within the text.
2. Inform is based at the London School of Economics, Houghton Street, London WC2A 2AE, www.inform.ac.
3. This hinges on a number of variables, charismatic leadership or the negotiability of a historical tradition being significant influences on the attitude toward changes and adaptation, as described in chapter two.
4. I shall, however, use the term "cult" or "NRM" when involving someone else's research or argument and language and when its meaning is similar to the way I use the term "sect" or "sectarian movement" or "community." This will be clear in the context of the discussion.
5. Sects are by definition minority religions (although some may disagree on definitions of religion employed), but minority religions are not necessarily sectarian.
6. In some cases support from the group, although undoubtedly with good intentions, has backfired, leaving the young member confused and pressured. This is understandable when leaders or parents try to get the young member to understand and conform to an "undeniable Truth"—this may be precisely what the young member is doubtful about or questioning.
7. Schiffauer (1999) also picked up on recognition as a theme in his research.
8. For more information about Inform, see www.inform.ac.
9. It is, of course, not an insurmountable problem. Inform frequently works with counselors and therapists by providing them information about a particular religious group, which helps them in their work.

CHAPTER I

1. Wallis (1996), for example, identified groups by the ideological positions they took vis-à-vis the world (world rejecting, world accommodating, and world affirming) and the resulting social consequences. Wilson (1982, 1990) emphasized that sects tend to have strong beliefs regarding salvation.
2. "Bruderhof" may also mean "place where brothers dwell," according to Rubin (2000). Membership numbers from the group's own website, http://www.bruderhof.org (accessed January 20, 2012).
3. I elaborate on this event in the following chapter, and describe it from some former members' perspectives throughout the following chapters.
4. Although these terms and distinctions were initially applied by one particular side in this debate, the terms were eventually used by both sides, including individual members. The former members I have spoken with used these terms to describe the schism at the time.
5. See, for example, Zablocki (1971), who described the Bruderhof as "The Joyful Community." Perhaps partly as a result of this image, the communities have never garnered much prominence beyond their geographic localities, and certainly are not as recognized as some of the other religious groups mentioned in this research.
6. This topic is covered in depth in chapter 6.
7. See, for example, Jentzsch (1994).
8. Allegedly Hubbard has written such levels up to 15—the levels after 8 not having been released by Scientology as of 2013.
9. This includes the churches, the International Hubbard Ecclesiastical League of Pastors, and Scientology Missions International.
10. This is in accordance with Scientology beliefs; members can then continue their mission when they are reborn (Atack 1990). Another interpretation is that this is a symbolic contract.
11. They have taken a vow to give undivided attention to their mission, a focus that, according to the organization, cannot be shared with the responsibilities of parenthood. According to some sources, children are asked to make the decision to join the Sea Org from the age of six, or even younger (see, for example, http://exscientologykids.com/astras-story/ [accessed July 16, 2014]). When I visited the Little Cadet School at Saint Hill in 2000 the youngest cadet was nine years of age.
12. Inform, from communication with Scientology official. These numbers may have included anyone who has taken courses or auditing with Scientology, which raises the question whether "clients," or anyone who has ever taken a course, may be counted as members alongside Sea Org members. In the last few years estimates have become vaguer.
13. Although many old religions are highly institutionalized and bureaucratized, new religious movements are generally stereotyped as having charismatic lead-

ers and looser structures. This is, of course, not necessarily the case, as explained by Barker (1995a)—one cannot generalize about the new religions.
14. See, for example, US v. Fishman NO. CR-88-0616 DLJ 1990 and US District Court, Mass., Flynn v. L. Ron Hubbard 1983.
15. There has been discussion about the way Hubbard defined ethics and the way the Scientology organization has possibly modified the meaning of the term over time. See, for example, Kent (2003).
16. See, for example, Hubbard (1992, 1993, 1998).
17. See, for example, http://www.lermanet.com/reference/77Granjurypart1.htm, where a copy of the case has been posted (accessed July 16, 2014) or Atack (1990: 218–241) for more details.
18. See, for example, reporting by Thomas C. Tobin and Joe Childs such as "Inside Scientology," in *Tampa Bay Times*, http://www.tampabay.com/specials/2009/reports/project/ (accessed July 16, 2014).
19. The website is at http://exscientologykids.com/ (accessed July 16, 2014).
20. The reboot mission consists of a number of documents, most of which have been posted on http://www.xfamily.org/index.php/Reboot_Documents (accessed July 16, 2014).
21. The level of sharing, as well as the interpretation of Berg's Mo letters, varied for each home and community throughout times of reorganization of the authority structures, when many of the members were relatively disconnected from each other. I elaborate such changes in chapter 2.
22. See, for example, the memoir of a former member, Williams (1998).
23. Inform estimated in 2002 that there were 25,000 members and approximately 500–600 in the United Kingdom . Around the same time David V. Barrett (2001) estimated that the UC had 4.5 million followers worldwide, 10,000 in the West. This discrepancy is not unusual as membership estimates are inherently difficult; one cannot always rely on the movement's own statistics and definitions of membership are not always clear. For example, Moon was politically quite powerful and had prominent guests who appeared at ceremonies, who in turn drew attendees, and it is not clear whether they are counted as "honorary members" or not.
24. Before marriage both men and women, referred to as brothers and sisters within the Unificationist family, are expected to be chaste.
25. This is called the four position foundation in Unification theology. Neither men nor women are complete without each other, blessed in a God-centered marriage, with children to complete the four points of love that travel vertically from God through the couple to their children, and horizontally between the married couple. See Barker (1983) for more on the ideal family in UC theology.
26. Radical changes to these requirements are discussed below.
27. See Moon (1973); Barker (1984), chapter 3.
28. For a more detailed discussion of "indemnity," see Barker (1984) and Moon (1973).

29. See, for example, the UC libel case against the *Daily Mail* in the United Kingdom in 1981, which the UC lost (Dennis Frederick Orme [plaintiff] v. Associated Newspapers Group Inc. [defendants] in the High Court of Justice, Queen's Bench Division, before Mr. Justice Comyn).
30. Brazilian and Paraguayan authorities investigated the property Moon purchased in their countries near their border after allegations of money laundering. The federal police in Brazil conducted a number of raids, and in Paraguay the UC had to return some land to locals after a series of land disputes.
31. Information from Inform.
32. See, for example, Muster (1997) on the controversy sankirtan caused at the Los Angeles airport.
33. "Godhead," here, refers to the original spiritual home of Krishna.
34. Krishna is believed to reside in his name and in his image. ISKCON temples are likely to have images and statues of other deities as well, such as Radha-Krishna, Gaura-Nitai, Visnu, Laksmi Narayana, and Sita Rama. They are generally thought to, at times of ritual, contain the spirits of the deities they represent.
35. See, for example, Bromley and Shupe (1981) and Beckford (1985).
36. To such an extent that some airports sought a ban on solicitation from ISKCON See ISKCON v. Lee, 505 U.S. 672 (1992).
37. The leadership of the sects and parents of the children do not always agree, and the birth of children may be an incentive for parents to leave the confines of the group. However, in general the plans for the children fall within the general worldview and doctrinal framework the members already adhere to, and consequently parents frequently follow the teachings relating to the following generations. My research focuses on those who have remained with the groups after the birth of their children, although in one case a mother left with her children when the daughter, who I later interviewed, was a young teenager.
38. From informal interviews with nine teenage members in 1997.
39. This idea is not unusual among evangelical Christians. Coleman (1999) has written about Livets Ord, an evangelical Christian group in Sweden, where the children born to church members are considered to be spiritually more advanced and mature than new converts. Therefore they have higher standing in the church. A ten-year-old may preach to the congregation and heal the sick.
40. Although some would disagree on whether the term is generally used in a derogatory way (and within Scientology it is not used in its originally racist context), "wogs" are at least disparaged for not using Scientology to better themselves and their surroundings. See, for example, Atack (1990).
41. This is comparable to beliefs that can be found in the New Age milieu, where some children are believed to be indigo children, crystal children, and star children. Indigo children are children who are believed to be intrinsically special and gifted, with an indigo aura considered unique to them (Carroll and Tober 1999: 1).

42. See, for example, Beckford's (2003) discussion of NRMs and their "identity spaces"; where he also acknowledges work by Kevin Hetherington.
43. See the appendix for information about the Oneida Perfectionists and Ananda Marga.
44. This changed once devotees started to become householders. I elaborate on this in chapter 2. Also, see Rochford (1997).
45. See the appendix for more information on the Sullivan Institute.
46. This is based on the tantric idea that the body is the primary vehicle of the divine, and that each individual is composed of four bodies: the physical body, the subtle body (made up of vibrations and energy), the causal body (which makes up the abstract mind), and the supercausal (in which lies the divine and universal self). See Coney (1999), chapter 2.
47. For more information on Osho see the appendix.
48. Over time the structure within the kibbutzim changed toward privatization within community, as did the approach to child care. See, for example, the differences between the accounts of Bettelheim (1969) and Spiro (1975), on the one hand, and Palgi (1997) on the other hand.
49. Term used by a teacher at the Bhaktivedanta Manor School in the United Kingdom, interview, 2001.
50. For example, parents within the New Age who believe their children are especially evolved as Indigo Children (see Carroll and Tober [1999, 2001]), are more likely to opt for alternative education options, including home schooling.
51. See http://www.bruderhof.com/community/education/(accessed January 20, 2012).
52. Palmer (1994b) has distinguished three ideal typical modes of interaction between men and women, or "sex identity," in religious communities: sex complementarity, polarity, and unity. The relationship hinges on whether men and women are individuals who complement each other, are only "complete as one androgynous being" once they are united (and are spiritually distinct and inessential or irrelevant to each other's salvation), or are essentially sexless spirits shrouded in a superficial (gendered) layer that obscures the immortal (1994b).
53. Although in both groups women have argued, after leaving, that gender bias and sexism were prevalent. See, for example, Williams (1998) regarding the Family and Hong (1998) regarding the Unification Church.
54. Of course, "society" is often constructed as an antithesis of the sect itself.
55. This changed significantly after the publication of the reboot teachings in 2010.
56. In the case of ISKCON this has changed drastically in the late 90s; I elaborate on this later.
57. The structure, lifestyle, and division of labor were conducive to traditional nuclear families and child rearing.
58. It was not until later in the movement's history that special communes and projects were developed for the children that took them out of the day-to-day Family activities. I elaborate on this in chapters 2, 3, and 5.

CHAPTER 2

1. The term "trial and error" arose in an interview with a second-generation Family member who discussed changes over time.
2. After the movement started spreading from Korea, however, it diversified under the leadership of different missionaries. The first centers, in the United States, United Kingdom, and Japan, were quite different from each other. It was not until 1971, when Moon conducted a large tour of the centers, that these disparate groups became an international movement.
3. Interview, Eric, 2000.
4. Several academics and theologians have written thorough analyses of Unification theology (e.g., Bryant and Richardson [1978]; Beverley [1994]).
5. Interview, Eric, 2000.
6. The Bruderhof attempted, for a time, to adhere to the Hutterite tradition, and ISKCON followed in the footsteps of the Caitanya tradition. In comparison, Moon, although he placed himself in the Christian tradition, reinterpreted many tenets in such a novel way that he was perceived, by the majority of other Christians, as not compatible with "their tradition."
7. See Mow (1991) and http://www.perefound.org/abt_rsb.html (accessed February 13, 2005).
8. From interviews, and see Oved (1996).
9. See, for example, Oved (1996) and Bohlken-Zumpe (1993).
10. The Great Crisis is a difficult chapter of Bruderhof history where the community was divided between those who supported the Arnolds and those who supported the Zumpes and the two parties' associated ideals. Hence Rubin's "Heini-ism" has a parallel with Heini supporters describing Hans Zumpe as creating an authoritarian and dictatorial regime. See, for example, Mow (1991). The exclusion by Heini of Eberhard's other son-in-law, Balz Trumpi, added to the feeling that Heini appeared to be carving out a hegemonic status for himself and the style of the North American communities.
11. See his open letter in the Bruderhof publication the *Plough*, no. 41, 2–6 (January 1995).
12. See http://www.perefound.org/jr_cn.html (accessed February 13, 2005) for Rubin's description of this development. Some Hutterite congregations disassociated themselves from the Bruderhof partly for this reason. See, for example, http://www.perefound.org/xcsob_90.html (accessed February 13, 2005).
13. I elaborate on this issue in chapter 6.
14. Their position has changed throughout the movement's history. In the late 1960s the American hofs began more involvement with their surrounding community and social-political issues such as the civil rights movement and the antiwar movement. For example, members were active in protesting against the death sentence of convicted prisoner Mumia Abu-Jamal (there have been ques-

tions around the fairness of the trial and resulting death sentence—in 2012 this sentence was commuted to life imprisonment without parole). Social contact with outsiders, however, is regulated—interested members of the public may visit communities, and members will do charity and outreach work in the community, but those who have left often cannot visit as freely.

15. For more information on this topic, see Muster (1997); Rochford (1995); and Rochford and Bailey (2006).
16. There were significant changes later, but not as a direct result of his death. I elaborate on these changes later in this chapter and in the following chapter.
17. One former president of the Society for the Scientific Study of Religion argued, during his presidential address, that aspects of religious belief, doctrine, and practice may be inherently abusive to children (Capps 1992).
18. See http://www.corpun.com/index.htm and http://www.religioustolerance.org/spankin6.htm (accessed August 4, 2005).
19. Interview, Stephen, 2001.
20. Interview, Stephen, 2002.
21. Not unlike reports a former Scientology member had to write while she was still part of the movement; her story is discussed in chapter 6.
22. Murmuring, in a biblical context, refers to voicing discontent and doubts, and is often seen as a lack of faith. See, for example, Ex. 15:24, 16:2–12, 17:3–7.
23. See, for example, accounts on www.movingon.org (archived on http://archive.xfamily.org/www.movingon.org/); Kent (1997); and Ward (1995: 94).
24. See the sources in note 23.
25. From a newsletter by Merry Berg (1999).
26. The Family teaches that individuals can be demonically possessed, and that this can be reversed through exorcism.
27. These publications are difficult to find as a result of literature purges (the destruction of some publications) when the Family was investigated and, in some cases, raided. However, in many cases old copies have been scanned and published on the Internet. See, for example, http://www.xfamily.org for a list of scanned and posted Family publications. *The Last State* is available on this site.
28. For further reading about disciplining in the gurukulas, see Raghunatha Dasa's *Children of the Ashram* on http://www.surrealist.org (accessed August 26, 2007).
29. This is similar to teachings in Osho and Sahaja Yoga.
30. See Rochford and Heinlein (1998: 49) and Muster on http://surrealist.org/*gurukula* (accessed August 26, 2007). This has, however, been debated, which I discuss in chapter 6.
31. See Muster on http://surrealist.org/*gurukula*/timeline (accessed August 26, 2007).
32. See Muster on http://surrealist.org/*gurukula*/timeline (accessed August 26, 2007).
33. Also available on http://surrealist.org/gurukula/timeline/children.html (accessed July 16, 2014).

34. The case attempted to use the Racketeer Influenced and Corrupt Organizations Act to corral allegations of abuse at several schools into one federal case, but it was dismissed by a Dallas district court in 2001 (see legal documents posted on www.wturley.com).
35. Although this was not a smooth process—by 1998 more letters about child abuse had been sent to the GBC, and a new guru was admitted to the GBC who advocated gurukula reform and the interviewing of former gurukula students as well as teachers—but he also favored keeping the matter a GBC secret. The minister of education, Jagadish, resigned, and the GBC reformed the existing Ministry of Education into a Board of Education. Jagadish became a member of the Board of Education.
36. See Anuttama Dasa, "Letter from Me," which was originally posted on chakra.org but has since been archived on http://oldchakra.com/mainpages/childabuse/ (accessed July 16, 2014). http://www.chakra.org/articles/2000/06/20/anuttama/index.htm.
37. Children of Krishna provides financial assistance for Krishna youth for educational needs and counseling.
38. Dasa, "Letter from Me." In the following chapter I elaborate on such acknowledgments and defenses using the Family as an example, and in later chapters further comparisons and analysis put such responses in a larger context.
39. By 2005 the office had reportedly received allegations of child abuse committed by more than 350 perpetrators; see http://www.childprotectionoffice.org/investigation.html (accessed January 20, 2012).
40. Raghunatha Anudasa, "Prabhupada's Magic Cure," initially published on chakra.org and now available from http://www.vnn.org/authors/raghunatha.html (accessed July 16, 2014).
41. Anudasa, "Prabhupada's Magic Cure," 2.
42. Anudasa, 7, "Prabhupada's Magic Cure," 7.
43. See Muster on http://surrealist.org/gurukula/timeline/index.html ((accessed July 16, 2014). In 1999 Dhanurdar was physically attacked by a former gurukuli. See http://www.vnn.org/world/WD9902/WD20-3113.html and http://surrealist.org/gurukula/timeline/docs.html (accessed July 16, 2014).
44. The results were posted on chakra.org, and have since been archived there, at http://oldchakra.com/articles/2000/04/14/survey.results/ (accessed July 16, 2014).
45. Interview, Janet, 2001.
46. Interview, Anna, 2001.
47. This shunning can be compared to silence restriction and isolation used on children and teenagers in the Family. Ward (1995: 111) describes a case in the Family where a young woman was put into isolation. Every morning she had to go to a caravan on the grounds of the home, isolated from fellow members. Some adults would visit her on occasion, and meals were brought to her. This isolation lasted seven weeks.

48. Interview, Janet, 2001.
49. Interview, Frank, 2001.
50. More discussion on this topic can be found on http://www.perefound.org/knsltrs.html (accessed August 17, 2007), where former members have addressed this topic on a number of occasions.
51. Interview, Anna, 2001.
52. Interview, Frank, 2001.
53. Comparisons can be made to other religious movements, including the Roman Catholic Church, where over time a structure developed in which priests who transgressed were protected within the institution over and above the welfare of children (Shupe 1998b; Jacobs 2007).
54. Some critics and former members, however, argued that academics and researchers only received access to special "PR homes" or "media homes" and only spoke with members who had been trained to deal with difficult questions (this was argued in interviews a number of times). They tended to see this, cynically, as a "PR whitewash" exercise. This may be the case, yet the end result is, nonetheless, that the group had opened up to some extent to outside scrutiny and, consequently, was not as isolated as it had been in the past. Of course this is not exactly what concerned the former members I interviewed, who were more preoccupied with "what version" I had been told.
55. For example, the *Loving Jesus Revelation*, where members are encouraged to see themselves as the bride of Jesus, and called to love and serve him with the fervor of a wife, and to include this "heavenly" relationship in their "earthly" relationships, was a controversial teaching. This concept is a radical form of "bridal theology"; the Family explains it as a logical part of the Law of Love, while critics describe it along the lines of "masturbating while praying."
56. The terms "flexible" and "rigid" do not make for sophisticated typologies; rather they are generalizations describing the group and its process of change and adaptation over time. The terms are meant to be descriptive within a context of charismatic and sectarian communities.
57. I speak of relative flexibility, in comparison with sects with strong traditional ties. Charismatic leaders can still create an environment where practice and doctrine are not negotiable, and they can have a strong "top-down" leadership. Yet as a result of their style of leadership, such leaders can implement dramatic changes overnight if they deem them necessary.

CHAPTER 3

1. Here I am relying on K. Erikson's (1966: 10–12) use of the term "boundary maintenance."
2. Sects are by definition minority religions (although some may disagree on definitions of religion employed), but minority religions are not necessarily sectarian.

3. Wallis (1979) introduced a classification system based on movements' views on and relationships with the world at large: world rejecting (who see the world as "evil"), world accommodating (who neither reject nor affirm it), or world affirming (who work with the system of the world).
4. One chapter in Wessinger's book (2000), however, deals with increased accommodation between an enclave, Chen Tao, and authorities after both sides worked to bridge the divide between them.
5. In the case of Cohen's work (1972), the important dynamic was between the social groups (Mods and Rockers) and the media. I argue here that the media had the role of an authority in the sense that the general public relied on them for information regarding perceived (and reported) moral panics.
6. Although the two sides are not always easily separated and identified; some academics denounce other academics for being easily fooled or even dishonest as well. Balch (1998) has questioned one particular research project.
7. This may be somewhat complicated as, because of the often international efforts of the sects, some or many minors may not be citizens of the state, at which point involvement of the state authorities is affected accordingly.
8. For more information on the Branch Davidians, see for example, Wright (1995) and Wessinger (2000).
9. See, for example, Clinton (1996), in which she argued that communities have a responsibility for the welfare of children, which immediately aroused opposition in the United States—namely, 1996 presidential nominee Robert Dole replied that it does not take a village, it takes a family to raise a child.
10. See Michael Bachelard, "Brethren Mother Ignores Court Order," *The Age*, January 27, 2007; and David Marr, "Leave Sect and Kiss Your Children Goodbye," *The Age*, July 12, 2009.
11. The group was founded in the late 1960s in Huntington Beach, California, where David Berg, the founder and leader, and a handful of followers were witnessing to people generally considered to be dropouts and hippies.
12. Also, by the end of the 1980s more members began returning to the United States after having been forced out of a few countries (Bromley and Newton 1994: 43).
13. Since these investigations, however, the Family has undergone further changes, which signal a return to the group's revolutionary days and seclusion from the system. I elaborate on these changes later in this chapter.
14. This was published as a DFO publication, which stands for Disciples and Friends Only. (There are also DO publications for Disciples Only.) Such literature was kept from the general public because of its sensitive nature.
15. There is a parallel to parts of the Pentecostal charismatic movement, as Martyn Percy (1997) argued.
16. See also Millikan (1994: 186).
17. In this chapter I regularly reference Millikan, a theologian who has extensively analyzed the Family's theology. He was one of the first to gain access to Family material as well as key individuals.

18. In the Family, acts of male homosexuality, referred to as "sodomy," was expressly forbidden; it was considered unbiblical. Female homosexuality, on the other hand, was not forbidden. As Berg wrote in *Women in Love*: "But I don't see and I've never been able to find any place in the Bible where it is forbidden to women" (1973: par. 2). However, he did, in the same publication, mention a woman who had never been with a man, and described this as "a form of perversion" (par. 5). Berg concluded that bisexual women were acceptable within the Family doctrine, as long as they were willing to share within the context of the Family's Law of Love.
19. Members explained this to me in interviews, and it is discussed in the Law of Love, which can be accessed online, http://www.thefamilyinternational.org/en/about/our-beliefs/gods-law-love (accessed January 20, 2012).
20. This book was quickly discontinued and is now very difficult to access (also because of an intentional "purge" of certain publications, where members were urged to destroy materials—the original call for this, the "Pubs Purge Advisory", has been scanned at http://www.xfamily.org/index.php/Pubs_Purge_Advisory_June_1991 (accessed July 16, 2014). Millikan, however, has a copy, and discusses it in his 1994 essay (240–241). Parts of it have been scanned and posted on http://www.xfamily.org/index.php/Story_of_Davidito.
21. Millikan (1994), and aspects of this are also discussed on http://www.movingon.org, archived on http://archive.xfamily.org/www.movingon.org.
22. It was first published as a series of individual chapters in 1977 and 1978, and these chapters were recompiled and republished as a book in 1982.
23. It was later archived on http://archive.xfamily.org/www.movingon.org/. This first posting on movingon.org was written using his name, Ricky, but later postings mentioned the name Davidito as well.
24. Ricky uses more disapproving and condemning language regarding Berg's behavior, among that of others, throughout his account; see http://archive.xfamily.org/www.movingon.org/, which has archived his post "Life with Grandpa—The Mene Story."
25. See, for example, Millikan (1994); Melton (1994a, 1994b); Palmer (1994a); and Bromley and Newton (1994).
26. In Argentina, the Family has been involved in eleven investigations since 1987; eight of these were court proceedings against Family members.
27. For more information on these raids, see Lewis and Melton (1994) and *The Family Vindicated* (1997).
28. I elaborate on this topic in chapter 6.
29. See, for example, Lewis and Melton (1994), where one essay refers to "the Inquisition Revisited" (Oliver 1994).
30. See, for example, the Love Charter. This Charter was periodically updated (Family 1998).
31. The Family's leaders have urged followers to destroy literature on a few occasions. Former members have reported drawing bikinis and clothes over pictures of naked followers in publications, and receiving "BAR pubs," burn after reading

publications—to be burned because of incriminating content. See discussions on www.movingon.com (archived on http://archive.xfamily.org/www.movingon.org/), the scanned "Pubs Purge Advisory" on http://www.xfamily.org/index.php/Pubs_Purge_Advisory_June_1991 (accessed July 16, 2014), and Penn (2000: 4). Some BAR literature has been scanned onto http://www.xfamily.org/index.php/Purge (accessed July 16, 2014).

32. Through prophecy, leaders as well as members receive messages from the spirit world (from Berg, Jesus, and other "spirit helpers") that guide them in their day-to-day lives. Such prophecy has assumed greater significance since Berg's death. See Bainbridge (2002).

33. Amsterdam (2002) argues that discipleship is like playing sports professionally, and "[t]o be a pro you have to give your sport everything" (par. 29).

34. See, for example, Williams's (1998) account.

35. Berg (1980) argues that, in contrast to what churches teach, the devil actually hates and fights against sex because it is the most beautiful creation of God.

36. The dance videos featured female members, including underage members, performing erotic dances for Berg. See, for example, Williams (1998) and Jones et al. (2007).

37. This court case is mentioned in chapter 2.

38. The demands posed by Ward (1995) also included limits regarding corporal punishment, silence restriction, isolation, and the use of open heart reports. His demands are listed in the concluding part of the statement.

39. In chapter 5 I elaborate on some types and techniques of denial still involved, and the consequences these have had for some former members.

40. "Denominationalization" was initially described by Niebuhr ([1929] 1957), who used the term to describe sects who accommodated over time (and with the maturation of the second generation) to the surrounding society.

41. There have been several different levels of leadership throughout the history of the Family. By 2007 there were five levels of commitment: Family disciples lived communally and were governed by the rules of the Charter, missionary members were bound by the rules of the Missionary Member Statutes (which has fewer requirements than the Love Charter), fellow members did not live communally and generally worked outside, but tithed 10 percent and lived by the Statement on Fellow Members, and active members and general members received the movement's literature and volunteered to help on specific projects. The 2010 reboot changed all this again.

42. The metaphor "bad apples" here is used differently than previous usage in this chapter. Here "bad apples," as used by the Family, refers to members with a lack of dedication who are weakening the community. Earlier the term has been used to describe those members who misinterpreted Berg's teachings and were abusive or neglectful toward children or other members, and tarnished the Family's reputation.

43. The Charter contained a range of available options for membership, on which I elaborate in a later chapter.
44. According to some, this was not a watertight system. For example, in *The Professionals*, the author of the letter tells the story of a young member who was reprimanded and disciplined despite there being no evidence of wrongdoing. A shepherd had asked God and reportedly received, through prophecy, information that this young member was guilty. The author of the letter, however, claims that he was there and knows firsthand that the young member was not involved in any wrongdoing (Amsterdam 2002).
45. Although there were no clear guidelines to distinguish between typical teenage attitudes and moods and "wrong attitude" or "bad spirit."
46. A reference to the biblical Gideon, who whittled down his army from over thirty thousand to three hundred dedicated soldiers. See D. Berg (1989).
47. I elaborate on this subject in the next chapter.
48. This was, after all, the term used by a second-generation member of the Family, as mentioned in chapter 2.
49. I elaborate on this topic in chapter 6.
50. Comparing the discourses at the time between Family-run websites such as http://www.myconclusion.com and others such as http://www.myreaction.net (created to provide commentary, mostly by former members, on articles posted on the former site) and http://www.movingon.org highlights this dynamic. Myconclusion.com has "taken a new direction" and archived its old material, myreaction.net is closed but present as an archive, and movingon.org has been closed and archived on http://archive.xfamily.org/www.movingon.org/.

CHAPTER 4

1. A response to *Mama's Moron Missives* archived on http://www.newdaynews.com/resource/ricky-3.htm (accessed January 20, 2012).
2. See, for example, Conway and Siegelman (1978); Hassan (1988); and Singer and Ofshe (1990).
3. There has been a significant evolution in socialization theory, which I elaborate on in a later chapter. For the moment, however, I concentrate on social-psychological and sociological approaches that focus on the ongoing interaction between the individual and society, which inherently engenders change. This interaction must be understood as a two-way interaction. In Wrong's (1961: 183) words, people are "social, though never fully socialised"; they may internalise social norms but they may also choose to not live up to these social norms.
4. Kai Erikson (1966) argues that deviancy is actually a necessary and important part of the ongoing process of the formation of communities, and of socialization, as individuals and communities then learn where the boundaries are drawn.

5. They may reach the status of clear or operating Thetan as freezoners or independent Scientologists (these are people who follow Hubbard's teachings outside the Scientology organization), but their status would not be accepted by those in the Scientology organization.
6. And are the opinions shared or divided? Such pressures can cause much tension within the group, and if opinions are divided, sectarian divisions may occur, causing much upheaval.
7. See, for example, Hong (1998).
8. One of the members I interviewed suggested that the first wave of children were somewhat neglected, and as a result they did not build the type of bond the younger children developed as a result of the camps, retreats and workshops that were later created for the second generation (interview, Justin, 1999).
9. See, for example, Rubin (n.d.) and his book on the Bruderhof (2000).
10. There are several levels of adaptation here; parents, teachers, and other community members disciplining individual children for transgressions, and leadership defining certain transgressions as deviant and institutionalizing disciplining measures to manage this deviancy. I concentrate on the social process of the institutionalization and management of deviance within these sects.
11. Interview, Justin, 1999.
12. Or, of course, the acts previously considered deviant could become part of the norm and no longer be considered transgressions.
13. In the next few chapters I describe how such labeling largely directs the interaction between the parents and the sects on the one hand and the children and young members on the other. The latter, as a result of their experiences and the associated labeling, also often grouped together to create a community of outcasts, either within or outside the religious groups.
14. The stereotypes as I have named them are admittedly simplistic (i.e., "baddie" and "goodie"), but they are the most representative of the explicit and implicit conveyed meanings of the polarized labels used by the parents and others within the religious groups.
15. Some might disagree with the statement that the adult children make "their own" decisions, arguing instead that they were indoctrinated from the start. However, this creates a tautological argument, as their actions and decisions are then dismissed as mere consequences of or reactions to ill-defined indoctrination. I align myself with the more interactionist theories that involve the child and young person as an active agent in the socialization process (Jenks 1996; James, Jenks, and Prout 1997), as no matter how sectarian the group, I have consistently found individuals who questioned the status quo of the culture in which they were socialized.
16. I noticed on occasion that when sitting in on gossip between young members I would hear stories about those who were baddies and had left, yet when talking with parents or leaders they would tell me about the same person but explain

their actions differently and describe the individual as troubled. I suspect that both labels may be used depending on the speaker and the audience.
17. High School Association for the Research of Principles, Collegiate Association for the Research of Principles, and related organizations.
18. The reasons for fund-raising changed over time, hence less indemnity did not safeguard the blessed children from fund-raising.
19. Interestingly, this was the terminology used by parents, leaders, and others inside the group. A former member described the goodies as "robotic"—especially those who had "gotten the victory" in Victor camps. He accused these members of having given up thinking for themselves (interview, Stephen, 2001).
20. Their use of language points to their awareness of where the first generation drew the line—the limits of what was considered acceptable behavior.
21. Here they are mostly behavioral aspects attributed to spiritual issues, as is the norm in the Family. But were these rebels to leave after failure to conform, I would expect the labeling to switch to them being troubled or baddies.
22. Although they will be allowed back once they show they have changed their ways, regained their faith, and found the way again. In other words, once they adapt.
23. An interesting comparison here is the literature about apostasy and apostates (Shupe and Bromley 1981; Shupe 1998a).
24. I elaborate on Vandaris in the following chapter.
25. I elaborate on this in the following chapter.
26. Interview, Anna, 2001.
27. Although it is important to note here that even the baddies have always the option to return, as long as they can change and adapt their attitude, behavior, and spiritual state.

CHAPTER 5

1. This relationship of pushes and pulls can also work exactly the other way for members who have had less positive or occasionally traumatic experiences and who wish to leave.
2. The topic of familiarity is important; it is something the "renegades" seek outside when leaving and often find with other former members. This theme has parallels to migrants—where familiarity is linked to settlement in an area where others from the same place have already established themselves and hence have prepared a haven of familiarity. Former members frequently make similar choices. I elaborate on this in the following chapter.
3. Nadine Pleil, another former member, provides a description of this library, shipped from England during the war, and which postwar received sizable donations from people in England, Germany, and America (1994: 64).
4. Interview, Anna, 2001.

5. This is an aspect of the implicit learning (of concepts, meanings, conduct, etc.) mentioned earlier in the discussion of socialization.
6. The strength and content of these idealizations of "goodness within" versus "badness outside" are likely to eventually change if members leave, depending on their experiences and fortunes "outside." Then, in hindsight, and within a different system of meanings, their autobiography may undergo significant changes.
7. Interview, Sam, 2001.
8. Note the use of the terms "sarcastic" and "pessimistic" in connection with nonmembers. This is interesting in light of discussion in the previous chapter, where a UC rebel was described in similar terms and criticized for his "negative attitude."
9. Purity is a very important doctrine in the church as a whole. Moon teaches that purity was lost in the Garden of Eden, as a result of the actions of Eve. As Eve tempted Adam, he lost his purity as well. But it was Eve who made Adam fall, and consequently she bears most of the responsibility—as do women, according to Moon. But his aim is to even out this inequality for the coming generations, and to restore purity in both men and women. The parents, through the blessing, have created a foundation on which the children could be born without "fallen nature," hence pure.
10. "Blessing and Ideal Family by Reverend Sun Myung Moon," chapter 1, part 2, *The Love of True Man and Woman*, http://www.unification.net/bif/bif-1-2.html, (accessed January 20, 2012).
11. This is, in Unificationist theology, the way to maintain one's purity. Marrying anyone other than a blessed child would be defiling, and it would break the purity of the lineage created by the blessing of the parents.
12. Although another reason he gives for wanting to marry within is: "And then, you don't have to explain your life as much."
13. This strong sense of community has not always been there for blessed children. I discuss this in a later chapter.
14. Part of the reason why the rebels challenge aspects of the groups is because they recognize the positive aspects and are not ready to leave the whole package behind.
15. Interview, Sally, 2000.
16. This is in stark contrast with the majority of the literature originating from other missionary groups and churches that describes the Family as heretical and cultic. See, for example, entries on apologetics websites such as www.apologeticsindex.org and www.watchman.org.
17. Interview, Nadine, 1998.
18. "Misunderstoods" are, according to Scientology teaching, the most important barrier to study, and "the only reason a person gives up a study or becomes confused or unable to learn" (*Basic Study Manual* [1990], preface).
19. Interview, Kevin, 2002.

20. The workshops were retreats, or camps, for young members to spend time together, bond, and learn about the Divine Principle.
21. There is an interesting similarity here to the literature about institutionalization (such as Goffman's [1968] *Asylum* and Clemmer's [1958] concept of "prisonization") that alludes to the way segregation in a closed environment can progressively incapacitate one for life outside the environment in question. Another striking parallel can be made with Punch's (1977) conclusions to his research into Dartington Hall School, a progressive boarding school, during the 1960s. Punch argued that the head of the school had created an "anti-institution" in his desire to innovate education and liberate pupils and enable them to become a new type of man or woman—a culture-free individual. Yet in the end, adjustments to the "realities" of the wider society proved "abrasive" to some respondents, and the head of Dartington had to admit that his modern school might be accused of having produced "neurotic misfits," incapable of adjusting to the world outside Dartington school.
22. The Pennsylvania-Dutch, as they are known, are perhaps more accurately described as Pennsylvania Deutsch or Dietsch, since they are of German origin, not Dutch.
23. See, for example, Hostetler (1993) and Kraybill (1989), as well as a documentary about Rumspringa (Walker 2003).
24. For more information on the authority structure of the Bruderhof, see Rubin (1993); Hostetler (1993); and Zablocki (1971).
25. She never did achieve the "success" she was aiming for, acceptance into the Brotherhood, which reinforces the view of adaptation as a process of trial and error into a possibly crudely constructed idealization—her view of the Bruderhof. I say here "crudely constructed" because clearly her idea of "success" and how to achieve this was different from that held by her elders.
26. I discuss this further in the following chapter.
27. I have met Family members who appeared more withdrawn and introverted, and it seems there is certainly room for a variety of personal styles, as there are a variety of tasks and responsibilities within the movement. There is, however, also evidence of what are referred to as "personality types" (treated as a personality issue rather than behavior) being deemed undesirable, as Maria has published letters denouncing "lazy" and "complacent" members for their attitude and spirit (e.g., Maria 1999).
28. For charter members and those in the mission field, life is communal and most goods are shared aside from allocated pocket money.
29. See, for example, Maria's letter *The Shakeup 2000* (1999b) and the following one, *Jesus Is Calling You Back to the Beginning* (1999a).
30. Maria's *Shakeup 2000* (1999b) is one such example.
31. For example, Moon's extramarital affairs would seem unacceptable according to the Divine Principle (where adultery is described as a grave sin). However, Moon's behavior has been justified by way of an old teaching that had not been officially disseminated before, P'ikareun. For more on this, see Hong (1998), chapter 1.

32. See, for example, Festinger, Riecken, and Schachter (1956).
33. There were also fund-raising and witnessing projects in London.
34. See Bainbridge (2002). This is a significant and interesting example of Weber's charismatic succession—ideas can still change as the result of one person's prophecy from Berg or other influential figures.
35. If second-generation adults reside in the same home as their parents, they can marry at the age of seventeen; otherwise the age of consent is eighteen.
36. This was a new membership level until 2011, which had evolved over time (from "tithing member" and "turf supporter" to "fellow member"). Since 2012 the organization of membership changed again with the "reboot."
37. See Geros Kunkel (European second generation blessing director), *The New Matching Procedure, the Joint Responsibility of Us Blessed Families*, lecture, Chamarande, France, November 3, 2002, http://www.tparents.org/Library/Unification/Talks/Kunkel/Kunkel-021103.htm (accessed January 20, 2012).
38. Many gurukula veterans, however, would argue that ISKCON has not adapted enough—or even that the organization has made the changes only to protect itself, as mentioned in chapter 2.
39. This conclusion is based on interviews in 2001 with teachers and members of the UK community, where the ashrams and schools have not had as problematic a history as some of those in the United States and India. As a result, the relations between the first and second generations in the United Kingdom are less polarized. Later chapters incorporate more data on some US members.
40. Interview, ISKCON teachers, United Kingdom, 2001.
41. In contrast, she argued, the first generation members are more judgmental toward each other.
42. This is reflected in discussions held at the time of the Turley case, where elder gurukulis were suggesting younger gurukulis were throwing the baby out with the bathwater (Dasa 1999). See also Parker (2001) and Anudasa (2000).
43. Similarly, Rochford (1999: 44) found that second-generation members who went to normal schools found ways of "passing" (fitting in with nondevotee children) and blending into the secular world, yet did not lose their religious identity in the process, even if they became less involved in the practice and lifestyle of Krishna consciousness.
44. Some are steadfast unbelievers, as I describe in the next chapter.
45. This is significantly different from groups with a Judeo-Christian tradition, where paths to salvation are not as negotiable and passed down to the next generation as "the way." Social and group dynamics, however, can change even the most relativistic of teachings and New Age groups can develop "absolutist" approaches to "the way things are done" and how to achieve one's spiritual goal.
46. Hardman (1999: 227–228) also argued that the members of the second generation are more likely to remain with the group as adults if they have been raised with this sense of absolutism—if their sense of self is constructed within a

framework of a belief in one absolute Truth, an external source of authority, and a notion of the child as essentially fallible and thereby requiring external correction and guidance.
47. Interview, Kevin, 2002.

CHAPTER 6

1. (Part III opening page text): For example, over twenty people contacted Inform between 1996 and April 2007 who were members of a sectarian community in the past but left. This number is problematic for several reasons: many inquiries to Inform are anonymous, and in the past inquiries were coded differently. Also, Inform is known first and foremost as an information center, not a support agency, hence people looking for support may not think of contacting Inform (and, after all, they don't need information about the groups they came from). However, those who did contact Inform were seeking advice and support. Similarly, the International Cultic Studies Association organizes workshops for former members, and since 2007 also workshops for second-generation former members.
2. This video can be found on http://www.xfamily.org/index.php/Ricky_Rodriguez_video in several formats.
3. This difference between the two "worlds" and the necessary adjustment work is also likely to encourage the former member to reinterpret past events, norms, and beliefs in an unfavorable light. I elaborate on this later in the chapter.
4. Personal communication and unpublished paper sent to me (2001).
5. God's Day is one of the main holidays in the UC, celebrated on the day of the Western new year.
6. Interview, Marianne, 1998.
7. Interview, Stephen, 2001.
8. Those who attended the camps make for an interesting parallel with Festinger et al.'s (1956) theory of cognitive dissonance. In the case of those who were not severely disciplined, the members did not have this incentive, as Stephen argues, to adjust their dissonance, and this, mixed with teenage disillusionment and differentiation from parents, eventually led to their rebellion.
9. Interview, Stephen, 2002. Berg's "One Wife" teaching redefined the family unit—everyone within the community being "one family" and, in a sense, married to everyone else.
10. Interview, Stephen, 2002.
11. Although Marianne left with her mother, she reported having been disillusioned as well and, in hindsight, argues that she was happy to leave the Family at the time.
12. Interview, Sam, 2001.
13. Interview, Janet, 2001.
14. Interview, Meredith, 2006. I discuss Meredith's experience in more detail later in this chapter.

15. XN publications are Family comic books for ages twelve and up. The definition of Vandaris comes from Maria, who claims to have received it through prophecy from David Berg.
16. Interview, Scientology staff member, 2000.
17. During a word-clearing action the student has to read text aloud while a tutor follows along and helps the student through usual "clearing" exercises (such as looking up the word and checking progress with the e-meter), until the student can read the text out loud without stumbling or hesitating.
18. Interview, Scientology staff member, 2000.
19. Interview, Meredith, 2006.
20. Interview, Meredith, 2006.
21. Interview, Frank, 2001. No person who is not a baptized member of the Bruderhof may participate in the Lord's Supper, a highly significant event within the community.
22. From an inquiry to Inform in 2005.
23. These are former members who left within a decade or two after the Great Crisis. See also Hostetler (n.d.).
24. From communication with a Family representative, September 19, 2007.
25. In Inform archive.
26. Of course one cannot generalize and individual families may have different interpretations of old doctrine, new teachings, and pedagogical suggestions. The Unification Church has members from a variety of cultural backgrounds, and these backgrounds account for differences in child-rearing practices as well—the Eastern cultural values being generally stricter than the Western ones. However, as one young member argued, there is now peer pressure from "hardcore BCs" which results in a lack of flexibility toward peers who attempt to stretch the boundaries and experiment with the accepted norms and practices. (See the discussion in chapter 5.)
27. I first heard the term "middle management" applied to parents at an American Family Foundation conference on May 29–31, 1998, titled "Children and Cults," in a talk by the late Margaret Singer. Singer argued, along similar lines to Landa, that in many cases parents in cults are not those who make the majority of pedagogical decisions for their children because they have relegated their parental authority to the leaders of their religious group. The foundation became the International Cultic Studies Association in 2004.
28. Her definition describes any "cult" as a religious or nonreligious organization with a "covert mission to accumulate wealth and/or power, to benefit its leadership." This is not exactly a value-free supposition, and suggests that cults are by definition immoral. Included in this discourse is an assumption that cults necessarily commit child abuse.
29. Not only does Landa frequently generalize from particulars, she does not offer a very precise definition of her subject matter (cults), making the article overall quite unclear. It is also contradictory in places. For example, on one hand Landa

argues that parents stand by and sometimes even aid abuse as a result of "learned helplessness" (9), yet on the other hand she later argues that deviant behavior incorporated into cult doctrine is considered normal by cult members (12). Following the latter argument, parents would not necessarily need to suffer from "learned helplessness" to allow, and be involved in, what is considered normal or even good behavior in the group, but deviant behavior in mainstream society.

30. Barker (2002) argues there are different types of cult-watching groups, each type having its own agenda, biases, and so forth—and consequently all types come to different conclusions.
31. In practice secular (nonsectarian) support organizations often suffer from lack of funding, which also affects the extent to which they can offer support.
32. Although, again, one cannot generalize. Former members have contacted Inform but would engage only after ensuring we had no religious agenda. One second-generation former Jehovah's Witness specifically complained about a particular support organization that, she claimed, tried to convert her to its particular interpretation of Christianity, which greatly upset her.
33. Although the use of the term is not always limited to accusations regarding methodology; polemics frequently enter the debate (Robbins and Robertson 1991; Barker 2002).
34. Those NRMs that came to the West and were controversial in the 1970s are demographically similar in the sense that their second generation grew up and started making their own decisions at around the same time, in contrast to nineteenth-century sects (such as the Church of Jesus Christ of Latter Day Saints and the Watchtower Society), who are now dealing with their third, fourth, and further generations.
35. The American Family Foundation, "Children and Cults"; Fecris, a pan-European cult-watching group, held a conference in Barcelona on May 15–15, 2002, similarly titled "Children in Cults."
36. Rock's research was on collective responses of bereaved people to the aftermath of violent death. Although the types of transgressions in my research generally cannot be compared to violent death, the collective responses and the creation of self-help groups, I believe, can be.
37. Some former members argue that this alientation is justified because of the abuse they suffered within the religious movement, and they do not want a dialogue unless the group or parents apologize and change.
38. The letter was posted on http://www.perefound.org/archives.html (accessed January 20, 2012).
39. For more information on the relationship between Children of the Bruderhof International and the Bruderhof, see Rubin (2002) and the court case, http://www.perefound.org/B_vs_3.html (accessed January 20, 2012).
40. See the 1997 New York Supreme Court case, Bruderhof communities v. the Peregrine Foundation, Ramon Sender, Julius H. Rubin and S. Blair Purcell, individually, http://www.perefound.org/B_vs_3.html (accessed January 20, 2012).

41. Bruderhof communities v. the Peregrine Foundation.
42. One of the defendants, also a former member of the Bruderhof, had been broadcast on a radio station, asserting: "We're out to destroy the Bruderhof" (Bruderhof communities v. the Peregrine Foundation).
43. Bruderhof communities v. the Peregrine Foundation. The academic involved, Rubin, was still the subject of a strategic lawsuit against public participation. This process is described in more detail in Rubin (2002). He has had an ongoing dispute with the Bruderhof as well; his 1997 essay *The Other Side of Joy* was included in an edited SPCK publication. The Bruderhof put pressure on the publishers to pull the chapter, which the publishers eventually did (Bruderhof communities v. the Peregrine Foundation).
44. Movingon.org was eventually closed down by the founder, who said she wanted to "move on with her life." Since then other former members have tried to revive the site. It has been archived on http://archive.movingon.org/ (accessed July 17, 2014).
45. See the section on high-demand organizations on the website http://www.safepassagefoundation.org (accessed September 12, 2007) for more information on this.
46. For example, in 2003 communication on movingon.org revolved around a Brazilian Family community that had been partially excommunicated. The foundation worked to mobilize people to help those who wanted to take this opportunity to leave the Family, and also sent information (via friends and relatives) to the members in Brazil with information on ways to best get funds together and leave the country, and where to go from there. The communication was archived on http://archive.xfamily.org/www.movingon.org/.
47. Although both the Safe Passage Foundation and movingon.org offer to help those in legal battles with the Family, individuals as well as authorities.
48. See, for example, discussion on http://www.myconclusion.com and http://www.myreaction.net and open letters, from the Family and to the Family, posted on the movingon.org website, archived on http://archive.xfamily.org/www.movingon.org/.
49. A few examples are Clambake on http://www.xenu.net, http://www.whyaretheydead.net and http://www.factnet.org/scientology-dianetics-0. More recently, www.exscientologykids.com has been an important resource for those born or raised in the movement to seek support upon leaving.
50. One of the creators is the niece of David Miscavige, the leader of Scientology (his official title is chairman of the Board of Religious Technology Centre). This website has grown and includes many discussions forums.
51. Tapestry against Polygamy was founded in 2000 as a nonprofit organization in Salt Lake City, Utah, that advocates against the human rights violations it considers inherent in polygamy. It provides assistance to individuals leaving polygamous groups. The organization had a site on http://www,polygamy.org (offline on January 20, 2012). Interestingly, soon afterward, http://www.anti-polygamy.org

was created, which, despite its name, is a propolygamy site that positions itself against Tapestry against Polygamy and other organizations like it, as it states: "unravelling the tapestry of anti-polygamy".
52. Winston (2005) has written about such "Hassidic Rebels."
53. See news articles on http://www.hillel.org.il/en/media (accessed July 17, 2014).
54. For instance, Tapestry against Polygamy wants to offer support for those who leave but it also campaigns against polygamy, and lobbies the government to act on what is, officially, an illegal practice in the United States. This, of course, causes great conflict between the organization and the polygamous communities.
55. This is reminiscent of Durkheim's (1893) argument that deviation performs a service by drawing people together in a common posture of anger and indignation, making them focus on what they have in common.
56. One might almost say that the stratification shows up the difference between, to generalize, the children of the new religious movement and the children of the denomination—the denomination being older and more experienced than the new religion, having adapted to the wider society. Interestingly, Barker has noticed, in her recent research (as of yet unpublished) on the Unification Church, that more members of the first cohort of the second generation have left than of later cohorts.
57. By "community siblings" I mean siblings in the sense that these children have grown up together, if not in each other's direct vicinity, then at least within similar communities and contexts. They often refer to each other as "brother" and "sister."
58. These discussions have been archived on http://www.chakra.org/discussions/gurukula.html and http://www.vnn.org/search/index.html. Good examples are Anudasa (2000) and Parker (2001).
59. Later in the same post the author writes to his or her contemporaries: "We simply can not hold it against our little brothers and sisters still in. They don't know any better. They aren't old enough to know the truth." On http://groups.able2know.org/xfamily/topic/48-3 (accessed on January 20, 2012.
60. Interview, Justin, KIT staff member, 2002.
61. Interestingly, according to Justin the younger cohorts of children also do not understand the Great Crisis.
62. Interview, Justin, 2002.
63. Interview, Joyce, 2002. Joyce has fostered several young adults from one particular religious community that is communal. In order to respect her confidentiality I will not mention the name of the religious community.
64. Inform had been helping individual young former members who had left, but was not founded for this particular purpose, and has been unable to secure funding for particular projects with this focus.
65. From an address by Secretary General Gro Braekken of Save the Children Norway, titled "Their Stories Made a Deep Impression," at the Go On conference on November 12, 2001, in Oslo, translated from Norwegian on location.

66. Address by Project Manager Turid Berger, "The Beginning and Objectives of Go On—and Experiences along the Way," Go On conference, Oslo, November 2001.
67. Berger, "Beginning."
68. Berger, "Beginning."
69. It was a small-scale project, and unlike research projects it had no stated or consistent methodology. Go On had in-depth contact with thirteen young adults and twenty adults, and received inquiries from approximately sixty to seventy others. Altogether it had contact with approximately one hundred people.
70. Michael, a former member of the Family, speaking at the Go On conference on November 12, 2001, on a panel where he was interviewed by Dag Hareide and Ellen Kartness.
71. From written communication to the author, 2001.
72. Michael Bachelard, "Brown Demands Sect Inquiry," *The Age*, December 27, 2006, and "Sect Asked for Power to Prevent Child Visits," *The Age*, December 27, 2006.
73. Michael Bachelard, "Brethren Chief Tells Girl to Disown Dad," *The Age*, December 26, 2006 .
74. I am not judging here whether the changes were sufficient and successful. Opinion has been divided on this subject, which I discussed at the end of chapter 3.
75. See, as mentioned before, www.myconclusion.com versus www.myreaction.net, both now archived.
76. Especially in online discourse. In in-depth interviews a more nuanced story emerges, but online discussions are rarely conducive to nuances.
77. Here I am not discussing what some may consider the "true" version, or the "Truth." The former members may be making money selling their story to the media (this may be because they do not have the necessary paperwork, skills, etc. for most employment and hence a salary), and the current members may be consciously or unconsciously embellishing good points while glossing over problems. This may be because they have a job and spouse and children in the movement who are dependent on them and are working to minimize any cognitive dissonance (Festinger et al. 1956). I am merely looking at the ways in which each party devalues the other.
78. This again is reminiscent of the work by Festinger et al. (1956) where a setback, in Festinger's case a failed prophecy, was followed by more intense proselytizing.
79. Interview, Family member, 2001.
80. From written communication to the author, 2001.
81. From written communication to the author, 2001.
82. From written communication to the author, 2001. "One Wife" is the term used in the Family to connote that everyone is married to anyone else; everyone shares one symbolic wife.
83. Interview, parent, 2001.
84. Of course here I am generalizing, but this has been the case with groups such as ISKCON, the Family, and the Unification Church. Groups such as the Bruderhof

and the Exclusive Brethren, on the other hand, have retained their social boundaries. The Bruderhof will allow contact, as long as a former member does not contact other former members or *KIT*. More research is needed on this topic.
85. Interview, Stephen, 2002.
86. Glazer and Strauss argue that "[a] prominent source of a passage 'going out of shape' is an incompetent or inappropriate agent" (1971: 77).
87. Interview, Stephen, 2002. The Latin word "limen" literally means "a threshold," and in the theories of rites of passage by Gennep (1960) and Turner (1986) this passage involves changes to the participants—especially in their social status. This stage comes, by definition, with ambiguity as one identity is dissolved in order to bring about a transition.

CHAPTER 7

1. The Hebrew title of Numbers, the fourth book in the Old Testament of the Bible, means "In the Wilderness." It continues the narrative, begun in the book of Exodus, of Israel's journey from Egypt to Canaan, the Promised Land. Douglas has used this title for a variety of works based on this narrative. In a separate article she studied Leviticus, where diet and bloodline are described in detail. At the time, she argued, these boundaries were important; the Israelites were moving from one culture to another, and while they were in limbo, "in the wilderness," they established new rules in order to unify their group and create boundaries in regard to "others"—hence create a group identity. Bloodlines tied them together and diet set them apart from others (Douglas 1970). This is interesting in light of chapter 6, where I described how the young former members frequently grouped together in new communities of opposition to the one from which they came. Similar themes have come up in migration studies.
2. According to biblical sources, murmuring reveals a "rebellious heart," i.e., Deuteronomy 1: 26, 27: "Nevertheless you would not go up, but rebelled against the command of the Lord your God. And you murmured." The murmuring of the Hebrews in the wilderness reportedly called forth the displeasure of God, which was only averted by the earnest prayer of Moses (Num. 11:33, 34; 12, 14:27, 30, 31, 16:3, 21:4–6, Ps. 106:25). Murmuring was forbidden by Paul (1 Cor. 10:10).
3. Nora, unpublished MS, 2001.
4. These are all "symptoms" mentioned throughout by K. Erikson (1994); he explores different ways people have reached a state of anomie. Having been raised in a sect is perhaps not entirely comparable to the types of disaster described by Erikson, but the resulting feeling of anomie can be compared. In both cases individuals believed they could not trust the world around them anymore, and that their rhythm of life had been totally turned upside down.
5. Interview, Joyce, 2002.

6. E. Erikson (1968) famously developed the term "identity crisis" to refer to persons who had lost a sense of personal sameness and historical continuity, and connected this to life stages where individuals' social roles had not been developed. Later theorists developed the crossovers between the psychological concepts of identity and the sociological concepts of social roles, and a more complicated image of identity emerged. See, for example, Goffman (1963); Mead (1967); Berger (1963); Deleuze and Guattari (1972, 1987); and Ricoeur (1994).
7. Nora, unpublished MS, 2001, and written communication with the author; emphasis in the original.
8. Nora, unpublished MS, 2001.
9. Although socialization is a lifelong process, I refer to primary and secondary socialization here to underline how different the two types of enculturation, child learning and adult learning, are frequently perceived to be for young people who have come out of sectarian communities.
10. I am here paraphrasing a theme from my interviews and research and will not elaborate on the reported assumption of an intrinsic identity, will, or individuality.
11. In this sense the young former members' sense of disconnection can be compared with that experienced by migrants and asylum seekers—the latter also being "in exile" and in unfamiliar territory. Interestingly, this is not a common comparison in the literature discussing cults and NRMs.
12. The best example of such a theory refers to a "sudden personality change" as "snapping" (Conway and Siegelman 1978).
13. But the debate does continue. See, for example, Zablocki and Robbins (2002).
14. Foucault put the emphasis differently, and described power as the capacity both to repress (negative) and produce (positive). Repression prohibits and constrains, setting limits to what agents do or might desire. Production creates, guides pleasure, forms knowledge, and produces discourse. More specifically, it produces "subjects," forging their character and normalizing them, rendering them capable of and willing to adhere to norms of sanity, health, sexuality, and other forms of propriety (see Foucault 1980: 119; Lukes 2005: 91). Foucault (1980) argues that these norms "mould the soul" and are "inscribed upon the body." But Lukes and Foucault disagree over the extent to which power can "mould" an individual. Lukes (2005: 92) argues that Foucault undermined the rational, autonomous moral agent.
15. Lukes describes a study by Hayward of two schools where social exclusion and feelings of social superiority were internalized by the pupils at the schools. Hayward is not arguing that the power lies with the teachers and the pedagogy, rather that it operates impersonally by "shaping the field of the possible" (Hayward qtd. in Lukes 2005: 104).
16. This is similar to Bourdieu's theory of the acquisition and maintenance of *habitus*—where people see their conditions as natural and even value them, failing to

recognize the sources of their desires and beliefs (2000). Lukes's concept of power also overlaps with the sociological theories of Berger and Luckmann (1967), who argue that people create and re-create their own realities—but these realities are a result of internalization of the objective (reified) structures around them.
17. These theories, again, are similar to Bourdieu's (1990, 2000) theory of *habitus*.
18. See chapter 5 for a more detailed introduction to her research.
19. This is a feeling also frequently described by what is generally referred to as "third culture kids," children who have been raised between cultures, such as missionary children or army children (Pollock and Reken 1999). There is, of course, also much comparison to migration.
20. Interview, Joyce, 2001.
21. Joyce described a similar sentiment when she spoke about Alan earlier in the chapter.
22. Inform.
23. Inform.
24. Interview, ISKCON teachers, 2001. More about this shift in lifestyle is discussed in chapter 2; for further information see Rochford (2001).
25. Interview, ISKCON teachers, 2001.
26. Interview, ISKCON teachers, 2001.
27. Written communication from Madhu, 2005.
28. Nora, unpublished MS, 2001.
29. Interview, Anna, 2001.
30. Interview, Janet, 2001.
31. Interview, Stephen, 2001.
32. Interview, Stephen, 2001. Stephen is referring to the powers Family children were supposed to gain when, according to their beliefs, Jesus returns in the new millennium. These powers include the ability to walk through walls, fly, travel through time, and more. In some cases children, teenagers, and young adults were taught they would have these powers in a matter of years.
33. Of course one can also resist a group identity, reject it, exchange it for another, and so on. Much of this research is about people who rebel against their identity, leave their identity behind, select a new identity, shape it, and so on. Although there is an aspect of labeling throughout this process, there is also an aspect of choice where the agents opt for one identity over another.
34. This is discussed at length in chapters 5 and 6.
35. In this example there is, of course, also a history of physical dominance, including violence, which will significantly affect one's choices and decisions.
36. In these cases violence has been a factor as well.
37. Nora, unpublished MS, 2001.
38. Go On conference, Oslo, November 12, 2001.
39. Interview, Stephen, 2001.
40. Interview, Stephen, 2001.

41. Interview, Stephen, 2002.
42. Interview, Marianne, 1998.
43. From written communication from Madhu, 2005, emphasis in original.
44. Although this is doctrinally the case, she reported she was sexually abused as a child.
45. Inform.
46. Originally on movingon.org, archived on http://archive.xfamily.org/www.movingon.org/article.asp%3FsID=3%26Cat=20%26ID=866.html (accessed January 20, 2012). Zerby is Maria's (whose given name is Karen) surname. Along the same lines, a video game named Vandari's Revenge allows the player to pelt the "King and Queen" with a number of items such as eggs and tomatoes (http://archive.xfamily.org/www.movingon.org/games/vgame.asp.html).

CONCLUSION

1. Interestingly, this is what some outsiders have accused them, the converts, of—being "victims" of the sect's "indoctrination" and "middle management," not able to be responsible for their offspring, and not "thinking for themselves."

References

ABBREVIATIONS IN FAMILY REFERENCES

DFO: Disciples and Friends Only
DO: Disciples Only
GN: General Newsletter
GP: Old designation for Mo Letters
ML: Mo Letter
XN: Designation for Family comic books

Amsterdam, P. (2002). *The Professionals—An Open Answer to an Open Letter*. World Services, the Family.

Amsterdam, P. and Apollos (1993). *Our Beliefs concerning the Lord's Law of Love*. The Family. GN 555/DO 2858.

Anudasa, R. (2000). "Nimala Has Stolen My Day in Court: An Open Letter to Mr. Turley." Retrieved September 18, 2006, from http://www.oldchakra.com/articles/2000/09/14/turley.responds/index.htm.

Apollos (1996). *The Loving Jesus Revelation*. World Services, the Family. ML #3077, GN 703.

Arnold, J. C. (1996). *A Plea for Purity: Sex, Marriage and God*. Farmington, PA: Plough Publishing House; Robertsbridge, UK: Bruderhof Community.

Atack, J. (1990). *A Piece of Blue Sky: Scientology, Dianetics and L. Ron Hubbard Exposed*. New York: Lyle Smart.

Bainbridge, W. S. (2002). *The Endtime Family: Children of God*. Albany: State University of New York Press.

Balch, R. W. (1998). "How the Problem of Malfeasance Gets Overlooked in Studies of New Religions: An Examination of the AWARE Study of the Church Universal and Triumphant." *Wolves within the Fold: Religious Leadership and Abuses of Power*. Ed. A. Shupe. New Brunswick, NJ: Rutgers University Press, 191–211.

Barker, E. (1983). "Doing Love: Tensions in the Ideal Family." *The Family and the Unificaiton Church*. Ed. G. G. James. Barrytown, NY: Unification Theological Seminary; Rose of Sharon Press, 35–52.

Barker, E. (1984). *The Making of a Moonie: Brainwashing or Choice?* Oxford: Basil Blackwell.

Barker, E. (1986). "Religious Movements: Cult and Anti-Cult since Jonestown." *Annual Review of Sociology* 12: 329–346.

Barker, E. (1995a). "Plus ça change…" *Social Compass* 42(2): 165–180.

Barker, E. (1995b). "The Scientific Study of Religion? You Must Be Joking!" *Journal for the Scientific Study of Religion* 34(3): 287–310.

Barker, E. (1995c). "The Unification Church." Miller 1995: 223–229.

Barker, E. (2002). "Watching for Violence: A Comparative Analysis of the Roles of Five Cult-Watching Groups." *Cults, Religion and Violence*. Ed. D. G. Bromley and J. G. Melton. Cambridge: Cambridge University Press, 123–148.

Barker, E. (2004). "General Overview of the 'Cult Scene' in Great Britain." *New Religious Movements in the Twenty-First Century: Legal, Political, and Social Challenges in Global Perspective*. Ed. P. C. Lucas and T. Robbins. New York: Routledge, 22–28.

Barker, E. (2007). "In God's Name: Practicing Unconditional Love to the Death." *Exercising Power: The Role of Religions in Concord and Conflict*. Ed. T. Ahlbäck and B. Dahla. Åbo, Finland: Donner Institute, 11–25.

Barrett, D. V. (2001). *The New Believers: Sects, "Cults" and Alternative Religions*. London: Cassell.

Basic Study Manual: Based on the Works of L. Ron Hubbard (1990). Los Angeles, CA: Bridge Publications.

Becker, H. S. ([1963] 1973). *Outsiders: Studies in the Sociology of Deviance*. New York: Free Press.

Beckford, J. (1985). *Cult Controversies: The Societal Response to the New Religious Movements*. London: Tavistock.

Beckford, J. A. (1995). "Cults, Conflicts and Journalists." *New Religions and the New Europe*. Ed. R. Towler. Aarhus, Denmark: Aarhus University Press, 99–111.

Beckford, J. A. (2003). *Social Theory and Religion*. Cambridge: Cambridge University Press.

Bednarowski, M. F. (1995). "The Church of Scientology: Lightning Rod for Cultural Boundary Conflicts." Miller 1995: 385–392.

Berg, D. (1969). *The Old Church and The New Church—a Prophecy of God*, The Children of God. GP#A.

Berg, D. (1973). *Women in Love*. The Children of God. ML 292.

Berg, D. (1977a). *Child Brides!* The Children of God. DO 902.

Berg, D. (1977b). "Prophecy for Davidito." *"It's a Boy!"—the Story of Little David Continued*, Children of God. DFO 619.

Berg, D. (1978a). *The Girl Who Wouldn't*. The Children of God. MO—DO 721.

Berg, D. (1978b). *The Real Meaning of "The Lord's Supper"!* The Children of God. DO 781.

Berg, D. (1980). *The Devil Hates Sex! But God Loves It!* The Children of God. DFO 999.

Berg, D. (1982). *Dream Queen! The Holy Ghost!* The Children of God. DFO 1304.

Berg, D. (1987). *The Last State? The Dangers of Demonism!* The Family. ML 2306; GN278.
Berg, D. (1989). *Trimming Down to a Gideon's Band.* The Family Home ARC / ML DO 2527. Retrieved July 16, 2014, from http://www.xfamily.org/index.php/HomeARC_ML_2527.
Berg, D. (1992). *Why Do Ye Stone Us?* The Family. DO 2835.
Berg, D. (n.d.). *It's Up To You! Mene's Farewell from the King's House*, The Family. ML 2524.
Berg, D. and Maria (1974a). *The One That Got Away! Part 1: On Unsuccessful Flirty-Fishing.* The Family. LTO 524.
Berg, D. and Maria (1974b). *The One That Got Away! Part 2: Jesus and Sex!* The Family. LTO 525.
Berg, M. (1992). "Merry's Story." *No Longer Children Newsletter* Retrieved April 7, 2007, from http://www.excult.org.
Berger, P. L. (1963). *Invitation to Sociology: A Humanistic Perspective.* New York: Anchor Books.
Berger, P. L. and T. Luckmann (1967). *The Social Construction of Reality: Everything That Passes for Knowledge in Society.* London: Allen Lane.
Bettelheim, B. (1969). *The Children of the Dream.* New York: Macmillan.
Beverley, J. A. (1994). *The Religious Teaching of Sun Myung Moon in the English Version of His Sermons and Related Esoteric Unification Documents (1965–1993).* Faculty of Theology. Toronto: St Michael's College.
Bohlken-Zumpe, E. (1993). *Torches Extinguished: Memories of a Communal Bruderhof Childhood in Paraquay, Europe and the USA.* San Francisco: Peregrine Foundation.
Bourdieu, P. (1990). *The Logic of Practice.* Stanford, CA: Stanford University Press.
Bourdieu, P. (2000). *Pascalian Meditations.* Stanford, CA: Stanford University Press.
Bourdieu, P. (2001). *Masculine Domination.* Stanford, CA: Stanford University Press.
Bromley, D. and S. Newton (1994). "The Family: History, Organization and Ideology." Lewis and Melton 1994: 41–46.
Bromley, D. G. and A. D. Shupe (1981). *Strange Gods: The Great American Cult Scare.* Boston: Beacon Press.
Bryant, M. D. and H. W. Richardson, eds. (1978). *A Time for Consideration: A Scholarly Appraisal of the Unification Church.* New York: Edwin Mellen Press.
Capps, D. (1992). "Religion and Child Abuse: Perfect Together." *Journal for the Scientific Study of Religion* 31(1): 1–14.
Carroll, L. and J. Tober (1999). *The Indigo Children: The New Kids have Arrived*, Carlsbad, CA: Hay House.
Carroll, L. and J. Tober (2001). *An Indigo Celebration: More Messages, Stories and Insights from the Indigo Children.* Carlsbad, CA: Hay House.
The Church of Scientology Moscow v Russia (2007). European Court of Human Rights, ECHR 258.
Clemmer, D. (1958). *The Prison Community.* New York: Holt, Rinehart and Winston.

Clinton, H. R. (1996). *It Takes a Village: And Other Lessons Children Teach Us.* New York: Simon and Schuster.

Cohen, S. (1972). *Folk Devils and Moral Panics: The Creation of the Mods and Rockers.* Oxford: Blackwell.

Cohen, S. (2001). *States of Denial: Knowing about Atrocities and Suffering.* Cambridge: Polity.

Coleman, S. (1999). "God's Children: Physical and Spiritual Growth among Evangelical Christians." *Children in New Religions.* Ed. S. J. Palmer and C. E. Hardman. New Brunswick, NJ: Rutgers University Press, 71–87.

Coney, J. (1999). *Sahaja Yoga.* Richmond, UK: Curzon Press.

Conway, F. and J. Siegelman (1978). *Snapping: America's Epidemic of Sudden Personality Change.* Philadelphia: Lippincott.

Cowan, D. E. (2003). *Bearing False Witness? An Introduction to the Christian Countercult.* Westport, CT: Praeger.

Dasa, D. S. (1999). "Please Don't Sue ISKCON." Retrieved September 19, 2006, from http://www.oldchakra.com/articles/99/11/18/why.not.sue/index.htm.

Davie, G. (1994). *Religion in Britain since 1945: Believing without Belonging.* Oxford: Blackwell.

Deleuze, G. and F. Guattari (1972). *Anti-Oedipus: Capitalism and Schizophrenia.* New York: Viking Press.

Deleuze, G. and F. Guattari (1987). *A Thousand Plateaus: Capitalism and Schizophrenia.* Minneapolis: University of Minnesota Press.

Douglas, M. (1966). *Purity and Danger: An Analysis of Concepts of Pollution and Taboo.* London: Routledge & Kegan Paul.

Douglas, M. (1970). *Natural Symbols: Explorations in Cosmology.* London, Barrie & Rockliff.

Durkheim, É. (1893). *The Division of Labour in Society.* New York: Free Press.

Elster, J. (1983). *Sour Grapes: Studies in the Subversion of Rationality.* Cambridge: Cambridge University Press.

Erikson, E. H. (1968). *Identity: Youth and Crisis.* New York: Norton.

Erikson, K. T. (1966). *Wayward Puritans: A Study in the Sociology of Deviance.* London: Allyn and Bacon.

Erikson, K. T. (1994). *A New Species of Trouble: Explorations in Disaster, Trauma, and Community.* New York: Norton.

Family (1998). *The Love Charter.* Zurich: The Family.

The Family Vindicated!—A Review of Legal Actions and Official Investigations involving the Family (1997). World Services, the Family.

Festinger, L., H. Riecken, and S. Schachter (1956). *When Prophecy Fails: A social and Psychological Study of a Modern Group That Predicted the Destruction of the World.* New York: Harper-Torchbooks.

Fichter, J. H. (1985). *The Holy Family of Father Moon.* Kansas City, MO: Leaven Press.

Foucault, M. (1980). *Power/Knowledge: Selected Interviews and Other Writings, 1972–1977.* London: Harvester.

Gelberg, S. J., ed. (1983). *Hare Krishna, Hare Krishna: Five Distinguished Scholars on the Krishna Movement in the West.* New York: Grove Press.

Gennep, A. v. (1960). *The Rites of Passage.* London: Routledge.

Gerth, H. H. and C. W. Mills, eds. (1946). *From Max Weber.* Oxford: Oxford University Press.

Glaser, B. and A. Strauss (1971). *Status Passage.* London: Routledge and Kegan Paul.

Goffman, E. (1963). *Stigma.* Englewood Cliffs, NJ: Prentice-Hall.

Goffman, E. (1968). *Asylums: Essays on the Social Situation of Mental Patients and Other Inmates.* Harmondsworth, UK: Penguin.

Goodstein, L. (2005). "Murder and Suicide Reviving Claims of Child Abuse in Cult." *New York Times* January 15.

Goswami, J. (1984). *Srila Prabhupada on Guru-Kula.* Los Angeles: Bhaktivedanta Book Trust.

Hardman, C. E. (1999). "The Ethics of Children in Three New Religions." *Children in New Religions.* Ed. S. J. Palmer and C. E. Hardman. New Brunswick, NJ: Rutgers University Press, 227–244.

Hassan, S. (1988). *Combatting Cult Mind Control: Protection, Rescue and Recovery from Destructive Cults.* Wellingborough, UK: Aquarian Press.

Holden, A. (2002). *Jehovah's Witnesses: Portrait of a Contemporary Religious Movement.* London: Routledge.

Hong, N. (1998). *In the Shadow of the Moons: My Life in the Reverend Sun Myung Moon's Family.* Boston: Little, Brown.

Hostetler, J. A. (1993). *Amish Society.* Baltimore, John Hopkins University Press.

Hostetler, J. A. (n.d.). "Expelled Bruderhof Members Speak Out." Retrieved September 12, 2007, from http://www.perefound.org/em-s_sp.html.

Hubbard, L. R. (1950). *Dianetics: The Modern Science of Mental Health.* Copenhagen: New Era Publications.

Hubbard, L. R. ([1981] 2007–). *The Way to Happiness.* Commerce City, CA: Bridge Publications.

Hubbard, L. R. (1992, 1993, 1998). *What Is Scientology?* Los Angeles: Bridge Publications.

Introvigne, M. (1994). "The Children of God and The Family in Italy." Lewis and Melton 1994: 113–120.

Jacobs, J. (2007). "Abuse in New Religious Movements: Challenges for the Sociology of Religion." *Teaching New Religions.* Ed. D. G. Bromley. Oxford: Oxford University Press, 231–244.

James, A., C. Jenks, and A. Prout (1997). *Theorizing Childhood.* Oxford: Blackwell.

Jenks, C. (1996). *Childhood.* London: Routledge.

Jentzsch, R. H. C. (1994). *A Description of the Scientology Religion Presented by the Church of Scientology.* Los Angeles: Bridge Publications.

Jones, K et al. (2007). *Not without My Sister.* London: HarperElement.

Kanter, R. M. (1972). *Commitment and Community: Communes and Utopias in Sociological Perspective.* Cambridge, MA: Harvard University Press.

Kanter, R. M., ed. (1973). *Communes: Creating and Managing the Collective Life*. New York: Harper and Row.

Kent, S. (1997). "Brainwashing and Re-education Camps in the Children of God/The Family." Paper presented at the annual meeting of the Association for the Sociology of Religion, August 8, Toronto.

Kent, S. (2003). "Scientology and the Human Rights Debate: A Reply to Leisa Goodman, J. Gordon Melton, and the European Rehabilitation Project Force Study." *Marburg Journal of Religion* 8(1). Available online at http://www.uni-marburg.de/fb03/ivk/mjr/pdfs/2003/articles/kent2003.pdf.

Kephart, W. (1982). *Extraordinary Groups: The Sociology of Unconventional Lifestyles*. New York: Saint Martin's Press.

Kraybill, D. B. (1989). *The Riddle of Amish Culture*. Baltimore: John Hopkins University Press.

Landa, S. (1991). "Children and Cults: A Practical Guide." *Journal of Family Law* 29(3): 1–28.

Lewis, J. R. and J. G. Melton, eds. (1994). *Sex, Slander, and Salvation: Investigating the Family/Children of God*. Stanford, CA: Center for Academic Publications.

Lukes, S. (2005). *Power: A Radical View*. Basingstoke, UK: Palgrave Macmillan.

Maria (1995). *An Answer to Him That Asketh Us*. World Services, the Family. 2989/DFO 3016.

Maria (1996a). *Loving Jesus Jewels*. World Services, the Family. 327 DO 3045.

Maria (1996b). *Mama's News and Views*. World Services, the Family. 335/DO 3054.

Maria (1997). *Overcoming the Generation Gap*. World Services, the Family. 415 CM/FM 3161.

Maria (1999a). *Jesus Is Calling You Back to the Beginning*. World Services/, Tthe Family. 503 CM/FM 3258.

Maria (1999b). *The Shakeup 2000*, World Services, the Family. 502 CM/FM 3257.

Maria and P. Amsterdam (2002). *Pray, Obey and Prepare!* World Services, the Family. 3420 GN 1007.

Mead, G. H. (1967). *Mind, Self and Society*. Chicago: University of Chicago Press.

Melton, J. G. (1994a). "The Family: Where Does It Fit?" Lewis and Melton 1994: 235–262.

Melton, J. G. (1994b). "Sexuality and the Maturation of the Family." Lewis and Melton 1994: 71–96.

Melton, J. G. (1995). "The Changing Scene of New Religious Movements: Observations from a Generation of Research." *Social Compass* 42(2): 265–276.

Melton, J. G. (1999). Anti-cults in the United States: An Historical Perspective. *New Religious Movements: Challenges and Response*. Ed. B. Wilson and J. Cresswell. London: Routledge, 213–234.

Mill, J. S. ([1869] 1989). "On the Subjection of Women." *J. S. Mill, On Liberty and Other Writings*. Ed. S. Collini. Cambridge, Cambridge University Press: 117–218.

Miller, T., ed. (1995). *America's Alternative Religions*. Albany: State University of New York Press.

Millikan, D. (1994). "The Children of God, the Family of Love, the Family." Lewis and Melton 1994: 181–252.
Mills, C. W. (1959). *The Causes of World War Three*. London: Secker & Warburg.
Moon, S. M. (1973). *Divine Principle*. Thornton Heath, UK: Holy Spirit Association for the Unification of World Christianity.
Moon, S. M. (1998). *The Way for a True Child*. Washington, DC: Family Federation for World Peace and Unification International.
More Madness from Mama Maria (1997). Pasadena, CA: Countercog.
Mow, M. (1991). *Torches Rekindled: The Bruderhof's Struggle for Renewal*. N.p.: Plough Publishing House.
Muster, N. J. (1997). *Betrayal of the Spirit: My Life behind the Headlines of the Hare Krishna Movement*. Urbana: University of Illinois Press.
Niebuhr, H. R. ([1929] 1957). *The Social Sources of Denominationalism*. New York: Meridian.
Nussbaum, M. C. (2000). *Women and Human Development: The Capabilities Approach*. Cambridge: Cambridge University Press.
Oliver, M. (1994). "Today's Jackboots: The Inquisition Revisited." Lewis and Melton 1994: 137–152.
Our Replies to Allegations of Child Abuse (1992). World Services, the Family.
Oved, Y. (1996). *The Witness of the Brothers: A History of the Bruderhof*. New Brunswick, NJ: Transaction.
Palgi, M. (1997). "Women in the Changing World of the Kibbutz." In *Women in Judaism*. 1(1). Accessed July 16, 2014, on http://wjudaism.library.utoronto.ca/index.php/wjudaism/article/view/163/209.
Palmer, S. (1994a). "Heaven's Children: The Children of God's Second Generation." Lewis and Melton 1994: 1–26.
Palmer, S. J. (1994b). *Moon Sisters, Krishna Mothers, Rajneesh Lovers: Women's Roles in New Religions*. Syracuse, NY: Syracuse University Press.
Parker, V. (2001). "Prabhupada Pure and Blameless." Retrieved September 19, 2006, from http://www.oldchakra.com/articles/2001/04/14/prabhupada/index.htm.
Penn, J. (2000). "No Regrets." Retrieved August 10, 2007, from http://www.xfamily.org/index.php/No_Regrets.
Percy, M. (1997). "Sweet Rapture: Subliminal Eroticism in Contemporary Charismatic Worship." *Theology Sexuality* 3(6): 71–106.
Pleil, N. M. (1994). *Free from Bondage: After Forty Years in Bruderhof Communities on Three Continents*. San Francisco: Peregrine.
Plummer, K. (1979). "Misunderstanding Labelling Perspectives." *Deviant Interpretations*. Ed. D. Downes and P. Rock. Oxford: Martin Robertson.
Pollock, D. C. and R. E. V. Reken (1999). *Third Culture Kids: The Experience of Growing Up among Worlds*. Yarmouth, MEs: Intercultural Press.
Prabhupada, H. D. G. A. C. B. (1978). *The Science of Self-Realization*. London: Bhaktivedanta Book Trust.
Pubs Purge Advisory. (1991). Retrieved February 22, 2007, from http://www.xfamily.org/index.php/Pubs_Purge_Advisory%2C_June_1991.

Punch, M. (1977). *Progresive Retreat: A Sociological Study of Dartington Hall School and Some of Its Former Pupils.* Cambridge: Cambridge University Press.

Puttick, E. (1999). "Osho Ko Hsuan School: Educating the 'New Child.'" *Children in New Religions.* Ed. S. J. Palmer and C. E. Hardman. New Brunswick, NJ: Rutgers University Press, 88–107.

Ricoeur, P. (1994). *Oneself as Another.* Chicago: University of Chicago Press.

Robbins, T. and R. Robertson (1991). "Studying Religion Today: Controversiality and 'Objectivity' in the Sociology of Religion." *Religion* 21.4: 319–337.

Rochford, E. B. (1995). "Hare Krishna in America: Growth, Decline, and Accommodation." Miller 1995: 215–222.

Rochford, E. B. (1997). "Family Formation, Culture and Change in the Hare Krsna Movement." *ISKCON Communications Journal* 5(2): 61–84.

Rochford, E. B. (1999). "Education and Collective Identity: Public Schooling of Hare Krishna Youths." *Children in New Religions.* Ed. S. J. Palmer and C. E. Hardman. New Brunswick, NJ: Rutgers University Press, 29–50.

Rochford, E. B. (2001). "The Changing Face of ISKCON: Family, Congregationalism, and Privatisation." *ISKCON Communications Journal* 9(1): 1–12.

Rochford, E. B. and K. Bailey (2006). "Almost Heaven: Leadership, Decline and the Transference of New Vrindaban." *Nova Religio* 9(3): 6–23.

Rochford, E. B. and J. Heinlein (1998). "Child Abuse in the Hare Krishna Movement: 1971–1986." *ISKCON Communications Journal* 6(1): 43–69.

Rock, P. (1998). *After Homicide: Practical and Political Responses to Bereavement.* Oxford: Clarendon Press.

Rodriguez, R. (2002). "Life with Grandpa—The Mene Story." Retrieved July 16, 2014, from http://www.xfamily.org/index.php/Life_with_Grandpa_-_the_Mene_Story.

Rubin, J. H. (1993). "The Abuse of Charismatic Authority within the Bruderhof." Retrieved 11/9/2007, from http://www.perefound.org/jhr_arch.html.

Rubin, J. H. (1997). "The Other Side of Joy: Harmful Religion in an Anabaptist Community." *Harmful Religion, an Exploration of Religious Abuse.* Ed. L. Osborn and A. Walker. London: SPCK, ch. 5.

Rubin, J. H. (2000). *The Other Side of Joy: Religious Melancholy among the Bruderhof.* New York: Oxford University Press.

Rubin, J. H. (2002). "Contested Narratives: A Case Study of the Conflict between a New Religious Movement and Its Critics." Zablocki and Robbins 2002: 452–477.

Rubin, J. H. (n.d.). "The Society Syndrome, Depressive Illness and Conversion Crises in a Christian Fundamentalist Sect." Unpublished MS, Retrieved July 16, 2014, from http://www.perefound.org/ssarch.html.

Schiffauer, W. (1999). "Islamism in the Diaspora: The Fascination of Political Islam among Second Generation German Turks." Oxford University, Transnational Communities Programme—Working Paper Series. Retrieved July 16, 2014, from http://www.transcomm.ox.ac.uk/working%20papers/Schiffauer_Islamism.PDF.

Shupe, A. (1998a). "The Role of Apostates in the North American Anticult Movement." *The Politics of Religious Apostasy: The Role of Apostates in the Transformation of Religious Movements.* Ed. D. G. Bromley. Westport, CT: Praeger, 209–218.

Shupe, A., ed. (1998b). *Wolves within the Fold: Religious Leadership and Abuses of Power.* New Brunswick, NJ: Rutgers University Press.

Shupe, A. D. and D. G. Bromley (1981). "Apostates and Atrocity Stories: Some Parameters in the Dynamics of Deprogramming." *The Social Impact of New Religious Movements.* Ed. B. Wilson. New York: Rose of Sharon Press, 179–216.

Shupe, A. and D. G. Bromley (1994). *Anti-cult Movements in Cross-Cultural Perspective.* New York: Garland.

Shupe, A. et al. ([2002] 2003). "The Cult Awareness Network and the Anticult Movement: Implications for NRMs in America." *New Religious Movements and Religious Liberty in America.* Ed. D. H. Davis and B. Hankins. 2nd ed. Waco, TX: J. M. Dawson Institute of Church-State Studies and Baylor University Press, 21–44.

Singer, M. T. and R. Ofshe (1990). "Thought Reform Programs and the Production of Psychiatric Casualties." *Psychiatric Annals* 20(3): 188–193.

Siskind, A. (1999). "In Whose Interest? Separating Children from Mothers in the Sullivan Institute/Fourth Wall Community." *Children in New Religions.* Ed. S. J. Palmer and C. E. Hardman. New Brunswick, NJ: Rutgers University Press: 51–70.

Speak for Yourself!—Your Thoughts, Reactions, and Replies to "The Professionals" (2002). World Services, the Family. FSM 388.

Spiro, M. E. (1975). *Kibbutz: Venture in Utopia.* Cambridge, MA: Harvard University Press.

A Statement on the Deaths of Angela Smith and Ricky Rodriguez (2005). The Family International.

Tönnies, F. ([1887] 1965). *Community and Society* (orig. title *Gemeinschaft und Gesellschaft*). 2nd ed. New York: Harper and Row.

Turner, V. (1986). "Betwixt and Between: The Liminal Period in Rites de Passage." *The Forest of Symbols.* Ithaca, NY: Cornell University Press.

Vandari Repellent—The Word (2003). World Services, the Family. XN 20.

van Eck Duymaer van Twist, A. (2010). "Children in New Religions: Contested Duties of Care." *International Journal for the Study of New Religions* 1(2): 25–48.

van Zandt, D. E. (1991). *Living in the Children of God.* Princeton, NJ: Princeton University Press.

Walker, I. (2003). *Devil's Playground.* Columbia Pictures.

Wallis, R. (1979). "The Elementary Forms of the New Religious Life." *Annual Review of the Social Sciences of Religion* 3: 191–211.

Wallis, R. (1996). "Three Types of New Religious Movements." *Cults in Context: Readings in the Study of New Religious Movements.* Ed. L. L. Dawson. Toronto: Canadian Scholars' Press, 39–69.

Ward, A. (1995). W 42 in the High Court of Justice, Family Division: Principal Registry in the Matter of ST (a minor) and in the Matter of the Supreme Court Act 1991.
Wessinger, C. (2000). *How the Millennium Comes Violently: From Jonestown to Heaven's Gate.* Chappaqua, NY: Seven Bridges Press.
Williams, M. (1998). *Heaven's Harlots: My Fifteen Years as a Sacred Prostitute in the Children of God Cult.* New York: Eagle Brook.
Wilson, B. (1982). *Religion in Sociological Perspective.* Oxford: Oxford University Press.
Wilson, B. (1990). *The Social Dimensions of Sectarianism: Sects and New Religious Movements in Contemporary Society.* Oxford: Clarendon Press.
Winston, H. (2005). *Unchosen: The Hidden Lives of Hasidic Rebels.* Boston: Beacon Press.
Wright, S. (1986). "Dyadic Intimacy and Social Control in the Three Cult Movements." *Sociological Analysis* 47(2): 137–150.
Wright, S., ed. (1995). *Armageddon in Waco: Critical Perspectives on the Branch Davidian Conflict.* Chicago: University of Chicago Press.
Wright, S. (1998). "Exploring Factors That Shape the Apostate Role." *The Politics of Religious Apostasy: The Role of Apostates in the Transformation of Religious Movements.* Ed. D. G. Bromley. Westport, CT: Praeger, 95–114.
Wright, S. A. (2007). "The Dynamics of Movement Membership: Joining and Leaving New Religious Movements." *Teaching New Religions.* Ed. D. G. Bromley. Oxford: Oxford University Press, 187–209.
Wrong, D. H. (1961). "The Oversocialized Conception of Man in Modern Sociology." *American Sociological Review* 26(2): 183–193.
Zablocki, B. (1971). *The Joyful Community.* Baltimore: Penguin.
Zablocki, B. and T. Robbins, eds. (2002). *Misunderstanding Cults: Searching for Objectivity in a Controversial Field.* Toronto: University of Toronto Press.

Index

Abuse, 182–5
   In the Family, 53, 78–9, 81–4, 86–9, 99
   In ISKCON, 55–9
Agent(s), 8–10, 152, 167, 187, 212, 214, 245n86
Alienation/Alienated, 8, 58, 96, 159, 168, 175, 186, 214
Alienating passage, 214
Amish, 14–5, 36, 59, 104, 122–3
Amsterdam, Peter, 22, 49, 85, 87–92, 97, 232n33
Ananda Marga, 32
Apollos, 85, 88, 92
Applied Scholastics, 18, 30, 36
Arnold, Christoph, 60
Arnold, Eberhard, 16–7, 46–7
Arnold, Heini, 46–8, 226
Ausschluss, 59–62, 211 (*see also* Exclusion)
Ausschluss, grosser, 46, 59–61, 108 (*see also* Exclusion)
Ausschluss, kleiner, 46, 59, 62, 108, 123 (*see also* Exclusion)

Bad apples, 85–6, 91, 95, 99, 107, 180–82, 188, 213, 215, 232
Baddies, 7, 108–12, 137–38, 142, 194, 198, 204, 206–7, 209–10, 234–5nn14, 16, 21, 27
Barker, Eileen, 6, 195, 222n13, 241n30, 243n56
Beckford, James, 6, 13–4, 42, 225n42

Berg, David, 20–2, 29, 49, 51–2, 71–99, 131, 136–37, 182, 184
Bhagwan Shree Rajneesh (*see* Osho)
Blessed, 25, 30–1, 106, 130, 223n25
   Children, 24–5, 31, 106–11, 116–22, 125–27, 130–43, 204, 210, 235–36nn18, 11, 13
Blessing, 24–5, 130–33, 236n9, 11
Boundary dynamics, 67–71
Boundary maintaining, 15
Brainwashing/ed, 3, 19, 22, 25, 63, 103, 181, 192–95, 214

Camp, rotten apple, 51
Camp, teen detention, 51
Camp, teen training, 51, 86, 146
Camp, Victor, 52, 129, 146–47, 235n19 (*see also* Victor Program)
Celibacy, 32–3, 37, 55
Child care, 33, 35, 39–40, 44–5, 53, 163, 225n48
Child rearing, 13, 34–5, 114, 225n57, 240n26
Child(ren), Blessed (*see* blessed children)
Child(ren), Fallen, 111, 133
Child(ren), Jacob's, 111, 132–33
Clearance(s), 61, 107, 138
Cognitive framework, 196, 212, 214
Cohen, Stanley, 98–9, 181–82, 230n5

Cohort(s)
   First, 7–10, 44, 107, 112, 138, 155, 172–76, 180, 243n56
   Second/later/younger, 7–10, 107, 138, 167, 172–76, 186, 243nn56, 61
Cold-hearted, 17, 47–9, 61
Collegiate Association for the Research of Principles (CARP), 121, 124–26
Communal living/lifestyle, 13, 19, 21, 37–9, 110, 114, 162, 164, 174, 237n28
Convert(s), 24–5, 130, 133, 192–3, 210, 224n39, 241n32, 248n1
Court case(s), 20, 91, 182, 241
Crisis (*see* Great Crisis)
Cultic Milieu, 14, 31

Davidito, 11, 29, 79, 103, 141, 183, 231n23 (*see also* Rodriguez, Ricky)
Davidito letters/*The Story of Davidito*, 11, 79, 87, 231
Demerits, 52
Denial, 56, 98–9, 158, 181–2, 215, 232n39
   Implicatory, 99, 181
   Interpretive, 99, 181
   Literal, 99
   States of, 98
Deviance/t, 6, 68, 104, 107–8, 137, 142, 161, 186, 212, 233–34nn4, 10, 12, 240–41n29
Discipleship Training Revolution, 53
Disciplining, 50–63, 107, 129, 146–47, 172, 179, 234n10
Divine Principle, 24, 121, 125, 130, 237n20
Douglas, Mary, 5, 31, 39, 202, 245

End time teens, 29, 50, 93, 106–7, 204
Erikson, Kai, 15, 108, 229n1, 233n4, 245n4
Exclusion, 16, 59–64, 114–15, 123, 151–52, 159, 163–64, 226n10 (*see also* Ausschluss)
Exclusive Brethren, 15, 59, 70, 170, 180
Exorcism(s), 52–3, 63, 227n26

Fallen nature, 24–5, 30–1, 136n9
Findhorn, 136–37, 196
Fitting in, 122, 238n43
   Not, 5, 190–91, 199, 212, 215
Flirty Fishing (FFing), 22, 73–8, 83, 90

Gemeinschaft, 113, 116
Gender, 37–8, 202–3, 225nn52, 53
Gesellschaft, 113
Go On, 177–78, 183, 204, 244n69
Goodies, 7, 108–10, 112, 118, 122–24, 138, 235n19
Governing Body Commission (GBC), 45, 49, 55–58, 228n35
Great Crisis, 16–7, 47–9, 61–2, 150–51, 159, 226n10, 243n61
Gurukula(s), 36, 54–9, 63–4, 106–7, 136, 198, 228n35, 238n38
Gurukuli(s), 56–8, 64, 106–7, 112, 134–36, 138, 142, 173, 182, 198–99, 228n43, 238n42

Ibatea community, Paraguay, 151
Identity crisis, 189, 197, 246n6
Identity, diaspora, 215
Indemnity, 25, 39–40, 44, 109, 130–31, 143, 235n18
Inform, 4–5, 9, 153, 175, 197–98, 239n1, 241n32, 243n64
Insertion, mode(s) of, 6, 13, 15, 42, 48, 63–71, 93, 97–8, 132
Isolation (as punishment), 51–2, 54, 228n47, 232n38

Jehovah's Witnesses, 59, 70, 153, 156, 170, 175, 197
Jumbo (Philippines), 51, 145–46

Kanter, Rosabeth Moss, 37, 43
Karmi(es), 56, 58, 111
Kibbutzim, 34–5, 38, 225n48

KIT (Keep in Touch), 168–72, 174–76, 245
Krishna Consciousness, 26–7, 30, 36, 54, 58–9, 238n43

Labeling, 107–8, 112, 137–38, 154, 181, 234–5nn13, 21, 247n33
Law of Love, 22–3, 37, 64–5, 73, 76–8, 83–6, 91–3, 99, 182, 229n55, 231n18
Law of Sannerz, 18
Leadership
  Charismatic, 42–9, 87, 221n3
  Traditional, 45–9, 64
Loving Jesus Revelation, 93–4, 182, 229n55

Marginal/ization, 13–5, 34, 55–7, 93, 108, 110, 149, 170, 186, 191
Maria (Karen Zerby), 11, 22, 29, 49, 53–4, 71–5, 79–98, 141–45, 153–55, 240n15
Matching/matched, 24, 111, 130, 133
Maya, 14, 27, 30, 36, 56
Mene, 52–3, 79, 103, 111
Millikan, David, 22, 75–9, 87, 90, 231n20
Mind, 18
  Analytical, 18
  Control, 162, 167, 179, 192–96
  Reactive, 18
Misunderstood words, 120, 157–58, 236n18
Mo letter(s), 22, 51, 74, 77–9, 145, 156, 223n21
Movingon.org, 79–80, 170, 210
Moon, Sun Myung, 23–6, 30–1, 40, 43–5, 49, 106, 117, 130, 223–24nn23, 30, 226nn2, 6, 236–37nn9, 31

New Religious Movements, 4, 6, 13, 165–68, 171, 211, 243n56
Normless/ness, 207, 212, 214

Oneida Perfectionists, 32, 37
Open heart report(s), 51, 138, 156, 232n38
Osho, 34, 227

P'ikareun, 237
Passage, 8, 152, 167, 187, 212, 214, 245nn86, 87
Passagee, 152, 167, 187, 212, 214
Passing, 197, 214, 238n43
Peregrine Foundation, 169, 171, 174
Prabhupada, A. C. B. S., 26, 30, 33, 36, 45–6, 49, 55, 58, 135, 173, 182
Primavera community, Paraguay, 16–7, 47, 62, 114, 150–52, 159
Providence
  Hometown, 44–5
  National Messiahs, 44
Possessed, demon, 61, 111, 198, 210, 227n26
Punishment, 50, 59, 62, 115, 123, 157
  (*see also* Disciplining)
  Corporal, 50, 52–4, 63, 179, 192
  (*see also* Disciplining)

Radical, 3, 6, 13, 16, 204, 215, 229n55
Raghunatha Anudasa, 56–8, 173
Raids, 64, 81, 224n30
Rebel(s), 7, 108–12, 118, 122, 124–29, 136–38, 209–10, 235–36nn21, 8, 14, 239n8
Reboot, 21, 91, 132, 225n55, 232n41, 238n36
Restriction(s), (*see also* Disciplining, Punishment)
  Conversation, 54
  Silence, 51–3, 228n47, 232n38
Rochford, E. Burke, 55, 58, 197–98, 238n43
Rodriguez, Ricky (*see also* Davidito), 79, 103, 141, 183, 231nn23, 24
Rubin, Julius, 48, 61–2, 222, 226, 242n43

Sabra(s), 29, 49, 62, 64
Safe Passage Foundation, 170, 176
Sahaja Yoga, 34, 227n29

Salvation beliefs, 14–5, 222n1, 225n52
Sankirtan, 26–7, 39, 56–7
Sea Org, 19, 30, 33, 36, 38, 40, 157–58, 222nn11, 12
Self-help groups, 8–9, 167–68, 176, 179, 214, 241n36
Sexual sharing, 23, 32, 37, 72, 75–8, 89–90, 93, 145, 172, 223n21
Sexuality, 22–3, 37–8, 60, 70, 74, 76, 84, 99
Silence restriction (*see* restriction, silence)
Social boundaries, 5, 15, 35, 48, 68, 72, 105, 107, 112, 132–36, 185, 195, 245n1
Socialization, 4, 31–2, 36, 63, 101, 103–6, 146, 171, 192–96, 205, 215, 233–34nn3, 15
   Primary, 191, 193, 196, 203, 209, 246n9
   Secondary, 101, 191, 246n9
   Segregated, 5, 211–12
Socializing forces, 31, 36, 38, 192, 195
Status (designation), 107, 109, 111, 115, 148, 152
Status Passage, 8, 152, 167, 187, 245n87
Stigma, 3, 7–8, 101, 108, 190, 197, 209, 215
Stigmatized, 5, 8, 55, 145, 178, 185–87, 210, 215
Sullivan Institute, 33–4
System, the, 22, 39, 81–7, 94–8, 118, 129, 170, 173, 186

Techi, 11, 29
Transcendental Meditation (TM), 136–7, 196
Trial and Error, 7, 43, 91, 98, 122, 226n1
Tribal Messiahship, 44
Troubled, 106, 109, 111–12, 136, 138, 181, 234–35nn16, 21

United Nations Convention on the Rights of the Child, 50, 69, 170, 192, 195

Victor Program, 50–4, 63, 96, 107, 129, 138, 146–48, 235n19 (*see also* Camp, Victor)
Vrindaban, New, 56

Ward, Lord Justice Alan, 51–2, 54, 63, 86–7, 91–3, 97, 182, 228n47, 232n38
Warm-hearted, 17, 47–9, 62
Wilderness, 188, 191, 193, 202, 209, 212, 214, 245n1
Wilson, Bryan, 5–6, 222n1
World Accommodating, 67, 222n1, 230n3
World Affirming, 67, 222n1, 230n3
World Rejecting, 67, 222n1, 230n3

Zerby, Karen (*see* Maria)
Zumpe, Hans, 17, 46–7, 226n10

www.ingramcontent.com/pod-product-compliance
Ingram Content Group UK Ltd.
Pitfield, Milton Keynes, MK11 3LW, UK
UKHW022241230426
12048UKWH00018BA/1402